To

Li

Thanks for keeping me
sane (ish!) ♡

Vi xxx

Secrets and Scandals
in Regency Britain

Secrets and Scandals in Regency Britain

Sex, Drugs and Proxy Rule

Violet Fenn

PEN & SWORD
HISTORY

First published in Great Britain in 2022 by
Pen & Sword History
An imprint of
Pen & Sword Books Ltd
Yorkshire – Philadelphia

Typeset by Mac Style
Printed and bound in the UK by CPI Group (UK) Ltd,
Croydon, CR0 4YY.

Pen & Sword Books Limited incorporates the imprints of Atlas,
Archaeology, Aviation, Discovery, Family History, Fiction, History,
Maritime, Military, Military Classics, Politics, Select, Transport,
True Crime, Air World, Frontline Publishing, Leo Cooper, Remember
When, Seaforth Publishing, The Praetorian Press, Wharncliffe
Local History, Wharncliffe Transport, Wharncliffe True Crime
and White Owl.

For a complete list of Pen & Sword titles please contact

PEN & SWORD BOOKS LIMITED
47 Church Street, Barnsley, South Yorkshire, S70 2AS, England
E-mail: enquiries@pen-and-sword.co.uk
Website: www.pen-and-sword.co.uk

Or

PEN AND SWORD BOOKS
1950 Lawrence Rd, Havertown, PA 19083, USA
E-mail: Uspen-and-sword@casematepublishers.com
Website: www.penandswordbooks.com

This book is dedicated to
an unknown Scottish girl who
died aboard the *Lady Juliana* in 1789.

And also to the memory of Boo,
who always listened. And
always understood.

Contents

Acknowledgements

I'd like to take this opportunity to thank the following people, without whom this book genuinely wouldn't exist:

Li Zakovics, who is, quite literally, the only reason I'm still sane; Gill Hoffs, for endless moral support and background cheerleading; Jo Austin, Myles Clarke and Silas, for their excellent detective work on the subject of London's confusingly renamed streets; Jay Émme, for being a living, breathing inspiration; Winston Gomez; Rachael Lucas, the Queen of Mindboggling Gossip; Sam Cleasby; Suzy Cavill; Lucy Chamberlain; Ruth Douglas; Sarah Wallace; Ricky Balshaw, my own personal scapegoat. If I've got anything wrong in these pages, it's entirely his fault.

Scott Wheeldon, my baby brother and partner-in-crime; Speedy Nan, who died just as I finished writing this book, having been a constant force in my life for more than fifty years; Mum and Pete, without whom, etc etc.

Eternal thanks to editor-extraordinaire Karyn Burnham, who is somehow still speaking to me. Also Claire Hopkins, Laura Hirst and all at Pen & Sword Books for their endless help and support.

Biggest thanks and appreciation as always goes to my beloved boys Jaime and Oscar, for coping with me turning absolutely feral whenever a deadline is approaching and, well, just for being there. I love you.

Introduction

In its most literal interpretation, the period known as the Regency lasted a mere nine years, from 1811, when George, Prince Regent, assumed power from his father to 1820, when King George III died and the Prince Regent himself became monarch. In reality, the 'Regency period' had its beginnings in 1788, when King George first began to show signs of mental illness.

Known primarily for losing both the American colonies (during the American Wars of Independence between 1775–1783) and his mind, King George III has often been dismissed as a comedy character who thought more about farming than of governance. This view diminishes his many other intellectual achievements, including establishing both the King's Library (now housed in the British Library at St Pancras, London) and the world famous Royal Academy of Arts on Piccadilly. However by the late 1780s it became impossible to ignore the fact that the king's faculties were not what they ought to be (although his health wouldn't go into terminal decline until the death of his youngest child, Princess Amelia, in 1810). King George III was the first of the Hanoverian monarchs to have been born in Britain and the first to speak English as his first language, so it's rather sad that his achievements have often been overshadowed in the history books by his periods of supposed madness (the causes of which have never been definitively established).

William Pitt was elected Prime Minister of Great Britain in 1783 and again in 1804. Often known as 'the Younger', to differentiate him from his father William Pitt, 1st Earl of Chatham, who had also held the role of Prime Minister during the mid-eighteenth century, Pitt was a mere 24 years old when he first came to power. King George's diminishing faculties were a golden opportunity for Pitt to take stronger control of the country, but at the same time, the situation held grave risk. It was clear that the king was unlikely to be able to retain full monarchal duties and Pitt needed a Regent on the throne in order to move the country forward. At this point in history a Prime Minister's role was tied so closely with that of the ruling monarch that should the incumbent king or queen die or otherwise relinquish their power, the PM was expected to leave with them and another be elected in their place. Pitt might have wanted King George out, but he wasn't planning to leave alongside his monarch. Luckily for Pitt, the first Regency Crisis resolved itself when King George recovered his health enough to carry on as monarch, at least for the time being.

When he was eventually put in charge, the Prince Regent was, as expected, mostly disinclined towards putting any real effort into ruling the country, and happy enough to leave most of the work to his government. Always preferring parties to principles, 'Prinny' seems to have viewed his role as regent as irksome, if not entirely unwanted. In essence, he wanted the power and wealth that ruling a powerful country brought with it, but didn't see any reason why he should have to work for the privilege. His was a boisterous court, which included such notorious society characters as Beau Brummell, who put as much effort into carousing as he did into refining his reputation as the epitome of the 'dandy'.

During the Regency period, the overcrowded and unhygienic slums of London and other developing cities grew apace, as their population increased faster than the supporting infrastructure. Many became known as 'rookeries', in reference to the way people lived jammed together like so many birds in a tree. Despite the rivers Fleet and Walbrook having been covered over and transformed into sewers, London was still half a century away from civil engineer Joseph Bazalgette's efficient sewerage system, which opened in 1865. At the beginning of the nineteenth century, raw human effluent – alongside waste from slaughterhouses and fish markets – was still regularly washed out into the streets and left to run down into the Thames.

Further north, by 1801, Liverpool's population was nearing 80,000 – sixteen times that of a mere century earlier. As the docks rapidly expanded and trade increased, so did the number of people working in the industry. Overcrowding and lack of basic facilities led to major health and social issues in most towns and cities, as people looking for work moved into the new bases of developing industry.

Life for the wealthy, on the other hand, was one of relative comfort and luxury, regardless of whereabouts in the country they lived. They made their money through the same industries without being involved directly in the physical work and, as such, were cushioned from its more deleterious effects. This doesn't mean that vast inequalities didn't also exist among the wealthier sections of society – women were still very much chattels who belonged first to their parents and then to their husbands, and only the first son of an aristocratic family could expect everything on a silver salver. But your chances in life still increased exponentially the further up the greasy class ladder you were. The rich and the poor may have lived in the same cities, but their lives were millions of miles apart – on the surface. Underneath the class-based public façades, humans have always been more similar than they might like to believe, and the Regency was no different. Secrets lurked behind even the most ornate of closed doors and the poorest in the land still had to deal with scandals of their own.

* * *

Author's note: Price comparisons were calculated in 2020, using the Bank of England's inflation calculator and do not take into effect changes in living standards, etc. The 'real' modern figures would in all likelihood be much higher.

Chapter 1

Poverty, Politics & Punishment

There would be no officially regulated system of law and order anywhere in Britain until 1829, when then Home Secretary Robert Peel founded the Metropolitan Police Service. Even then, only London had any formal 'policing' system (and had done so since 1749, when Henry Fielding had hired six men as 'thief-takers' and formed the Bow Street Runners), the rest of the country having long been left to fend for itself when it came to matters of law and order. In 1786, Fielding's half-brother John established a weekly newspaper called *The Public Hue and Cry*, which contained announcements of stolen property and lists of crimes and their suspects, the first real example of a national register of criminal behaviour. Even so, this method wasn't taken up by others and remained limited to a relatively small area of London.

Most victims of crime who wished to see justice done had to do so privately – everything from investigations through to prosecutions were a paid-for service with professional standards that varied depending on the abilities of the person one managed to hire. Every parish was obliged by law to have at least one constable, but it was a voluntary post that the appointee would do in their spare time for the extra money, rather than a dedicated career. One could hire a constable to investigate a crime, but all expenses would have to be paid and there was no guarantee of a positive result.

As with any unregulated industry, it was all too easy for those of a less altruistic nature to set themselves up in business with the aim of making a profit on both sides of the legal fence. 'Thief-takers' were unofficial constables who worked purely for financial reward in much the same way as bounty hunters and were hired directly by the victims themselves. This created a situation in which it was often worth a supposed thief-taker setting up crimes themselves in order that they could then be paid to 'solve' them. On some occasions they would take on a genuine commission and find the person responsible, only to then extort protection money from the criminal in return for not handing them over, a situation that perpetuated the general air of lawlessness. Jonathan Wild, perhaps the most famous of all thief-takers, had himself been hanged for theft in 1725, having spent years running criminal gangs and extortion rings.

The lack of a cohesive court system in the late 1700s added to the difficulty of controlling crime. Even if a person was clearly and unarguably guilty, it was very difficult to arrange for them to face any kind of formal justice. The official punishment of crimes was still centrally based (power wouldn't devolve to individual areas until the Local Government Act of 1888 created county councils for the first time) and relied on a rolling court system that heard cases at only a few set times of the year. 'Petty sessions' were local courts which were headed by magistrates and held to try minor crimes such as theft, assault and drunkenness (hence our modern usage of 'petty crime'). Quarter session courts sat, as the name suggests, four times a year in each region. These were for those crimes more serious than those heard in the petty sessions, but not severe enough to require a hearing at the assizes. They also on occasional heard cases that had been sent to appeal from the magistrates at petty sessions.

The Courts of Assizes heard the most serious cases. These were presided over by judges who travelled around six separate court circuits – Home Circuit (the Home Counties), Midland Circuit, Oxford Circuit, Western Circuit, Norfolk Circuit and Northern Circuit. These courts passed judgment on those most serious of crimes that risked capital punishment, such as treason, rioting or murder.

High treason – disloyalty to the monarch and/or Crown – carried the most severe punishments of all because it was a direct threat to the state, rather than to individual members of its populace. The Treason Act of 1351 had been the first attempt to clarify just what 'treason' meant, but even then it was a murky definition, which included having sex with the husband or wife of a monarch. Both Anne Boleyn and Catherine Howard's death sentences were for the conveniently 'treasonous' act of supposedly having been intimate with men other than King Henry VIII. Queen Mary I abolished the crime of treason entirely in 1553, only for it to be restored within the year, but this time applying to certain forms of counterfeiting. The Treason Act of 1743 brought the crime back into the realms of personal betrayal, threatening death to anyone found consorting with or supporting in any way the sons or employees of James

Francis Edward Stuart, the 'Old Pretender' who had attempted to claim the British and Irish throne.

Counterfeiting was the charge that brought Mrs Catherine Murphy and her husband Hugh to the Old Bailey dock in September 1788, from their cells in Newgate. The prison itself sat on the corner of Newgate Street and Old Bailey Street, the latter giving its name to the adjacent criminal court that had first been established in the mid-sixteenth century. Found guilty of 'coining' – counterfeiting gold or silver coins – both Catherine and Hugh were sentenced to death for high treason. Their sentences were carried out on 18 March 1789, with Hugh being hanged at Newgate alongside seven other male convicts.

As a woman, Catherine was subject to an even more archaic and cruel punishment – she was to be burned at the stake. After the men had been put the death, Catherine was forced to walk past the hanging bodies – including that of her own husband – and made to stand on a small, low platform in front of a tall stake fitted with an iron ring through which ropes could be threaded. The executioner tied Catherine to the stake, making sure to run the rope around her neck. Bundles of straw were then packed around the base; before the fire was lit, the platform was kicked out from under Catherine's feet. She was left to strangle for thirty minutes before the fire took hold. In theory, this method was used to ensure a woman was already dead before she was burned, but in reality things didn't always work out that way – in 1726 Catherine Hayes, having been convicted of murder, had burned alive in front of horrified onlookers when the fire beneath her caught hold so fiercely that the executioner didn't have time to pull the strangling rope.

Whether Catherine Murphy was dead or alive by the time the flames took her, she was the last woman in England to be officially burned at the stake – it was abolished as a method of execution by the Treason Act of 1790.

Back in the realms of more 'average' crime, things were rather less dramatic but often just as harshly punished. By the end of the 1700s, there were approximately 200 crimes that were theoretically punishable by hanging. So extensive was the range of capital offences that magistrates began taking matters into their own hands and it's now believed that around 60 per cent of recorded death sentences of the time were quietly commuted to either transportation or imprisonment. On some occasions, the judge would reframe the crime itself, in order to bring it down into a slightly less severe category. If the accused had stolen an item worth more than five shillings – the threshold for capital punishment in theft cases – a more lenient judge might claim that the item was overpriced to start with and reduce its supposed value to an amount that carried a lesser punishment. Although tens of thousands of death sentences were handed down by British courts during the Regency period, it's estimated that perhaps only 20 per cent of them were actually carried out.

The threat of capital punishment for what we would now consider to be trifling crimes – if indeed they were crimes at all – wasn't restricted to those of the lower classes. On 29 March 1800, Mrs Jane Leigh Perrot, an aunt of Jane Austen, appeared at the spring assizes in Taunton, Somerset, having been accused of stealing a 'card of lace' from Elisabeth Gregory's haberdashery shop in Bath. During the previous August, Jane had bought a card of black lace from Gregory, but the shopkeeper alleged to have found a similar card of white lace in the accused's possession, which had not been paid for. The price of the supposedly stolen lace was £1 – a value that carried with it huge potential punishment. If found guilty, Jane could have potentially been put to death or transported to the Australian penal colonies for fourteen years of hard labour. She insisted that it must have been accidentally handed to her by the store clerk while finalising her purchase, but both Gregory and her assistant, a man by the name of Charles Filby, stuck to their story.

Perrot spent nearly eight months in Ilchester County Gaol, awaiting trial for the supposed theft of a small piece of lace. Given Jane's wealth and social standing, she wasn't required to see out her time in the gaol proper; rather she lodged in the house of the prison-keeper, a Mr Scadding, with her husband John staying by her side. When the case finally came before the assizes court, it took the jury very little time to dismiss Gregory's accusation and find Jane Leigh Perrot not guilty of the theft. She had, however, spent a very long time being imprisoned – albeit it in a genteel manner – before the slow cogs of the eighteenth-century court system finally clunked around to examining her case, all with a potential death sentence hanging over her head. One can only imagine how many people with less support (of both the financial and emotional kind) and social standing found themselves either on the gallows or forced onto an overcrowded ship heading for the other side of the globe, on the basis of nothing more than unprovable accusations and unreliable witnesses.

In an era when the behaviour of most of society was expected to be 'pure' because they were supposedly being watched by God rather than being supervised by any form of structural policing system, the threat of punishment was the only real weapon that the authorities had. Because of this, the 'using a sledgehammer to crack a nut' method was the simplest way for them to control the populace. But of course, not everybody is going to be controllable, regardless of the potential consequences. Given the inherent feeling of 'us against them', so endemic during a time of extremes – in both poverty and wealth, some aspects of criminality were viewed by the British public as heroic and courageous, rather than activity to be discouraged. Rotten Row, an avenue that stretched between St James's Palace and Kensington Palace in London, had become the first artificially lit road in Britain as far back as 1630, when King William III decided that he'd had enough of the highwaymen who regularly lurked on their horses in dark corners, ready to confront anyone who looked as though they might be carrying – or simply wearing – items of value.

The numbers of highwaymen were on the decline in Britain by the turn of the nineteenth century, as cities expanded and open spaces decreased accordingly. The increase in traceable currency as banknotes took over from gold also made a highwayman's nefarious deeds far harder to carry out. The main enemy of the would-be highwaymen, however, was the rapidly increasing population, who left fewer places unwatched and therefore restricted the opportunities for thieves on horseback to ply their trade without being caught.

There was still, however, an air of romance about the idea of highwaymen; this was a time in which the poor were feeling increasingly downtrodden by the rich and the inequalities with which they were being forced to live were becoming ever more bitter pills to swallow. Under such conditions it's not surprising that tales of the plucky anti-hero stealing from those who could easily afford it became the stuff of legend – especially when the suspects were even more unexpected than usual. An incident that had occurred in the mid-eighteenth century is a good example of unlikely but fascinating secret lives.

The Right Reverend Philip Twysden, Lord Bishop of Raphoe, died in November 1752, four months before the birth of his daughter, the future

Lady Jersey. The cause of the 39-year-old Reverend's death was given as inflammation of the bowel, but the truth may have been rather more intriguing. An alternative explanation soon sprang up, suggesting that Twysden had, in fact, died from shotgun wounds received during an ill-fated attempt to rob a stagecoach on Hounslow Heath, then a desolate and dangerous area of open heathland on the outskirts of West London (other reports suggest that the incident possibly happened on Wrotham Heath, near Maidstone in Kent). Reports of the incident differ, but in the nineteenth century, politician and author the Hon. George Charles Grantley FitzHardinge Berkeley, writing as 'Grantley Berkeley', mused,

> The Lord Bishop Twysden, of Raphoe, a member of the old Kentish family of that name, was found suspiciously out at night on Hounslow Heath, and was most unquestionably shot through the body. A correspondent of the *Gentleman's Magazine* asked, 'Was this the bishop who was taken ill on Hounslow Heath, and so carried back to his friend's house … where he died of an inflammation of the bowels?'

It does seem most likely that Twysden's 'bowel inflammation' was, in fact, a gunshot wound caused when the intended victim – a local doctor – retaliated on being attacked. Berkeley's information had originally been reported by a witness who had stumbled upon the scene while walking home from dinner with none other than Twysden's own brother. This most unlikely of highway robberies may have been a desperate attempt by Twysden to save himself and his family from financial ruin, as he had recently been made bankrupt.

The prison system of the Georgian era was big on punishment and low on rehabilitation. Gaols were run as private concerns by anyone with the space and money to do so, from tiny lockups in villages to large cellars and even castle dungeons in larger towns. Conditions were almost universally appalling – prisoners were expected to pay for anything other than the bare minimum and those who couldn't afford to do so often died of disease or malnutrition (or simply succumbed to the wet and cold conditions inside their cells). There was little segregation for differing severities of crime and no thought to prisoner's safety in such overcrowded spaces – minor debtors could be held in cramped cells next to murderers, and men and women were all forced in together. Children often accompanied their parents if there was no one else to care for them at home. The largest gaols, such as Newgate in London, were infamous for the terrible conditions in which their prisoners were kept.

Originally nothing more than a few prison cells built into the old walls of the city, Newgate spread like a virus, being rebuilt and extended over the decades until by 1778, it could hold 460 prisoners. Executions were always a popular event at Newgate, with hundreds of people packing the streets around the gallows in order to witness justice being done. Brisk trade was done at the Magpie & Stump public house – which is still trading to this day – across the road. A trip to the hangings was a social event, children tagging along with parents in order to be shown just what happened to those who didn't follow the law. But, just occasionally, the crowd gathered for the opposite reason – to protest against what they perceived to be a miscarriage of justice.

Just such an event took place on 23 February 1807. Owen Haggerty and John Holloway were due to be hanged for murder, alongside another convicted killer, Elisabeth Godfrey. While Godfrey's case might have not been entirely fairly heard – she was convicted of murdering a fellow resident in her lodging house, despite claiming self-defence – it was at least clear-cut, with several witnesses declaring that she was indeed guilty of her crime. Haggerty and Holloway's case, however, was different. The pair had been sentenced to death for killing a man during a robbery, based only on the testimony of their accomplice, Benjamin Hanfield (charges against Hanfield had been dismissed in return for his agreeing to testify against his friends). Both men proclaimed their innocence to the last. Crowds of almost 40,000 people crushed into the tight space around the scaffold, with cries of 'murder!' being shouted at those in charge of carrying out the execution. The mass hysteria that was brewing grew ever more intense as Holloway made a final plea on his way to the scaffold – 'Gentlemen all! I am innocent! No verdict – We are innocent, so help me God!'

Despite his last desperate exhortations, Holloway – along with Haggerty and Godfrey – were dropped to their deaths; later described colourfully by *The Sun* (a London-based political newspaper that ran from 1792–1896, rather than the modern tabloid of the same name) as, 'precisely at ten minutes past eight o'clock, all three were launched into eternity'. The dramatic romance of the situation was such that one young woman was said to have applied the deceased Haggerty's hand 'to her naked knee' and several other women also had the dead men's hands 'passed over' them (there being a belief at the time that the touch of a hanged man could cure various ailments). But the terrible drama wasn't over yet. As the convicts dropped, the enormous crowd surged forwards for a closer view of their convulsing bodies (although some contemporary reports suggest the they were actually trying to get away from the scene). According to a report in *The Sun* it rapidly turned into a scene of utter carnage:

> It has been said that the whole of this horrid calamity was occasioned by the fall of a man who sold pies, but as the crowd was so great, it is probable that a similar circumstance must have happened in several places, though the origin of the unhappy event has not yet been ascertained. Not only the whole of the area in the Old Bailey was as full as possible, but all the adjoining streets to a considerable extent, and every moment the crowd was augmenting at every avenue to the fatal place. The pressure was so great, that in all parts the cries of 'murder' were heard, accompanied with the most terrific screams, particularly from the female part of the spectators, many of whom were seen in almost expiring situations, without the possibility of the least assistance, every one being compelled to exert himself for the preservation of his own life.
>
> In one part the violence of the pressure was so strong, that the greatest scene of confusion ensued—a large body of the crowd, as in one convulsive struggle for life, fought with the most savage fury with each other; the consequence was, the weakest, particularly the women, fell a sacrifice. Screams were heard from the poor sufferers, and from the persons who witnessed the scene from the different windows. Help was called for; but the crowd was so great, that no person could penetrate it for some time. About fifty persons in all were trampled underfoot, ten of them women, A considerable time elapsed before the constables could clear the way; at length they effected a passage: on raising up the poor sufferers, some were found with broken limbs; others with dreadful bruises; many were quite dead. One of the women had a child in her arms; finding it

impossible to save herself, she threw the infant from her; alighting on the heads of the multitude, the child was saved; but in an instant the unfortunate mother was literally trampled to death. On the side of the platform next Ludgate-Hill, about seven fell down, and were trampled to death....

Persons within twenty or thirty yards of the platform were squeezed, till with fear and pressure they could not breathe; it was extremely warm, the weakest fainted and dropped, others fell over them; the shrieks and confusion were tremendously horrible. The doors of some houses in the street were burst open, hundreds rushed in, panting, speechless, and almost expiring.

The report goes on:

As soon as the general terror had begun to subside, and the crowd began to retire from the scene of horror, several of the dead bodies were carried to St Sepulchre's Church [St Sepulchre-without-Newgate, which still stands on the corner opposite Old Bailey, on Holborn Viaduct]; others to neighbouring public-house, and the greater part soon after to St Bartholomew's Hospital. Language is not adequate to express the feelings of those who thronged around the Church and the Hospital, demanding, with breathless solicitude and anxiety, a sight of the unfortunate sufferers, in whom they expected to discover a brother, sister or father, or some other dear and natural friend.

Hundreds were bruised, some more or less, limbs broken, the flesh torn off the legs of others, &c. When the mob was cleared away, several hundred pairs of shoes were picked up in the streets, with boots, cloaks, bonnets &c., beyond number.

A report from St Bartholomew's Hospital announced that twenty-four men and three women had been declared dead by their doctors, and they were still treating thirteen injured men and two women. The *Star* newspaper gave the final death toll as twenty-four men, three women and five children.

The *Sun* again:

> Among the unfortunate victims was a youth between twelve and fifteen, of Somers Town. He was with his father, who felt him slip from him in the crowd. The father was also brought senseless to Hospital; but is since somewhat recovered and is continually enquiring if his son has escaped. … The Hospital has been a scene of the deepest distress; as the relations and friends of the deceased, on discovering who they were, were thrown into a state more easily imagined than described. … After all effort for the recovery of the 27 dead had proved fruitless, they were removed to an empty ward, and there arranged with every regard to decency. The bodies had been washed, and laid out in a row of beds on each side of the room, with the clothes of each tied in a bundle, under the head of each, and the faces so placed as to give the spectator a full opportunity of examining the features. Some of the faces were quite black, others were dreadfully cut and disfigured. The bodies being thus arranged for the purpose of being recognised by their relatives and friends; at two o'clock the outer gates were opened, and the impatient trembling mass that besieged them, were admitted twenty at a time. They consisted of women and men, whose children, apprentices, or friends, were missing. On their entrance, some flew to the melancholy scene, others trembled, and were afraid to approach the place to which they had been so anxious to obtain access. Among the first of these unhappy inquirers, was a man who came to seek his apprentice, and found his only child a mangled corpse.

Despite this tragedy, public executions continued at Newgate until 1868. The tide was, however, turning against both capital punishment and the prison system in general. Prison reform began to gather momentum towards the end of the eighteenth century. Not only was there a growing understanding of the levels of barbarism involved in hangings, it was clear for all to see that, as a method of deterrence, it was failing for the most basic of reasons. Because punishments were so severe for even relatively small crimes, courts were often loathe to convict if it meant invoking a death sentence – this resulted in many smaller scale criminals going entirely unpunished.

John Howard's 1777 report, *The State of the Prisons in England and Wales*, had been scathing in its criticism of the way the prison system was organised at the time. His main complaints were short and to the point – prisoners were not being segregated by either their gender or the severity of the crime of which they were accused; too many were dying of sickness and disease; there were not enough warders and/or other security staff to keep ether the inmates or prisoners safe; gaolers themselves were too often corrupt; and the release fees required at the end of a prisoner's sentence – known as the 'gaoler's fees' because they were the only income the gaoler's were given for the job – were more than many prisoners could afford and thus they were kept imprisoned long past their official release date. Howard also introduced the idea of solitary confinement as both punishment and a method of keeping those prisoners who were perhaps more troublesome than usual away from the other inmates.

In 1785, Sir George Onesiphorus Paul had secured an Act of Parliament enabling him to build a new gaol at Gloucester. This 'model prison' was designed to be safe and secure and also to take all of Howard's suggestions into account. Men, women and children were segregated, all prisoners had regular health checks, wore a uniform that was provided for them, were fed to an acceptable standard and offered at least some education in basic literacy. But Gloucester would be the outlier for quite some time – the vast majority of prisons were still places into which no one would want to step foot unless they had no other choice.

*   *   *

* The current Central Criminal Court of England and Wales, still popularly known as the Old Bailey after the street on which it still sits, covers most of the footprint of the old Newgate Prison.

Chapter 2

Back to Bedlam

On the evening of Thursday, 15 May 1800, the Drury Lane Theatre was playing host to King George III, who was due to take his place in the royal box alongside Queen Charlotte and other members of his family. The royals were, along with the rest of the large audience, expecting to see a production of the comedy *She Would, and She Would Not,* by Poet Laureate Colley Cibber. As the orchestra played the National Anthem to herald the king's entrance, musician Joseph Calkin looked out over the audience from his position in the orchestra pit and saw a man 'above all the rest' holding a pistol. Before Calkin had chance to raise the alarm, the man fired.

James Hadfield was an ex-soldier who had been badly injured during the Battle of Turcoing in 1794. He was hit over the head several times with a sabre while being captured by the French, injuries which are thought likely to have been the source of his later battles with mental illness. Having joined a religious cult, Hadfield had somehow come to believe that the second coming of Christ was imminent, if only he could manage to get himself killed by the British government. The only logical way to do this, went Hadfield's thinking, was to make a threat to the king's life in the hope of being hanged for treason.

Hadfield was identified at the scene of the attempted assassination by the king's brother Prince Frederick, Duke of York, who recognised the accused as being a member of the duke's own regiment that had fought at Turcoing. When questioned, Hadfield confirmed that he had indeed been with the duke since the day after 'the battle of Farmar' (although there is no formal record of a battle of this name). Giving evidence in Hadfield's trial at the Court of King's Bench, Westminster on 3 July of the same year, the duke gave his own views on Hadfield's state of mind at the time:

He said his life was forfeited; that he was tired of life, and that he regretted nothing but that his wife would only be a wife to him a few days longer. He said, once or twice, 'The worst has not happened yet.' During this time he did not portray the least appearance of derangement; he was as collected as person possibly could be. After his Majesty was gone, I remained to see the house searched. A perforation was traced 14 inches higher than where his Majesty sat, and on looking about a slug was found in the orchestra; there was a smell of powder about it.

Hadfield claimed insanity as a defence, but his apparently rational composure at the time of the event – along with the forethought needed to commit such an act – led the court to dismiss his plea. It was then decided that the accused's head injuries were the cause of his behaviour. Hadfield's own sister-in-law had given evidence to the court stating that he had threatened to kill his own child but that 'on other occasions he was extremely fond of the infant'. Hadfield had also informed his family that Jesus Christ was a 'bastard', and the Virgin Mary a 'whore'. This and other testimonies were enough for the court to dismiss the treason charge on the basis that Hadfield was not of sound mind – the verdict finally returned was one of 'Not Guilty, being under the influence of insanity at the time the act was done'. In such cases, the prisoner was often returned to the care of what family they might have, there not being facilities for the criminally insane within the British penal framework at the time.

In Hadfield's case, however, there was some nervousness as to the king's future safety, should he be allowed back into society. He needed to be kept somewhere secure, for the safety of both king and commoner – but where?

*   *   *

But is there so great Merit and Dexterity in being a mad Doctor? The common Prescriptions of a Bethlemitical Doctor are a Purge and a Vomit, and a Vomit and a Purge over again, and sometimes a Bleeding, which is no great mystery.

Alexander Cruden,
The London Citizen Exceedingly Injured, 1739

The doctors to which Cruden – a staunch moralist – was referring were those who staffed the Bethlem Royal Hospital, which in 1676 had moved from its original site in Bishopsgate to a much more prestigious purpose-built home in Moorfields. The area's reputation in the late 1700s can perhaps be summed up by the fact that the path that now runs along the south side of Finsbury Park was at the time known as *Sodomites Walk*, in acknowledgement of its popularity as a cruising area for gay men. Home to brothels, pickpockets and highwaymen, Moorfields was also the site of violent unrest during the Gordon Riots of 1780 when anti-Catholic sentiment boiled over, Moorfields' large Irish immigrant population and the open public spaces behind the Bethlem buildings making it an easy target for protestors.

The imposing building in which the second iteration of Bethlem Hospital was housed belied the misery within. The hospital's formal name had been corrupted to 'Bedlam' via colloquial pronunciation since the mid-1600s and the word itself would go on to become the accepted term for general lunacy. Built with the aim of impressing onlookers and potential donors rather than with the health and wellbeing of its unfortunate inmates in mind, Bethlem Hospital may have featured impressively airy corridors and huge viewing galleries, but these were for the use of visitors rather than patients, who were confined to small unsanitary cells for most of their time. The practice of allowing sightseers to pay a small entrance fee in return for viewing the patients much as animals in a zoo had been abandoned as inhumane in 1770, but the lack of public visiting had an unexpected and unpleasant side effect – with few people supervising them, the warders could abuse inmates freely without any risk of repercussion.

Patients were committed to Bethlem for conditions such as epilepsy (then known as 'falling sickness') and dementia, and some simply had what we would describe today as learning disabilities. 'Treatment' in Bethlem was harsh and based more on fear than rehabilitation; corporal punishment for anything seen as bad behaviour was common. Particularly restless inmates would have their activities restricted with manacles and chains, or be put into solitary isolation in the hope it would help them 'come to their senses'.

Stone pillars either side of the entrance gates to Bethlem carried carved stone figurines titled 'Melancholy' and 'Raving Madness', presumably intended to both advertise and warn of the perils that lay within. Rather than keeping the building compact and efficient, it was decided that the new hospital should be an example of architectural extravagance in order to impress those who might be persuaded to donate to the hospital's funds. Built as 'single pile', the corridors had rooms down only one side rather than both, in order to allow more space to those walking along them. Unfortunately for the patients under the hospital's care, it was rarely them using the extra space in Bethlem; they were more often than not restricted to their very bare and basic rooms. The new Bethlem was so grand and so similar to the French Tuilleries in its design that there was a (quite possibly apocryphal) rumour that Louis XIV took such offence at the association that he requested 'a plan of St James's Palace to be taken for offices of a very inferior nature' in response. By the turn of the nineteenth century the impressive building was all but uninhabitable, in no small part because it had been built over an area known as the 'City Ditch'. Part of the City's medieval defence system, the original ditch had been covered over in the sixteenth century after becoming filled with toxic waste. Known locally as the 'Hounds-ditch' because of the amount of dog carcasses dumped in it (canine skeletons thought to date back to Roman times were excavated as recently as the 1980s); there is still a street of the name today, connecting Bishopsgate and Aldgate. Sitting on top of centuries of filth and with no proper foundations of its own, the hospital's roof was leaking and the walls were slowly falling in on themselves. Bethlem was crumbling before it was even half-a-century old.

In the case of James Hadfield, there was no law that allowed authorities to imprison him 'just in case', because a verdict of insanity was, in effect, the equivalent of an acquittal. Any move to keep him in custody would, in any case, have been subject to a new and separate case in the civil courts. The Vagrancy Act of 1774 had occasionally been used to keep hold of those people that made the authorities nervous, but in Hadfield's situation the usual procedure would have been to release him into the care of his family.

Parliament therefore speedily introduced the Criminal Lunatics Act of 1800, which stated:

If [the jury] shall find that such person was insane at the time of the committing such offence, the court before whom such trial shall be had, shall order such person to be kept in strict custody, in such place and in such manner as to the court shall seem fit, until His Majesty's pleasure shall be known.

Hadfield was thus sent to Bethlem Hospital, then still based at Moorfields. When the hospital moved yet again, this time to St George's Fields in Southwark, Hadfield's continued presence led to a wing for the 'criminally insane' being built to house both men and women declared insane by the state. The new building was designed by James Lewis; later additions, including the central domed roof that gives what remains of the building its distinct look to this day, were the work of renowned architect Sydney Smirke.

In a section titled 'St George's Fields' in *Old and New London: volume 6*, published by Cassell, Petter and Galpin in 1878, Edward Walford describes Bethlem thus:

On entering the grand hall, the eye of the visitor is immediately attracted by the spacious staircase, which ascends from the ground-floor to the council chamber above. On either side passages run laterally through the building, the one to the right leading to the male, the other to the female wards. The basement and three floors are each divided into galleries. The basement gallery is paved with stone, and its ceiling arched with brickwork; the upper galleries are floored with wood, and the ceiling plated with iron.

One is struck on entering the female wards, not so much with the exquisite cleanliness of everything as with the air of taste and refinement which may be met with on either hand. The wards are long galleries, lighted on one side by large windows, in each of which stand globes of fish, fern-cases, or green-house plants; while the spaces between are occupied by pictures, busts, or cages containing birds.

The whole air of the place is light and cheerful; and although there is, of course, sad evidence of the purposes of the institution in some of the faces, as they sit brooding over the guarded fires which warm the corridors at intervals of about fifty yards, there is a large per-centage of inmates who look for the most part cheerful, and are either working at some business, reading, writing, or playing with the cats or parrots, which seem wisely to be allowed to them as pets.

Edward Wakefield was a leading campaigner for reform in the treatment of mental health, who made several inspection visits to Bethlem in 1814, when it was still at the Moorfields site. His report on conditions therein made for damning reading. He claimed that, among other issues, patients were mixed together in enclosed units with no thought to the safety of those meeker souls trapped with those who were more aggressive and disturbing in their behaviour. Wakefield made particular note of a man by the name of William (or John – records differ) Norris, an American soldier who had been kept in restraints – including an iron ring around his neck which was bolted into the wall – for at least twelve years.

Wakefield's reports, alongside earlier ones describing similar conditions at York Asylum, led to the establishment of the 1815 House of Commons Select Committee on Madhouses. Although the committee's inspection focused largely on the new and as yet uninhabited Bethlem site at St George's Fields rather than the dilapidated Moorfields buildings, they still found much of concern.

> Your Committee cannot however hesitate to suggest, with the utmost confidence, from the Evidence they now offer to the House, that some new provision of law is indispensably necessary for insuring better care being taken of Insane Persons, both in England and Ireland, than they have hitherto experienced; the number of whom appear to be very considerable; as the inquiries of the Committee have convinced them, that there are not in the Country a set of Beings more immediately requiring the protection of the Legislature than the persons in this state; a very large proportion of whom are entirely neglected by their relations and friends. If the treatment of those in the middling or in the lower classes of life, shut up in hospitals, private madhouses, or parish workhouses, is looked at, Your Committee are persuaded that a case cannot be found where the necessity for remedy is more urgent.

The report's comments on the design of the brand-new building illustrate just how deeply the negative attitudes towards the treatment and human requirements of psychiatric patients were ingrained.

> On entering the Gallery on the principal Floor, they [the inspection party] observed that the windows were so high as to prevent the Patients looking out; with the unfitness of which Your Committee were struck, ... that the greatest advantage might be derived from the Patients having opportunities of seeing objects that might amuse them. An alteration might be made in this respect ... at little expense, and with no risk of injury to the building; as it was stated ... that these windows were at first so constructed, but were afterwards built up at the lower part, on a suggestion that it would be inconvenient to expose the Patients to the view of passengers what passengers this might refer to is not specified; which inconvenience it is conceived might be very easily obviated.

> ...

> In the Sleeping Apartments the windows are not glazed, which Your Committee think deprives the Patients, generally, of a reasonable comfort, ... still more important, there are no flues constructed for the purpose of conducting warm air through the house, except in the lower Galleries.... This appears to be deserving of serious consideration, because it is represented that the Patients suffer sensibly from cold; and Doctor Munro, the Physician to the Hospital, stated, that it had not been thought advisable to administer medicines in the winter, on account of the cold of the house.

> ...

> In the Infirmary for Female Patients, there are only three small windows, at a great height, ... something should be done for ventilation, which might easily be accomplished.
>   The construction of the Privies appears to be very objectionable; ... And it seems doubtful, whether the drain passing under the beds, is on such a construction as will answer the intended purpose.
>   There is no room set apart for the reception of the dead bodies....

The Committee also notes that, although the new hospital benefited from being sited in the middle of large open grounds, very little of it was initially intended to be used for the benefit of patients, an issue which the report addresses quite sharply:

> There are eight acres of ground occupied for the Hospital, including the of the building, the airing-grounds, and one acre and an half intended for a kitchen garden; and there are nearly four acres more adjoining, which it is the intention of the Governors to turn to profit…. The Committee, however, think it may be expedient to submit to the considerate of Parliament, the propriety of enabling the Governors to devote this ground to the general purposes of the Hospital, from a conviction of the benefits the Patients derive from exercise, and in many cases from labour.

Regardless of the report's clear view that conditions should be drastically improved for psychiatric patients, it would be a very long time before patients saw any real change. Doctor Monro himself, once a consulting physician to King George III and mentioned in the Committee's report, was forced to resign in 1816 following allegations regarding his inhumane approach to patients under his care in Bethlem. The central block of the St George's Fields iteration of Bethlem has been the home of the Imperial War Museum since 1936, the reminders of mental insanity having been replaced by reminders of the insanity of war.

Chapter 3

The Killing Field

In a time of high unemployment and huge poverty, general unrest was growing alongside demands for the reformation of parliamentary representation. On 16 August 1819, cavalry troops armed with sabres charged into a crowd of thousands who had gathered to protest at St Peter's Field, Manchester. 'The Peterloo Massacre', as it became known, has been described as 'a political earthquake in the northern powerhouse of the Industrial Revolution'.

The Guardian newspaper is such a mainstay of modern British culture that it has spawned its own lexicon. '*Guardian* reader' is now a byword for anyone who is perceived as being even remotely left-leaning in their politics. Many of its current readership would perhaps have no idea that the newspaper that prides itself on reasoned liberal thinking was borne out of one of the greatest tragedies of the nineteenth century.

On the morning of 16 August 1819, crowds began to gather at St Peter's Field in Manchester. The protest had been organised to demonstrate against the grinding poverty and lack of democracy that was then endemic through most of British society. The intention from the start was that the demonstration should be as peaceable as possible; to that end, many women wore white clothing, men wore Sunday best and the crowd sang God Save The King, in order to demonstrate that their protests did not equate to anti-monarchism. Many children also attended.

The crowd had gathered to listen to famed political orator Henry Hunt, who was due to speak from the back of a cart being used as a makeshift hustings on the perimeter of the open space, near to Windmill Street (the Radisson hotel now stands on the site and has a blue plaque on its wall in memory of the event). Hunt was a wealthy farmer turned Radical, notorious for his belief in equal rights and suffrage for all. He had been invited by the *Manchester Observer*, a newspaper established by a group of radicals including James Wroe, the newspaper's only editor (and who would go on to coin the name 'Peterloo'). The *Observer's* liberal agenda did not sit well with those in authority, who were threatened by its growing influence.

By the time Hunt finally began addressing the crowd, there was approximately 60,000 in attendance. Many carried banners proclaiming their desire for 'Love', 'Suffrage' and 'Reform'. The authorities were convinced that Hunt's crowd was a potential threat, regardless of their peaceful stance and the many women and children involved. One only has to read the list of the military units in attendance that day to see that those in charge were intending to crack down hard as soon as they had what they perceived to be good enough reason. The Manchester Yeomanry were stationed in two separate groups to both the west and east of the crowds, ready to be called in. Again to the west, the Cheshire Yeomanry was at St John's Street with the 15th Hussars on Byrom Street. The 31st Regiment was to the north, on Brazennose Street. Closer still to the gathering crowds were the Royal Horse Artillery, tucked in on Lower Mosely Street near its junction with St Peter's Square. The 88th Regiment waited on Dickenson Street. In addition, a large contingent of special constables was in the Square itself. Reports of the numbers of military involved vary, but there were certainly many hundreds – if not a thousand or more – officers of varying rank around and in the crowd.

Local magistrates were watching proceedings from the windows of a house on Mount Street and, despite the crowd being generally well behaved, became alarmed by the sheer volume of people that were gathering. Leaning out of a window, they read the Riot Act to the crowd.

Rather than being nothing more than the turn of phrase we know today, in the nineteenth century, it referred to a literal 'reading of the Riot Act'. The Riot Act of 1714 gave officials the power to disperse anything considered a 'riotous gathering', on condition that warning was given and the gathering allowed an hour to disperse. The wording of the Riot Act was:

Our sovereign lord the King chargeth and commandeth all persons, being assembled, immediately to disperse themselves, and peaceably to depart to their habitations, or to their lawful business, upon the pains contained in the act made in the first year of King George, for preventing tumults and riotous assemblies. God save the King.

Several prosecutions under the Riot Act had been thrown out of court, due to the proclamation being read incorrectly or having had some words omitted (often the 'God save the King' section). There was also often confusion as to whether the warning had been issued at all, particularly in the face of noisy crowds. This was an era long before amplification, so a lone voice shouting a legal statement was often lost in the noise of the melee. Regardless, when the hour was up, officials were permitted to remove the crowd with force. More importantly, anyone given the task of doing so was immune from prosecution for any accident or injury caused to those being 'encouraged' to move on. This, unsurprisingly, gave free rein to aggressive behaviour that was often politically motivated. One of the most notable examples of this had already happened in 1780, when the Gordon Riots had taken place in St George's Fields in Southwark, South London and resulted in the deaths of at least six people. It would be nice to think that lessons had been learned, but those who had gathered to protest were about to have their peace shattered in the most horrific manner.

At approximately 1.40pm, shortly after Hunt began his speech to the waiting crowd, the magistrates gave orders for the Yeomanry to move in and seize the speakers. Reportedly led by Hugh Hornby Birley, a local mill owner and magistrate, the Yeomanry was made up of other mill and shop owners, many of whom had scores to settle with the leading protestors. One report claimed that a reporter from the *Manchester Observer* was spotted in the crowd by one of the Yeomans, who called out, 'There's Saxon, damn him! Run him through!' More than one contemporary report claimed that a large proportion of the Yeomanry were drunk when they went on the attack.

The crowd linked arms in an attempt to stop the arrests, but the armed Yeomans forced their way in on horseback – a terrible mistake, as the horses became panicked in the pressing crowds and began to rear and attempt to leap around. Unbalanced and trapped, the yeomanry hacked blindly at the crowd around them with the sabres they carried. Some reports say that an officer of the 15th Hussars attempted in vain to stop the bloody attack, but other officers viewed the Yeomans as the ones at a disadvantage and determined to attack the crowds themselves in order to aid their fellow officers' escape.

By 2pm, it was all over (although rioting by those furious at the authorities over the attack went on in nearby streets until the next morning). The final death toll for the Peterloo Massacre is generally accepted to be eighteen, including the unborn child of one Elizabeth Gaunt, who was held without trial for eleven days after the massacre and suffered a miscarriage as a result. Magistrates avoided blame wherever possible, including in the case of 2-year-old William Fildes, who was being carried across the road by his mother when they were both struck by a trooper from the Manchester Yeomanry, riding his horse at speed towards St Peter's Field. William's death was officially recorded as 'died from a fall from his mother's arms', with no mention of the incident. Another whitewashed death was that of John Rhodes, who died three months later, having suffered a sabre wound to the head in the attack. Magistrates insisted that Rhodes's body be dissected in an attempt to prove his death bore no relation to Peterloo, despite his head injury – the coroner duly recorded a verdict of 'natural causes'.

Having reported the massacre in detail at the expense of the authorities – and, via Wroe, giving it the name 'Peterloo' – the *Manchester Observer* was a constant target for malicious prosecutions from that day forward, brought on behalf of the authorities who saw it as a threat to the establishment. It ceased publication in 1821 after the Wroe family had suffered endless prosecutions and imprisonments. The *Manchester Guardian* (the foundation stone of today's *Guardian*) having just been established, the *Observer*'s last editorial included the following recommendation:

> I would respectfully suggest that the *Manchester Guardian*, combining principles of complete independence, and zealous attachment to the cause of reform, with active and spirited management, is a journal in every way worthy of your confidence and support.

Henry Hunt was arrested for high treason and later found guilty of the lesser charge of seditious conspiracy. He was sentenced to thirty months in Ilchester Gaol. The motives behind his incarceration were almost certainly concerned more with the potential threat from his radical beliefs on the business and financial interests of the establishment, rather than his personal involvement with the terrible events of a summer's day in Manchester.

Chapter 4

The Foundling Factories

About fifty miles south of Dublin, Ireland, sits Carlow, a county town that during the fourteenth century served as the country's capital. But 400 years later Carlow was a very different place, the Great Famine wiping out much of its population and leaving many people in abject poverty and desperate for any way to survive. Even so, the case being heard at Carlow Assizes on 4 April 1801 was shocking in the extreme. The defendant, Mary Doyle, was being tried on charges of taking babies into her care in order to gain the payments offered for their care – and then purposely letting them die.

The Dublin Foundling Hospital had been established in 1704, with the intention of giving some hope of salvation to those babies and children whose parents could not care for them. And they were many, for not only had poverty and famine ripped through Ireland, society and cultural standards of the time were strict by any standards and tied to the country's Catholic religion. The hospital might have begun with good intentions, but it was soon being overwhelmed by the sheer volume of children handed into its care via the no-questions-asked policy. The shame and stigma that came with illegitimacy – along with strict religious policies against birth control – meant that it wasn't long before savvy middlemen and women realised that they could charge a fee for collecting unwanted babies and delivering them to Dublin. For the reluctant mother who had no way of keeping her child, this would have seemed a preferable option to the more usual method of simply abandoning the child in the open to take their (very small) chance with nature.

The children were treated as a product to be moved by the carriers, rather than living creatures in need of care and tenderness. They would be bundled together in a large basket and bounced along the road to Dublin either on horseback or by cart, and many tales were told of babies arriving at the hospital either with broken bones or already dead. Those children who did survive the journey would not find themselves in a much better position even after they were admitted to the hospital. Conditions were dire, with sickly children left to die and those who survived often treated very harshly.

In November 1799, a young woman named Margaret Collins was accepted by the hospital as 'nurse' (more akin to what we would today describe as a foster carer) for Michael Slain, a baby boy of only a few months old. On the recommendation of a local priest, the Reverend McNeil, Margaret was to take on Michael as her own and would be paid a small stipend for doing so. Along with the baby, she was given what clothes he had, as well as five shillings towards her expenses. Margaret took Michael with her to lodge at the home of Ann Vignes, telling her that the baby was her own. The pair stayed with Ann for just a few days before leaving on their travels – a move which Ann presumably didn't find surprising, as she already knew Margaret under her real name of Mary Doyle – 'a woman of infamous character', and of no fixed abode.

What clearly did startle Ann was Mary's reappearance a month or so later, this time with a different child in tow. Doyle was more open about the baby's origins on this visit, telling Ann that his name was John Ball and he had been procured from the Foundling Hospital. Ann was horrified by the condition John arrived in, describing him as 'naked and nearly dead from starvation and cold'. Mary freely admitted to having been given 'two suits of clothes and a yard of diaper' for the baby's care, which she had immediately sold. Upset at hearing John crying from hunger during the night, Ann resorted to keeping back some of what food she had for her own baby and feeding John as well, in the hope of saving him. Despite Ann's protestations, Mary insisted on taking John with her to beg on the streets and, when Ann pleaded with her not to take him out in the cold again, replied, 'The Devil's cure to it!' and said she would simply sell him and get a replacement from the hospital. Mary attempted to sell John for a crown (the equivalent of twenty-five pence at the time, or something just above £10 in today's currency – but a much more sizeable amount in 1800, when it was the equivalent of a day's wage for a skilled tradesperson), but no one was willing to pay her. It's likely that most simply didn't have the money, let alone the financial and emotional wherewithal to take on the responsibility for a tiny infant so close to death's door.

In desperation, Ann herself eventually gave Mary just under four shillings and took John from her. She found Reverend McNeil, and when he heard what had happened, he brought clothes for John. Despite all efforts, John weakened further and died, even though Ann had weaned her own baby in order to feed him herself as his wet nurse. In the meantime Mary had also confessed to Ann the events that had befallen baby Michael, the first child she'd brought with her to the Vignes house the previous December. She had intended to take him to Dublin and began the journey there with her sister, but the two women had quarrelled along the way and one of them had laid Michael down in the snow. He had rapidly died from the cold and Mary claimed they buried him in a nearby churchyard – but not before removing his clothes, which she then sold. She then spoke of another child previous to the two already known about, saying she'd also had a baby of her own at the time and as she wasn't producing enough milk for two infants, they had both died.

While giving evidence in court, Ann Vignes produced an identity badge from the foundling hospital. She said she had found it in her house after Mary had left, and believed it to have belonged to Michael Slain. Called to identify the badge, the hospital's apothecary William Lindsay confirmed that it indeed corresponded to the details held in the hospital's records.

The Sun reported the charges against Mary with – perhaps justifiably – hyperbolic horror:

procuring Infant Children from the Foundling Hospital, under false pretences, as a nurse; robbing them of the covering with they received from the ... institution; then starving the unfortunate infant, to render its miserable appearance an object to excite compassion; and, when famine and nakedness had reduced it to the last extremity, selling it to some person who would carry it to town ... leaving it afterwards to perish.—Mary Doyle had practised that traffic, which disgraced the very name of the human species : the most ferocious of the brute creation protected their young; but Mary Doyle, though in human form, destroyed the innocent infants which she was bound by humanity, duty and trust, to protect and nourish.

The Sun (London), Saturday, 18 April 1801

The problem the court faced was that, however negligent Mary had clearly been towards the children in her care, there was no proof that she had definitively intended them to die. Frustration with the case is evident in records of comments made by the judge, Lord Norbury, who described Doyle as a 'wretch who was clearly guilty of the most barbarous and inhuman conduct', and proclaimed his sorrow that her offence could only be tried as a misdemeanour. Norbury did what he could within the restrictions of the law – Mary was sentenced to 'stand three times in the pillory', followed by a year's imprisonment, after which she was to be deemed a vagabond and transported for life.

Chapter 5

The Shores of Botany Bay

Those such as Mary Doyle who were deemed unworthy of being kept in their home country would often be labelled a 'vagabond' – a vagrant, of no fixed employment or abode – and shipped out of the country as an inconvenience to be moved elsewhere. The history of the wholesale transportation of convicts from Great Britain to its colonies – most notably Australia – is a well known one, but what is often forgotten is just how easy it was to be convicted of a transportable offence. This author's own many-times-great uncle was transported to Australia in 1832, for the crime of larceny. In contrast to burglary (breaking into a structure in order to steal) or robbery (taking from a person with the use of force), larceny was (and still is) theft without force against either people or property. Many of the convictions for larceny in the eighteenth and nineteenth centuries involved theft of items that we today would consider trivial – a loaf of bread, perhaps, or a few coins from someone's table. Stealing has always been frowned upon for obvious reasons, but the temptation to do so is perhaps more understandable when we consider the context of the conditions in which the poorest sections of society were living at the time. Theft of any item worth more than five shillings was punishable by transportation. If your only choice is to starve to death – or watch your children starve – then it is perhaps forgivable that you might decide to take your chances in stealing food, or a few coins, in order to buy bread. But theft was theft, and punished as such.

Simply being without a home was also a crime in itself. The Vagrancy Act is still in force across England and Wales to this day, although pressure to repeal it has grown in recent years (both Scotland and Ireland have long left it behind). Generally, modern-day policing and other social structures interpret the Act liberally in comparison to the Georgian era (even the current law dates back to 1824, when the Vagrancy Act replaced the Vagabonds Act of 1597). But in the late 1700s and early 1800s, the laws available to the courts to rid areas of what the locals might consider to be 'undesirables' were being used to their fullest extent.

The 'Bloody Code' isn't a phrase that anyone would have recognised at the time, but it has since become shorthand for the period towards the end of the 1700s when upwards of 200 different crimes were punishable by death. The sheer scale of offences that could earn the culprit the death sentence made the system cumbersome and almost impossible to enforce. The amount of capital offenders was so high in itself that the wider public were beginning to question the number of death sentences passed in Britain and to wonder whether there wasn't perhaps a better alternative. Transportation had already been widely used during the eighteenth century, when tens of thousands of British men, women and children convicted of crimes of varying severity were shipped out to the Americas. But by the end of the century, the American Revolutionary War had put paid to Britain's use of its land as a dumping ground for the unwanted and alternatives had to be found. Prisons had fallen into being used as not much more than holding pens for those awaiting trial and/or execution, and as such were wholly unsuitable for long-term containment.

Those prisoners still sentenced to transportation – but with nowhere to be transported to – were held on prison 'hulks'. These were disused warships moored at various points in London, as well as Portsmouth, Plymouth and Chatham in Kent. Conditions were appalling and only got worse as time went on, making the need for somewhere else to hold prisoners more urgent than ever. Even the renowned battle ship *Victory*, having done her duty with Vice Admiral Nelson, did a stint as a prison hulk moored off Gosport in Hampshire between 1813 and 1817. Conditions on board the moored ships were appalling, with an estimated 25 per cent of prisoners dying every year, either from disease or as a result of the violence that was endemic in such crowded and tense situations.

Captain James Cook had travelled to the southern hemisphere in the summer of 1768 on an expedition to track the transit of Venus across the sun, in order to establish the distance between sun and earth. As a sort of side quest on his journey, he had also been tasked with investigating the possibility of the existence of *Terra Australis Icognita* – 'undiscovered southern land'.

On 13 May 1787, the 'First Fleet' set off for this new continent. The fleet was made up of a retinue of eleven ships (two Royal Navy escort vessels, three supply transports and six convict transports) carrying several hundred officers, crew and their families along with 789 convicts and their children (exact figures have never been established due to lack of formal records, but what is certain is that the numbers had dropped by the time the ships arrived, due to deaths en route). Australia was now the destination of (little) choice of those who Britain no longer wished to house on its home shores, but who didn't quite deserve the death penalty.

Many of those convicts may have wished fervently that they had, indeed, been sentenced to death – transportation took upwards of 250 days, mostly in appalling conditions. Regulations for the treatment of convicts did exist, but were not always heeded – and those ships carrying female prisoners were often hotbeds of sexual transactions and transgressions on the part of both prisoners and their captors. The *Morning Chronicle* reported in 1819 of the practice – by then supposedly forcibly phased out – of officers and seamen picking out the women with which they wished to 'associate' during the long journey to the Australian colonies. It is unlikely that the women had any choice in the matter, although it was often the safest option – being 'attached' to a man aboard the ship, whether an officer or a fellow convict, gave a measure of security in very difficult conditions. Although the female convicts were sometimes referred to as 'courtesans', prostitution wasn't a transportable offence and most had merely been convicted of either petty theft or disorderly behaviour.

One of the most notable ships that carried female convicts was the *Lady Juliana*. She and her human cargo left Plymouth on 29 July 1789 and didn't arrive in Port Jackson until 3 June 1790, making her journey of 309 days one of the longest of any among the convict ships of the time. Surprisingly, given the length of time she was at sea, conditions on board the *Juliana* were better than one might expect. Of the 226* women who boarded the ship in England, 222 were still alive to disembark when she finally arrived at her destination. In fact there were at least one or two very small passengers disembarking at Port Jackson who *hadn't* been on the ship when she first set sail. A ship crewed by thirty-five men and carrying over 200 women as its cargo was inevitably going to see its share of intimate behaviour. The men onboard the *Juliana* were said to have each chosen a 'wife' of their own from the assembled convicts, in order to provide company and entertainment for the journey, and some of these couplings inevitable resulted in offspring.

Sarah Whitlam was, on paper at least, a shoplifter. In her late teens or early twenties, she was convicted at Lincoln Assizes of stealing 'cloth and clothing', despite her protestations that she had, in fact, simply borrowed a 'mantle' (a cloak or shawl) from an acquaintance who had then accused her of theft. Whatever the truth behind her supposed crime, Sarah found herself on the *Lady Juliana*, where she met Scotsman John Nicol, a member of the crew. Whitlam conceived and gave birth to Nicol's son during the journey, but the couple were separated on arrival at Port Jackson, Nicol returning to Britain with his ship and Whitlam being sent on to Norfolk Island along with her infant. Presumably pragmatic about the minimal options available to improve her chances in a new land, Whitlam married a fellow convict soon afterwards. John Nicol went on to write his autobiography, which includes much about his experiences on the *Juliana*. His first-person account is a strange mixture of unexpected kindness and a flat straightforwardness about the realities of managing a ship full of women of varying standards of virtue.

We lay six months in the river before we sailed [Nicol is referring to the time the ship spent moored at Plymouth before she began her journey], during which time all the jails in England were emptied to complete the cargo of the *Lady Juliana*. When we sailed there were on board 245 female convicts.** There was not a great many very bad characters. The greater proportion were for petty crimes, and a great proportion for only being disorderly, that is, street-walkers, the colony at the time being in great want of women.

One, a Scottish girl, broke her heart and died in the river. She was buried at Dartford [...] The poor young Scottish girl I have never yet got out of my mind. She was young and beautiful, even in the convict dress, but pale as death, and her eyes red with weeping. She never spoke to any of the other women or came on deck. She was constantly seen sitting in the same corner from morning to night. Even the time of meals roused her not. My heart bled for her—she was a countrywoman in misfortune. I offered her consolation but her hopes and heart had sunk. When I spoke she heeded me not, or only answered with sighs and tears. If I spoke of Scotland she would wring her hands and sob until I thought her heart would burst. I endeavoured to get her sad story from her lips but she was silent as the grave to which she hastened. I lent her my Bible to comfort her but she read it not. She laid it on her lap after kissing it, and only bedewed it with her tears. At length she sunk into the grave of no disease but a broken heart.

The captain and crew of the *Lady Juliana* were clearly not without empathy, and allowed some limited visiting during the months the ship was moored at Plymouth. Nicol recounts the story of a mother and father who had been searching for their missing daughter:

One day I had the painful task to inform the father and mother of one of the convicts that their daughter, Sarah Dorset, was on board. They were decent-looking people, and had come to London to inquire after her. When I met them they were at Newgate. The jailor referred them to me. With tears in her eyes the mother implored me to tell her if such a one was on board. I told them there was one of that name. The father's heart seemed too full to allow him to speak but the mother with streaming eyes blessed God that they had found their poor lost child, undone as she was.

I called a coach, drove to the river and had them put on board. The father with a trembling step, mounted the ship's side, but we were forced to lift the mother on board. I took them down to my berth and went for Sarah Dorset. When I brought her the father said in a choking voice, 'My lost child!' and turned his back, covering his face with his hands. The mother, sobbing, threw her hands around her. Poor Sarah fainted and fell at their feet. I knew not what to do. At length she recovered and in the most heartrending accents implored their pardon. She was young and pretty and had not been two years from her father's house at this present time, so short had been her course of folly and sin. She had not been protected by the villain that ruined her above six weeks, then she was forced by want upon the streets and taken up as a disorderly girl, then sent on board to be transported. This was her short but eventful history. One of our men, William Power, went out to the colony when her time was expired, brought her home and married her.

The vast majority of women transported on the *Lady Juliana* and ships like her were in similar situations to that of Sarah Dorset. Nicol himself says, 'the far greater number were harmless unfortunate creatures, the victims of the basest seduction'. Nicol appears to acknowledge the imbalance of power between the ship's male crew and its human cargo, already broken and rejected for simply, well, being human. That's not to say that onboard relationships weren't often engaged in for genuine reasons.

> When we were fairly out to sea, every man on board took a wife from among the convicts, they nothing loath. The girl with whom I lived, for I was as bad in this point as the others, was named Sarah Whitlam. She was a native of Lincoln, a girl of modest reserved turn, as kind and true a creature a creature that ever live. I courted her for a week and upwards, and would have married her on the spot had there been a clergyman on board. She had been banished for a mantle she had borrowed from an acquaintance. Her friend prosecuted her for stealing it, and she was transported for seven years. I had fixed my fancy upon her from the moment I knocked the rivet out of her irons upon my anvil, and as firmly resolved to bring her back to England when her time was out, my lawful wife, as ever I did intend anything in my life. She bore me a son in our voyage out. What is become of her, whether she is dead or alive, I know not.

The convicts were not above making their own fun, by any devious means necessary. Occasions of misbehaviour were punished by the culprit being confined to the hold, but this appeared to be of little deterrent, Nicol commenting that 'they became in turns outrageous, on purpose to be confined'. He soon found out why:

> I, as steward, found it out by accident. As I was overhauling the stores in the hold I came upon a hogshead of bottled porter with a hole in the side of it and, in place of full, there were nothing but empty bottles in it. ... I immediately told the captain, who now found out the cause of the late insubordination and desire of confinement.
>
> We were forced to change the manner of punishing them.... I was desired ... to take an old flour barrel and cut a hole in the top for their

head and one on each side for their arms. This we called a wooden jacket. Next morning, Nance Ferrel, as usual, came to the door of the cabin and began to abuse the agent and captain. They desired her to go away between decks and be quiet. She became worse in her abuse, wishing to be confined and sent to the hold, but to her mortification the jacket was produced, and two men brought her upon deck and put it on. She laughed and capered about for a while, and made light of it. One of her comrades lighted a pipe and gave it to her. She walked about strutting and smoking the tobacco, and making the others laugh at the droll figure she made. She walked a minuet, her head moving from side to side like a turtle.

She began to get weary and begged to be released … but in a few days was as bad as ever. There was no taming her by gentle means. We were forced to tie her up like a man, and give her one dozen with the cat-o'-nine-tails, and assure her of a clawing every offence. This alone reduced her to any kind of order.

There was fun to be had, despite everything, but as always Nicol's accounts are tinged with reminders of the harshness of life on board a convict ship, especially one carrying women. On the occasion of crossing the Equator, he writes,

In crossing the line we had the best sport I had ever witnessed upon the same occasion. We had caught a porpoise the day before the ceremony which we skinned to make a dress for Neptune with the tail studded. When he came on deck he looked the best representation of a merman I ever saw, painted, with a large swab upon his head doe a wig. Not a man in the ship could have known him. One of the convicts fainted, she was so much alarmed at his appearance, and had a miscarriage after.

Whitlam and Nicol's child wasn't even the youngest on board the *Lady Juliana* by the time she docked in Port Jackson – that honour went to the baby daughter of Mary Pardoe, another convict who had become pregnant by seaman Edward Scott. Scott had also been forced to leave with the ship on its return journey, leaving Mary another single mother in a new country. Mary would go on to have three more children with

Peter Hibbs, a member of the First Fleet who had stayed on after his own arrival on the southern continent. Ten years Mary's senior, Hibbs met his convict wife after she was sent to Norfolk Island soon after her arrival. The pair eventually married and were still together at her death in 1844, when she was approximately 77 years old. Mary and Peter are buried together in the Wisemans Ferry Cemetery in Laughtondale, a suburb of Sydney, New South Wales.

The female convicts on board the *Lady Juliana*, along with many women who were convicted and transported on other ships during the period, are often recorded as having been prostitutes, but even those such as Nicol seemed to be aware that this was unlikely – it didn't stop the *Lady Juliana* becoming known as 'the floating brothel'. It was said that, when the ship called in at ports along its journey to Australia, seamen from other ships moored in the area would be 'entertained' by the women and that the ship's crew made no attempt to quell such activities.

There was business-minded logic behind the transport of convicts, as well as the desire to remove them from the home country. Rather than being incarcerated on home soil at the government's expense, the logic ran, better to send those convicted of crimes to the colonies and put them to work building new outposts for the burgeoning British Empire. Sentences of transportation were for seven years, fourteen years or life, dependent on the severity of the original crime, and those who had completed their sentence could, in theory, return to Britain. The expense of a return journey was, however, beyond the realms of possibility for the vast majority of ex-convicts and as a result, many of them stayed on and built a life for themselves in Australia. It's estimated that, as of 2020, approximately 20 per cent of Australians can trace their family tree back to a convict ancestor.

* * *

* Exact figures for those transported on the *Lady Juliana* are difficult to confirm. When she set off from Plymouth she was officially carrying 226 convicts, five of whom died en route.

** John Nicol's contemporary account states that the ship transported 247 women, while convict records available today list 246 names, some of which are possibly duplicates.

Chapter 6

Breaking News

Newspapers had been in existence in Britain since the late 1600s, but really started coming into their own in the eighteenth century with the launch of the *Daily Courant* which, as the name suggests, was the first 'daily' paper. By the time of the Regency there were several dailies in existence, and with the launch of the *Observer* in 1791, media became a seven-day a week presence. As printing presses developed, it became cheaper to produce larger and more regular newspapers – as circulation increased, advertising began to take up more space, turning the media into the beginning of the commercial industry we know today. Although most covered general news and commerce, by the end of the century certain publications were beginning to show political bias. By 1772, John Wilkes's campaign for increased freedom of the press led to newspapers gaining the right to publish parliamentary records.

Born the son of a Surrey farmer, William Cobbett might have had a very different life had he not, at the age of 20, decided to take a spur of the moment trip to London. His jaunt turned into several months working as a clerk at Gray's Inn, before spending nine years in the army, his last and longest posting being a stint in New Brunswick, on the east coast of what is now Canada. Cobbett returned home to Britain in 1791 carrying the rank of sergeant major, along with a major grudge about the venality he had witnessed among his fellow officers. Such corruption was widespread in much of public life and office, but Cobbett was a rarity in being someone who actually wanted to do something about it. His first steps into the world of radical pamphleteering was with the publication of *The Soldier's Friend* in 1792, which laid out his thoughts on corruption in the armed forces. Despite a growing public awareness of the issues – or perhaps because of it – the officers Cobbett laid accusations against brought counter-charges against him. Initially fleeing to France to avoid being court martialled, Cobbett's arrival coincided with the swelling fury of the French Revolution – Louis XVI would be beheaded in January

1793, followed rapidly by the National Convention threatening war on Britain – and it was not a good time for an Englishman to be travelling in newly republican France. Cobbett quickly made arrangements to sail to America and settled in Philadelphia.

Cobbett made his name as a journalist with the publication of *Observations on the Emigration of Joseph Priestley*, a sharply barbed attack about the circumstances surrounding the arrival of radical scientist Priestley on American shores. On Priestley's large claim for damages after the Birmingham riots of 1791 (now generally known as the 'Priestley Riots') resulted in the destruction of his manuscripts, Cobbett wrote, 'if they were to be estimated by those he had published for some years before, their destruction was a benefit instead of a loss, both to himself and his country'. Cobbett's reputation as a viciously conservative writer developed over the years as he published ever more polemics railing against American democracy, earning him the nickname 'Peter Porcupine', but after being fined heavily for libel, he returned to England in 1800.

William Pitt's Tory government saw their opportunity and offered to subsidise Cobbett's work, but regardless of his political beliefs, he refused to be beholden to others. In 1802, Cobbett launched the *Political Register*, which initially supported Pitt's government but rapidly developed its own political voice. In the meantime, Cobbett found time to establish a collection of transcripts of Parliamentary debates going back to the eleventh century, before yet another run-in with authority (in the form of a critical 1810 article in *The Register* against the flogging of soldiers who had refused to pay for their own equipment as they were also due missing wages) saw Cobbett in court on charges of treasonous libel. Sentenced to two years in Newgate, Cobbett didn't let imprisonment quieten his voice and the *Political Register* continued to be published throughout his incarceration.

Financial difficulties on his release from Newgate left Cobbett with no option but to sell the one thing of value he owned – his collection of political records. This archive is now better known under the name of the man who bought it from Cobbett – T.N. Hansard.

Chapter 7

The Art of Falling Apart

Political cartoons are commonplace nowadays, appearing in most newspapers, with their sharpness of humour defined by the political and intellectual wit of the end audience. Criticism of the monarchy and political systems, either by ourselves or others, is something we have come to expect as our right. But despite the thousands of words and hundreds of pages of newsprint expended on reporting such events on a daily basis, a simply drawn cartoon often makes the clearest point. Artists such as Gerald Scarfe and Steve Bell are seemingly able to disseminate an entire governmental crisis with a few sharp strokes of their pen, their talent for mimicry and caricature slicing through the fat and down to the very heart of the matter in hand.

The history of political caricature is a long and educated one; it would be possible to learn almost all one really needs to know of modern British history simply by scanning through newspaper cartoons of the last 300 years. One of the best known of these is William Hogarth, whose serialised works *Marriage a-la-Mode* and *A Rake's Progress*, cast sharp opinion on the behaviour of others without a word being written. *Gin Lane*, another of Hogarth's most famous works, is itself a potential example of bias in media representation, Hogarth having supposedly been persuaded into producing the work – along with its sister-piece, *Beer Street* – as propaganda for the Gin Act of 1751, in which sales of the imported spirit were restricted in order to promote the consumption of British ale.

James Gillray was one of Hogarth's biggest fans. Born to a strictly Protestant household, the young Gillray had been sent to a boarding school run by the Moravian Brethren when he was only 5. If the strictly regulated surroundings were not enough to prompt some level of rebelliousness in the young boy, then the death of his older brother Johnny there at the age of 8, along with the Brethren's beliefs that he had gone to a happier place despite his tender age, surely did. Gillray became apprenticed to an engraver in Cumbria when he was 14 and showed a talent for painting and drawing. Eventually returning to London when he was 19, he developed a working relationship with renowned printmakers William Humphrey and his sister Hannah that would last the rest of his life.

After a stint at the Royal Academy, and having honed his etching and printing skills with the Humphreys, Gillray began to stretch out into caricature. 'Stretch out' is a misnomer, as caricatures of the time relied on wit rather than excessive artistry, but Gillray used elements taken from Hogarth in order to add to his imagery. By the time he produced his infamous work *Temperance Enjoying A Frugal Meal* in 1792, the acerbic detail is astounding, with seemingly every inch of the print containing a barbed jibe at the king and queen. Their purported miserliness is illustrated in everything from the unlit fire, to the scales (commonly used at the time for weighing guineas) on the mantel. In contrast, the pair to the image – *A Voluptuary Under the Horrors of Digestion* – shows George, Prince of Wales, as an over-indulging profligate who's immoderate ways and their consequences are illustrated by the array of remedies for various intimate ailments that sit on a shelf close by. If the tablets 'for the piles' and the bottle of 'Leake's Pills' (a quack remedy for sexually transmitted disease) weren't enough, the chamber pot that Gillray illustrates as overflowing onto a pile of unpaid bills illustrates the opposing public images that the king and his eldest son had at the time.

As with almost everything Gillray produced during his career as a cartoonist, *Temperance* was printed and published by Hannah Humphrey on behalf of the family firm. Hannah would display Gillray's work in the shop window, outside which people would gather to view his latest savage judgment. Rumours abounded as to the true nature of James and Hannah's relationship, but given that Gillray's portrayal of Hannah as an elderly lady in *Two-Penny Whist* (1796) is believed to be accurate, one must assume that the age gap was either too extreme for there to be any intimate relationship, or if there was, they kept it well hidden precisely because they knew it would be frowned upon.

Gillray had complained to a friend as early as 1795 – when he was only 39 years old – of being troubled by what he thought was rheumatism. By 1807 it was said that he was struggling with failing eyesight, but his work continued to be of high standard. What is perhaps more likely is that Gillray was beginning to suffer with mental health issues, possibly exacerbated by drinking; his pace of work slowed down dramatically and he didn't always meet deadlines with the reliability he had once managed. He was certainly beginning to struggle with life, whatever the reasons behind it – in 1811, he attempted to jump out of an attic room window above the Humphreys' shop, only for his head to become jammed in the iron bars. He was rescued after the alarm was raised by a gentleman coming out of White's Club and, according to newspaper reports of the time, had 'proper persons appointed to take care of him' (presumably Hannah Humphrey).

In his 1965 biography of Gillray, the American political cartoonist Draper Hill said of this period, '[he] lapsed into a state of insanity that continued, with only occasional lucid intervals, until his death in June of 1815'. Despite being of sound enough mind to occasionally start new art works, Gillray rarely finished them before lapsing back into mental illness. On one occasion he insisted that he was actually the famous painter Rubens. There are reports of Gillray making at least two more attempts on his own life, before he eventually succeeded. One day in late May 1815, he again threw himself out of an upstairs window onto St James's Street and was, again, nursed by Hannah Humphrey until he died a few days later on 1 June at the age of 58. Other than a brief paragraph in a gentleman's magazine, Gillray's death went entirely unnoticed.

Chapter 8

Pride Comes Before a Fall

The advent of the magazine industry brought 'fashion trends' as we know them today to a wider audience and later in the Regency era, industrial sewing began in earnest, bringing mass-produced clothes within reach of more people then ever before.

With revolution in France and rumblings on home shores, ostentatious clothing began to make way for more understated fashions as the upper classes realised it wasn't always wise to look eye-catchingly wealthy. Clothing became simpler in both shape and fabric – for men as well as women – but there was still potential for awkward situations. Some women carried a bourdaloue, or 'carriage pot' with them on journeys or trips to the theatre – the portable chamber pot would be slipped beneath the lady's long skirts in order to enable reasonably discreet ablutions when away from one's own chamber.

This was the age of the dandy, during which fashionable gents thought nothing of spending literally hours getting dressed. By far the best known of these dapper chaps was Beau Brummell, whose dedication to the decadent cause was such that he allegedly liked to have his boots washed with the best champagne.

George Bryan Brummell was born in 1778. The boy who would eventually become the most famous of all dandies found his place in society through his father, William Brummell, who had been private secretary to Lord North before becoming High Sheriff of Berkshire in 1788. The grandson of a shopkeeper – albeit one who rented lodgings to the aristocracy – Brummell developed his particular style at a young age. Using his time at Eton to hone both his wit and his networking skills, Brummell furthered his study at Oriel College Oxford, but left after only one term in order to take up a commission with the 10th (Prince of Wales's Own) Light Dragoons regiment. More commonly known as the Royal Hussars, the regiment was renowned for the extravagant uniforms required of its officers and the heavy financial cost for the prestige of being a member. Although commissioned as a cornet, the lowest rank of officer in a cavalry troop, Brummell would still have been expected to live up to the regiment's reputation for profligacy in both fashion and finance.

Brummell's taste for the finer things in life was helped along by the death of his father in 1794, which brought with it an inheritance of £20,000 (equivalent to more than £2.5 million in today's money). He certainly cut a dash in military circles, despite an unfortunate incident soon after he joined the Hussars, in which his horse threw him off in front of a large audience at a military parade in Brighton, breaking his nose and making his profile 'interesting' rather than purely handsome. Brummell's ostentatious habits brought him to the attention of the Prince of Wales and the two men rapidly became close friends – indeed, Brummell was one of those friends that Caroline would later blame for ruining her honeymoon by encouraging her new husband's drunkenness. This royal connection enabled Brummell to flout the rules while still being promoted up the ranks – a situation which infuriated the older and more experienced members of the regiment. Brummell's military career was, however, short-lived. When his regiment transferred to Manchester in 1797 he resigned his commission, declaring that he 'had not enlisted for foreign service'.

Regardless of his wealth and social influence, Brummell put great superstitious store in a 'lucky' sixpence that he insisted on always carrying about his person. There are different stories as to whether a friend originally gave it to him or whether he in fact found it in the gutter of Berkely Street in Mayfair while walking home from an evening's gambling. What *is* known is that Brummell soon became convinced that his good luck at the gambling table was down to its presence in his pocket. And then, late one night after a lengthy drinking session, Brummell took a hackney cab home – and accidentally used his lucky shilling to pay the fare.

High tastes and social contacts weren't enough to prevent Beau Brummell's eventual fall from grace. He had a habit of coming out with witty comments at the expense of those around him and even Prince George's royal status wasn't enough to save him from the dandy's acid tongue. The most popular story among the litany of incidents leading to Brummell's downfall tells of him being ignored by the prince at Watier's (an exclusive gentleman's club in Piccadilly that had been founded by Prince George) in 1813, prompting Brummell to remark sneeringly to

Lord Alvanley, who was standing with the prince, 'Alvanley, who's your fat friend?'

No member of royalty was going to let a comment like that slide without some form of retaliation, but it's unlikely that the Watier's incident – however rude – was the sole reason Prince George turned his back on Brummell. The far more likely nail in the fraternal coffin was Brummell's continuing attitude towards the prince's mistress, Maria Fitzherbert. Whether Maria took against him because of his influence over her royal lover or simply because of his generally unpleasant attitude isn't clear, but Brummell certainly went out of his way to ruffle her feathers as often as possible. Newspaper reports of the time note that Brummell was even attempting to sully her name with the prince himself. Perhaps the dandy simply didn't like sharing the royal attention. He didn't bother to hide his disdain for Maria, even when dining privately with the lady herself, alongside her Prince. When George commented in amusement, 'So I hear they've given me the soubriquet 'Big Ben',' Maria responded, 'Perhaps they will find one for me next.' Rather than taking the sensible route through the conversation and staying quiet, the acerbic Brummell responded, 'yes, they may call you 'Big Benina''. Whatever the motives behind it, the tension between Brummell and Mrs Fitzherbert was such that George had personally intervened and on at least one occasion had asked his friend to be kinder to his mistress.

After finally falling out disastrously and irrevocably with the Prince Regent in 1816, Brummell fled to Calais. Now all but penniless, he survived on the generosity of friends, including Lord Alvanley (who himself eventually ran out of money and was forced to sell the family estates in order to survive). Brummell's personal belongings were sold at auction to pay his debts after his exile abroad and when the auctioneer opened a particularly fine snuffbox, a note fell out. A snark to the end, in Brummell's own handwriting was allegedly written, 'This snuff-box was intended for the Prince Regent, if he had conducted himself with more propriety towards me.'

Beau Brummell, once the accepted leader of glamorous society and fashion, died in poverty-stricken insanity (caused by the effects of end-stage syphilis) in 1840 at Le Bon Saveur Asylum, Caen.

Chapter 9

Venus in Furs

Saartjie (sometimes styled as 'Sara') Baartman, was born in 1789, near the Gamtoos River in what is now the Eastern Cape of South Africa. Despite being generally known by variations on the Baartman name, she was actually named Ssehura by her parents. Khoikhoi by birth, Ssehura lost her mother when she was 2 years old, and her father was killed when she was still an adolescent. The young girl had a condition called 'steatopygia' – an excessive build-up of body fat, which causes hugely protuberant buttocks (and also, in Ssehura's case, exceptionally enlarged labia). This undoubtedly made her more noticeable than most girls of her status as the time. As an older teenager, Ssehura was persuaded to move to Cape Town by a 'free black' trader called Pieter Cesars, and eventually ended up working in the household of his brother, Hendrik. It's thought that she gave birth to two children during her time in Cape Town (most probably fathered by a Dutch soldier, although details are scant), but both died in infancy.

In 1810, the illiterate girl was persuaded to sign a contract with English ship surgeon William Dunlop, in which she agreed to travel with him to England in order to appear as a human exhibition. Dunlop had a sideline in supplying animal exhibits to British showmen and clearly saw an opportunity to up his game. Although she had agreed the contract, Ssehura refused to travel to Britain without Hendrik Cesars. Cesars wasn't keen, but was eventually persuaded by the prospect of making money from Ssehura's unusual physiognomy. Dunlop had requested permission to take her out of the country (as was required at the time) from the governor of the Cape. Permission was granted, but then-governor Lord Caledon would later go on record as saying that, having since discovered the true purpose of the trip, he regretted allowing her to travel.

Dunlop knew when he was onto a good thing and the prospect of using Ssehura as an exhibition piece was, to his mind at least, a very good thing indeed. Large buttocks were very fashionable and highly desirable at the time and British women were genuinely envious when she first went 'on display' at the Egyptian Hall in Piccadilly Circus, London, in November 1810. Ssehura was advertised as the *Hottentot Venus* – although 'Venus' is in itself relatively inoffensive, referring to the goddess of love, 'hottentot' was a derogatory name from the Dutch for those of Khoi or San descent which has long fallen out of use. She refused to ever appear fully naked in public and wore tight, flesh-coloured clothing onstage that was decorated with beads and feathers, in order to give the impression of nudity while saving her modesty. It's said that the wealthier of her admirers were offered the chance to pay Ssehura's 'management' for the privilege of viewing her in private demonstrations within their own homes and, on those occasions, viewers were allowed to touch her.

Slavery was still relatively commonplace within the British Empire at the time, the slave trade itself only having been abolished in 1807. Attempts to prosecute Ssehura's managers for holding her against her will failed – in no small part because she actually testified in their favour. Cesars declared that Ssehura was free enough to be entitled to choose how she earned her living, even if that was to be through selling herself as entertainment. When questioned, Ssehura stated clearly that she had come to Britain of her own free will and had not been abused. It's difficult to know whether she really was 'free' or had been conditioned into believing she was, when in actuality she was nothing of the sort. She may simply have been too intimidated to feel able to do anything other than defend them. Because of his ethnicity, Hendrik had been assumed to be the potential ringleader of any slavery issue and was kept out of the room while Ssehura gave evidence, but Dunlop – who in reality was the one in charge – was allowed to remain. Whatever the truth of the matter, it certainly couldn't have been an equal professional relationship, regardless of how it was viewed by its participants.

Ssehura's physical differences were more of a draw than her African background, London having already been a melting pot of different ethnicities for a very long time. As the novelty of her appearance waned – and Dunlop died, loosening her ties to London – Ssehura came under the influence of a man called Henry Taylor. Although there is little information to be found about Taylor, there is a possibility that they were married in Manchester in December 1811. Whether this was by choice, one can only wonder. Taylor took Ssehura to Paris in September 1814, where he promptly sold her to an animal trainer called Réaux.

Réaux had taken her on as he would any other animal and treated her as such; exhibited at the Palais Royal for the next fifteen months, Ssehura was now truly enslaved. The way she was treated became more overtly racist, on a pseudo-scientific level. She was poked, prodded and inspected by endless scientific investigators, all keen to debate the physical characteristics of her ethnicity.

As her standards of living declined, so did Ssehura's health. She died on 29 December 1815, at somewhere around 40 years of age, the cause of death recorded as 'inflammatory and eruptive disease'. Opinions on what this actually meant have varied over the intervening two centuries, although alcoholism and/or syphilis are possible contenders, as is pneumonia.

Georges Cuvier was a naturalist who had met and danced with Ssehura at a party and who, after her death, claimed her body for scientific investigation. Having made a full plaster cast of her body, he then dissected it. Her skeleton was preserved and her brain and genitals pickled, before being put on display at the Musée de l'Homme in Paris, where they stayed until 1974. Ssehura's remains were only repatriated in 2002, after several years of campaigning by the then President of South Africa, Nelson Mandela.

Chapter 10

The Princess Who Wasn't

Samuel Worrall was a county magistrate who lived at Knole Park House in Almondsbury, Gloucestershire, with his American-born wife Elizabeth. On the evening of 3 April 1817, the Worralls were visited by a Mr Hill, the local 'overseer of the poor', whose job it was to administer welfare aid to those in need. It just happened to be Maundy Thursday, the religious holiday celebrating the Last Supper, during which Jesus commanded his disciples to forgive sins and love one another. Hill had with him a young woman dressed in shabby but unusually exotic clothing, who spoke only incomprehensible mumblings and had been found wandering in the street by a local cobbler. Samuel and Elizabeth took the woman into their house at Knole Park and attempted to decipher what she was trying to tell them. By means of hand gestures and odd words, it was ascertained that the woman called herself Caraboo. Samuel was wary enough of the unknown girl to want her transferred immediately to the local workhouse, but Elizabeth Worrall was more sympathetic. She arranged for a maid to accompany Caraboo to a local inn, where she could stay while they decided what to do next. When Caraboo and her chaperone arrived at The Bowl Inn, the young woman apparently recognised a botanical painting of pineapples on the wall, announcing '*Nanas!*' as 'nanas' was known to mean 'pineapple' in many foreign languages, this – along with Caraboo's interest in Chinese artwork in the Worrall's home – was enough for a theory to begin circulating that she was, in fact, a lost foreigner from exotic climes.

Caraboo had arrived with the Worralls not only destitute, but also carrying a counterfeit sixpence, which Samuel considered to be a step too far. Despite the intrigue, she was admitted as a vagrant to St Peter's workhouse in Bristol. While incarcerated at St Peter's, Caraboo was befriended by a Portuguese sailor called Manuel Enes (sometimes reported as 'Eynesso'), who announced that he both spoke her language and could translate her story. This he did, explaining that the supposed beggar was actually an escaped survivor of piratical kidnapping who had overcome the odds to end up lost and friendless – but at least alive – in the genteel surroundings of Gloucestershire. According to Enes' translations, the young prisoner was actually Princess Caraboo of Javasu, an island in the Indian Ocean. She apparently alleged that she had been kidnapped from her father's garden by pirates and held captive onboard their ship as it sailed towards Britain. The plucky young woman had leaped overboard in the Bristol Channel and swam ashore, dragging herself out onto the Gloucestershire coastline and wandering until she had finally landed in Almondsbury.

The presence of the newly discovered princess caused such disruption at St Peter's that the Worralls decided to take her back into Knole Park. News had travelled about this exotic stranger who had arrived apparently out of nowhere and people began to visit the Worralls in order to view their exotic houseguest. Princess Caraboo lived up to the reputation her story had given her, dancing for the family's friends, shooting a bow and arrow in the parkland, and praying to a god she called 'Allah-Talla'. She insisted on sleeping on the floor and on at least one occasion was known to have swum naked in the lake when left to her own devices.

In order to reassure themselves of Princess Caraboo's provenance, it was arranged that she should be examined by a Dr Wilkinson, who had travelled widely and would therefore, it was hoped, be able to identify her origins. Wilkinson identified Caraboo's language as definitively oriental, using Edmund Fry's *Pantographia* as the source of his research. Published in 1799, the '*Pantographia; containing accurate copies of all the known alphabets in the world; together with an English explanation of the peculiar force or power of each letter*', was exactly what it declared itself to be – a collection of Fry's knowledge of foreign alphabets and their construction. Wilkinson backed up his belief by examining marks found on the back of the woman's head and confirming that they could only be the result of work by oriental surgeons.

All was going swimmingly for the princess, until a housekeeper by the name of Mrs Neale visited Knole Park and, taken aback by the young woman's presence, announced, 'Ah, Mary Baker, how come you're here?'* Neale went on to say that she had suspected for some time just who 'Princess Caraboo' really was. In the face of such hard evidence, the princess's facade crumbled. She immediately switched to speaking English with complete fluency and admitted she was, indeed, Mary Baker – and rather than being a foreign princess, she was in reality the daughter of a Devon cobbler.

At about the same time, Samuel Worrall had received word from Oxford that Wilkinson's conviction about Caraboo's linguistic origins was quite possibly not as accurate as he'd have liked. Archbishop Whately, on being presented with a sample of her handwriting for analysis, had declared it to be 'unmeaning scrawls ... the writing of no known language'. Furthermore, the scars on the back of Caraboo/Mary's head had not been caused by foreign surgery after all – they were in fact marks left by a wet cupping procedure** that was supposed to relieve 'overheated' brains and which had been carried out on the girl while she was living in a London poorhouse. Despite all concerned being widely mocked in national newspapers of the time, the Worrall's were clearly kindly people – when Mary said she'd like to go to America, they arranged a passage for her to Philadelphia, complete with a chaperone. Even then, Mary wasn't done with her celebrity status – a letter appeared in the *Bristol Journal* in September 1817, suggesting that 'Princess Caraboo' had caught the eye of none other than the exiled Emperor, Napoleon Bonaparte. Purportedly written by Sir Hudson Lowe, Governor of St Helena and Napoleon's de facto gaoler, the letter claimed that the 'Princess' had jumped ship while sailing close to the island, rowed herself ashore and made acquaintance with Napoleon, who declared her to be 'enchanting'. Marvellous as this story is, there is no trace of any evidence to support it.

Mary's celebrity was rather less appreciated in America than she may have hoped, and traces of her fade away for the next few years. In 1824 she returned to England and briefly set herself up as an exhibit once again, without much success. By 1828 she is on record as living as a widow in Bedminster, under the name Mary Burgess – as she was actually using the name of one of her cousins, it's likely that the widowhood, too, was fake. She did, however, marry – she and her husband Richard Baker had a daughter in 1829.

With some irony, given her earlier career living off her tall tales, Mary eventually settled in Bristol and made a living from selling imported leeches. She died on Christmas Eve 1864 and was buried in an unmarked grave in Hebron Road cemetery, Bristol.

*   Quote is taken from a report in Gloucestershire Notes and Queries, vol. 3, 1877. It is uncertain whether Mrs Neale actually referred to Caraboo as Mary Baker, as she would have still been Mary Willcox at that time.
** 'Wet cupping' is an alternative health treatment during which suction cups are placed on the skin – most commonly on the patient's back – and blood drawn out into the cups through small incisions made with a scalpel (dry cupping the same treatment but without the incisions). Although the medical benefit is debatable, it has existed as a treatment at least as early as Ancient Greece.

Chapter 11

Terror at the Theatre

After Charles I was executed in 1649, Britain came under the austere rule of Oliver Cromwell and the Puritans. Popular entertainments such as the theatre were banned for being 'places of lascivious mirth and levity', that were considered unfitting for true followers of Christ. The eventual restoration of the British monarchy in 1660 brought the dead king's son out of foreign exile to take his place on the throne as Charles II. Theatres were re-established with Charles's full support during the Restoration period; however, the new entertainment venues were restricted in the types of performance they could stage. Only the 'patent' theatres – those granted 'letters patent' to do so by the king – were allowed to put on serious dramatic productions, with all other venues restricted to more light-hearted comedies and pantomimes. Even the patent theatres would intersperse their dramas with comedic interludes, for fear that their audience might become bored. A trip out to see a show was a popular choice of entertainment in Regency Britain and most large towns had their own theatre. By 1805 it's estimated that there were upwards of 280 such venues across the country, alongside countless 'penny gaffs' – more casual venues such as the back room in pubs, where raucous entertainment would be put on with minimum investment and maximum entertainment value for guests from the lower classes.

By the end of the eighteenth century, patent theatres had opened in Dublin, Cork, Liverpool, Bristol and Birmingham, as well as three in London, all of which bore the name 'Theatre Royal'. One of them – the Theatre Royal in Drury Lane – still exists on the site it has inhabited since 1663, when it was first established by Thomas Killigrew's King's Company. Killigrew had been the very first to establish a patent theatre in 1660, at Gibbon's Tennis Court on Vere Street, but quickly moved his company to Drury Lane where the facilities were of high enough standard for him to compete with his rivals. The second of the patent theatres to be established was run by William Davenant's Duke's Company at Lincoln's

Inn Fields, which opened in 1661, the company later being absorbed into the Drury Lane site. In 1728, John Rich, then actor-manager of the Duke's Company, commissioned the poet John Gay to write *The Beggar's Opera*, the spectacular success of which earned Rich enough money to build a theatre of his own. The Theatre Royal, Covent Garden, opened its doors in 1732.

The Drury Lane and Covent Garden patent theatres had a tradition of closing during the summer months and, in order to fill the gap in London's public entertainment, Samuel Foote was granted a patent for a third Theatre Royal at Haymarket in 1766, where he staged plays during the summer. During 1793–94, the Drury Lane theatre was being rebuilt and the company had moved into the Haymarket for the duration, from where they had been given permission to perform under Drury Lane's patent license. On 3 February 1794, King George and Queen Charlotte were in the audience. When the theatre doors were finally opened to allow the audience in, the vast swell of people toppled forward into the auditorium, pushing those at the front down into the orchestra pit. An estimated fifteen people were trampled to death and twenty more seriously injured. Unbelievably, the evening's performance went ahead, with the royal visitors blithely unaware of the appalling tragedy that had befallen many of the audience. Theatres in those days were not quiet places and one can only assume that those sitting in ignorance of the calamity simply assumed the excess noise to be part of the crowd's enjoyment. In fact it was the tortured cries of people being tramped underfoot by others who must have realised what they were stepping on but had no way of stopping themselves being propelled forward. The king and his family had no idea what had happened until they returned home later that evening and were given the news that they had inadvertently sat through the deaths of so many people. The regal horror was such that it would be another ten years before the Haymarket was allowed to host a royal visit.

The composer George Frederic Handel was closely associated with the Covent Garden theatre company where he presented, among other things, the first London performance of *Messiah* in 1743. On his death, Handel's organ was bequeathed to the company's actor-manager John Rich, who had it installed in a prominent position on the main stage.

Which is where it stayed, until – along with many of Handel's original manuscripts – it was destroyed by fire on 20 September 1808.

By this time being run by John Kemble as actor-manager, the Covent Garden Theatre Royal had presented a performance of the five-act tragedy *Pizarro* on the night of 19 September. The story of Francisco Pizarro González's expedition to conquer Peru on behalf of the Spanish in 1532 had proved a popular one with audiences keen to broaden their cultural minds and it was staged with full effects, including mock gunshots and a collapsing set. Monday night's show had gone well and just after midnight, the theatre housekeeper Mr Brandon did his customary rounds of the building. Finding nothing untoward, he saw that the night watchman was on duty and went to bed. The watchman took his dog on patrol, checking the theatre's auditorium, stage and backstage area. Again assured that nothing was amiss, he then settled in for the night and fell asleep. Around 3.30am, he awoke with a feeling of suffocation and realised that he was surrounded by smoke. Running first to Brandon's apartments and then to anyone else he could rouse, he raised the alarm and help began to stream in from the entrances on both Hart Street and Bow Street.

The company's treasurer, a Mr Hughes, was woken by an alarmed maid around 4am, who informed him that the entire theatre was now on fire. Grabbing the company's takings from his office, he packed it into two bags and gave it to the maid for safekeeping. Running from the building in nothing more than her underclothes and petticoat, she carried the money to Mr Boyce, the company's tax gatherer, in nearby York Street. Unfortunately, Mr Boyce's servant was understandably taken by surprise at the sight of a frantic woman turning up on the doorstep at such an ungodly hour and refused to let her in on the assumption that she was some kind of madwoman. The poor maid had no option but to sit on the money bags in the doorway for fear of being robbed – and there she stayed in her nightwear until Mr Hughes himself turned up and explained the situation to those within.

Because the fire had started in the upper area of the building it was behind the rooms of those who lived within it, enabling them to make their escape. By this time it was said that the crackling of the fire could be heard on the Strand, several streets away. Covent Garden Market was already busy with people at that time in the morning and many ran to help, but because the fire had first caught in the remote extremities of the building, it had managed to spread for some time before the alarm had been raised. By 4.30am fire tenders were arriving from all over London, only for the men to discover that there was no mains water available – the theatre's water supply had been cut off just the previous day, in order to allow repair work to a problem with an intermittent supply. This meant that water had to be brought in from elsewhere to quell the growing blaze, which contemporary reports estimated to take another hour. By the time the fire tenders had a reliable water supply, the entire theatre was fully alight. Amid the panic, people found time to rescue a horse, which had become trapped with fear at the back of a nearby mineral water warehouse. Quick-thinking bystanders tied a cloth around the terrified animal's eyes so it couldn't see the flames and led it to safety. Houses opposite the theatre on the other side of Hart Street began to catch light from burning embers being blown in the air, but the gathered volunteers managed to quench the flames before they caught.

A few hundred yards down the road, people rushed to save the Drury Lane theatre from a similar fate as the wind sent burning embers flying towards it. Some climbed onto the roof in readiness to open the safety reservoir that was stored in the roof space, while others packed the windows with wet cloths. Occupants of neighbouring houses came flying out in their nightclothes, carrying what belongings they could and dragging children and animals behind them. It was said that the fire was so fierce that it lit the sky with 'the brightness of meridian day'. The theatre was at some elevation in comparison to much of the rest of the city and the scene was described in *The Star* newspaper the next day as having looked as though 'the whole quarter of the city, from St Martin's Lane to Temple Bar was wrapt in flames'. Firefighters managed to drag an engine inside the building and aimed the water jets at what they believed to be the heart of the fire, standing under what they assumed was a stone arch in a passageway. This being a theatre, the arch turned out to be fake. The combined force of fire and water broke the structure and it fell in on the men, burying them under burning lumps of papier mâché. Newspapers later reported that eleven bodies were eventually removed from the ruins of the building and laid out in the grounds of St Paul's Church nearby. Rescuers poured buckets of water over the burned and injured bodies in the hope of identifying the dead. Sixteen more rescuers were badly injured, including a man who was so delirious with pain that he was reported to have torn the flesh from his own burned arm in frantic agony.

Not all the personal damage was physical. One of the theatre's musicians, a violinist named Mr Ware, had left his violin behind in the theatre overnight for the only time in two years. Worth £300 (the equivalent of seven years' wages for a skilled tradesperson at the time), it was completely destroyed in the blaze, along with almost all of the theatre's contents. The orchestra as a whole estimated to have lost £20,000 worth of musical instruments, most of them irreplaceable. It was said that a few fake weapons, a model of a Roman Eagle and a Mother Goose costume were among the few items to survive the inferno. The damage was estimated by newspapers to be in the region of £150,000 and it appears to have been widely known that the theatre was only insured for a maximum of £50,000. A fundraising drive was organised for the restoration of the ruined Covent Garden theatre, headed by King George III, the Duke of York and the Duke of Northumberland.

The rebuilding of Covent Garden Theatre Royal was a massive project, undertaken at huge cost to a design by renowned architect Robert Smirke (who had, the previous year, designed what is now known as the Johnson Smirke Building as part of the Royal Mint). The foundation stone was laid on 31 December 1808 by the Prince of Wales, with all due pomp and ceremony. According to the *London Sun* newspaper on the day,

A brass-box, as usual on similar occasions, filled with coins of the present reign, and a record of the event, were deposited in the stone. A silver trowel, of beautiful workmanship, was presented to the Prince of Wales, whose affability and elegance of manners were conspicuous on the occasion.

This massive undertaking was completed in only ten months and the theatre was due to reopen to the public on 18 September 1809 with a production of *Macbeth*, starring Sarah Siddons – elder sister of John Kemble and a renowned actress in her own right. Ahead of opening night, the following statement from the theatre management appeared in the *Morning Post* newspaper (the *Morning Post* later became the *Telegraph*):

The Proprietors having completed the New Theatre within the time originally promised, beg leave respectfully to state to the Public the absolute necessary that compels them to make the following Advance on the Prices of Admission:-

FIRST PRICE – Boxes, 7s. Pit, 4s

HALF PRICE – 3s 6d. [Pit] As usual

...

When it is known that no less a sum than one hundred and fifty thousand pounds has been expended in order to render this Theatre worthy of British Spectators, and of the Genius of their native Poets; when, in this undertaking, the inevitable accumulation of, at least, a sixfold rentage is positively stated to be incurred; and when, in addition to these pressing incumbrances, the increased and rapidly increasing prices of every article indispensable to dramatic representations come to be considered – the Proprietors persuade themselves that in their proposed regulation they shall be honoured with the concurrence of an enlightened and liberal Public.

The proprietors had, unfortunately, persuaded themselves wrong. There was a distinct belief at this time that the theatre was an entertainment that should be available to everyone, not just the wealthy. A crowd of thousands turned up for opening night, but only a fraction managed to pack their way into the theatre. When Kemble appeared onstage he was applauded, but as soon as he opened his mouth to speak, he was drowned out by the jeering boos of aggrieved protesters. The company ploughed on with *Macbeth*, but were fighting against the noise of the crowd. Kemble called the local magistrates in to read the Riot Act, in order to allow him to have the troublemakers forcibly removed, but the magistrates found themselves in a dilemma when they realised that the audience had valid tickets for the performance and therefore were technically entitled to be on the premises. The protestors refused to leave and stayed in the theatre singing until 2am. From the second night onwards, the rioters entered at 'half price time' – a point well into the performance when those who wished to could join the audience for half the standard ticket price – and the inside of the theatre was adorned with banners and slogans in support of the Old Price protests. The rioting continued night after night – on one occasion a coffin was carried ceremoniously into the theatre with 'Here lies the body of the New Price' written on it.

The Old Price Riots were markedly different from other incidents of unrest, in that they were generally good-humoured and all but devoid of any serious intent to damage. These rioters came from across the class divides and all had but one aim – to ensure access to the theatre stayed available to all. The riots went on for three months, until Kemble finally gave in to the unending pressure and returned the ticket prices to their previous levels.

Drury Lane was not to be without its own drama. On the afternoon of Friday 24 February 1809, while the theatre was closed to the public and mostly empty of staff, a fire that had been left burning in an upper-floor coffee room somehow ignited the building's woodwork. The flames grew and spread during the afternoon and early evening, but the fire itself wasn't discovered until some time after 11pm. According to a report in *The British Press* the next day,

At a quarter past eleven o'clock last night, this magnificent Edifice appeared a blaze of fire. The night was dark, but in a moment the atmosphere was illuminated, and the light was as strong on the steeples and the roofs of the houses for miles around as in the brightest sunshine. The fire-bells, bugles, and drums instantly gave the alarm. The Volunteers mustered in force, and the engines crowded from all quarters to the spot. Their exertions to save the Theatre, we saw with regret, were ineffectual. The fire had seized every part of the building, and blazed with irresistible fury. Such was the fierceness of the flames, the immense mass of fuel which this superb pile afforded was almost exhausted before two o'clock this morning, when the volume of flame that issued from it was not greater than what might be produced by an ordinary building. The advantage of having a great public structure of this kind in an isolated situation was apparent upon this awful and melancholy occasion. Altho' the engines could not arrest the progress of the flames in the Theatre, they were able to play upon the surrounding buildings, and thus saved the neighbourhood from destruction. In contemplation of fire, there was a reservoir full of water on the top of the building, which fell in. Of its quantity, and that supplied by the engines, some idea may be formed from the appearance of the streets in the vicinity. The whole line from the Theatre, down to St Clement's Church, which had been perfectly dry only an hour before, was scarcely passable at two o'clock, from the depth of water upon it. Several of the houses in the vicinity, particularly those in Vinegar-yard, had caught the fire, and the neighbourhood was thrown into great confusion; but the activity of the engines prevents any considerable mischief outside the Theatre. Neither the burning of Covent-Garden Theatre, nor the late fire at St James's Palace, can be compared in terrible grandeur with the fire of last night.

After witnessing the destruction of the Covent Garden theatre the previous year, the owners of Drury Lane had taken extra precautions with their own venue, installing large water tanks in the roof space and a heavy iron safety curtain on the stage. Despite this, the fire took hold with ferocious speed and it was said that the owner of Drury Lane, Richard Brinsley Sheridan, realised that there was no saving the theatre and resigned himself to drinking a glass of port while watching the flames rip through his beloved building. Turning to a friend, he said that he should be 'allowed to take a glass of wine by his own fireside'.

Chapter 12

Tears of a Clown

One of the most popular productions staged at the Covent Garden Theatre was 'Mother Goose', the well-loved pantomime. Its star was Joseph Grimaldi, an English actor and comedian whose great-grandfather had migrated to Britain from Italy in 1730 and passed down his love of amateur dramatics. Born in 1778 in Clare Market, London, Grimaldi's parents were an unlikely match. His father Guiseppe was in his 60s when Joseph was born, his mother Rebecca only 14. Having taken Rebecca as an apprentice dancer and performer, he rapidly moved her into the role of mistress. The birth of Grimaldi's first son did nothing to curb Guiseppe's appetite for women and he welcomed the arrival of a second son the same year by a another mistress, Anne Perry (it's believed that Guiseppe Grimaldi would eventually accrue at least ten children by several different women). Rebecca raised Joseph alone for the first few years of his life, the two of them living in Clare Market while Guiseppe spent the majority of his time with Anne and their child. This clearly didn't put Rebecca off her erstwhile employer/lover, as she gave birth to Joseph's brother, Jean Baptiste, in 1780.

Upon the arrival of his second son, Guiseppe left Anne and their daughter, returning to Rebecca and moving with her and the two boys to High Holborn, central London. It is unlikely to have been the happiest of families, Guiseppe having a fondness for beating his children if they were perceived to have disobeyed him in any way. He also had a habit of pretending to drop dead in front of his – presumably terrified – children, in order to see how they would react. Guiseppe had a deep-seated fear of premature burial and allegedly had a clause added to his will that requested his eldest daughter to behead him after death in return for a larger inheritance, as a morbid safety measure.

Joseph made his stage debut at only 2 years old, appearing at Sadler's Wells Theatre in late 1780 for what Guiseppe called his 'first bow and first tumble'. Just over a year later on Boxing Day 1781, Grimaldi appeared as

'Little Clown' in *The Triumph of Mirth; or, Harlequin's Wedding*, at Drury Lane. He rapidly became a popular child actor and although he did spend some time at Mr Ford's Academy, a boarding school that specialised in taking in children from performing families, what education he managed to scrape together took second place to theatre commitments. Joseph's stage appearances weren't always without risk, despite his tender years. On one memorable occasion he was playing the part of a monkey on a chain held by his father, who swung the young boy around with such force that the chain snapped and sent Joseph flying into the orchestra pit. Between them, the Grimaldis were by now earning enough to move out of the Clare Market slum into a much more presentable house in Holborn.

When Guiseppe died of dropsy (the very unspecific term used for what we would now call oedema – fluid retention and swelling – the severity of which depends on which part of the body it affects) in 1788, Grimaldi junior became the family's main breadwinner at only 9 years old. Already working two separate contracts at both Drury Lane and Sadler's Wells, the manager of Drury Lane paid him an above average wage for the time and also took Rebecca (still only in her mid-20s) on as a dancer, in order for mother and son to work together. Sadler's Wells, however, were notably less supportive and cut Joseph's wages by four fifths, leaving the family with no option but to leave the Holborn house and move back to the slums, this time in St Giles. Soon afterwards, Joseph's younger brother John Baptiste – aged 9 – signed up as a cabin boy aboard a frigate whose captain clearly didn't check very carefully for fraudulent proof of identification and quite literally sailed off into the sunset, leaving Rebecca and Joseph to continue the family's theatrical tradition alone.

In 1796, Rebecca Brooker introduced her son to Maria Hughes, the daughter of Sadler's Wells' proprietor, Richard Hughes. The pair fell in love and married the same year, making their home in Pentonville. Over the next two years, Joseph gained a reputation for his acting and comedic abilities, and particularly his individualistic portrayal of the Clown, a long-standing theatrical tradition. During 1800 Joseph appeared in four different productions at Drury Lane, including playing a gravedigger alongside John Kemble's star turn as *Hamlet*. To top off what was shaping up to be a very successful year, Maria was expecting their first child. Sadly for the expectant father, things didn't go to plan – both Maria and the baby died in childbirth on 18 October 1800. Grief-stricken, Grimaldi

– still only 22 years old – threw himself into his work, often running the two miles between Sadler's Wells and Drury Lane in order to appear in performances at both theatres on the same night.

Grimaldi's portrayal of the Clown began to develop a legendary reputation with his appearance in Kemble's production of *Harlequin Amulet*, the first pantomime staged at Drury Lane for three years. Popular enough to be brought back for a second run over Easter 1801, the role established Grimaldi as the foremost Clown of them all. He established his own catchphrases, some of which are still used today. When a clown cheekily turns to their audience before doing something amusingly ridiculous and asks, 'Shall I?' before waiting for the audience to shout 'Yes!' in response, it's Grimaldi's spirit that they're invoking.

Just as Grimaldi's reputation was growing, he accidentally shot himself in the foot while onstage and was confined to bed for several weeks. The injury, along with the prolonged confinement with nothing but his thoughts about his dead wife and child for company led him to sink into such depths of despair that his mother worried for his health. In desperation, Rebecca hired Mary Bristow, a fellow dancer from Drury Lane, to nurse him through it. Whether it was her nursing abilities or merely her presence that comforted him, Grimaldi not only recovered, he went on to marry Mary at St Pancras Old Church on Christmas Eve 1801. By 1802, Grimaldi's reputation was such that he allegedly earned £300 for two days' work in pantomime, a vast amount of money (to put it into context, Grimaldi's 48-hour stint earned him the equivalent of five years' wages for a skilled tradesman of the time). He and Mary also welcomed their son Joseph Samuel – known as 'JS' to his parents – that same year. Joseph continued to appear in ever more successful stage productions, as always appearing at both Sadler's Wells and Drury Lane. In 1806 he moved to the Covent Garden Theatre and was feted for his role as Clown in *Mother Goose*, which would establish itself as one of the most successful pantomimes. Grimaldi was described as 'a genius...' by famed actress Dorothea Jordan, companion of the future King William IV, but the Clown himself disagreed, convinced that his performance was one of the worst of his entire career.

Grimaldi moved to Haymarket with the rest of the Covent Garden theatre company after the fire of 1809, and was part of the cast who appeared in the revival of *Mother Goose*. For the next few years Grimaldi enjoyed continued success with various theatre companies – but life very nearly came crashing down around him once again.

Grimaldi's wife Mary had taken to their newly lavish lifestyle with gusto – and to spending their money without a care, enjoying the kudos that came with being accepted into social circles that included such luminaries as Lord Byron. Byron is often quoted as having been in awe of the famous clown at their first meeting, declaring his 'great and unbounded satisfaction in becoming acquainted with a man of such rare and profound talents'. But according to Grimaldi's own memoirs, this might not have been quite as genuine a sentiment as has been reported. He wrote (in the third person, see footnote), 'Perceiving that his lordship was disposed to be facetious at his expense, Grimaldi felt half inclined to reply in a similar strain; but, reflecting that he might give offence by doing so, abstained – resolving, however, not to go entirely unrevenged for the joke which he was evidently playing him: he returned all the bows and congees threefold, and as soon as the ceremonious introduction was over, made a face at Colonel Berkeley, expressive of mingled gratification and suspicion, which threw those around into a roar of laughter; while Byron, who did not see it, looked round for the cause of the merriment in a manner which redoubled it at once.'*

Sadly, Grimaldi's biggest mistake in life turned out to be in putting his trust in his own son. Perhaps wishing to establish a more successful family dynasty than his own father had managed, Grimaldi pushed for JS to be involved in the theatres as much as possible. This plan must have seemed to come to perfect fruition when father and son appeared in *Don Juan* in 1814, with Joseph taking the title role and JS appearing second on the bill as Scaramouche. The performance was a great success and the pair would go on to perform together in many productions around the country.

Grimaldi's popularity was such that it perhaps didn't seem *too* terrible an idea for him to appear as 'Grimaldicat' in the Sadler's Wells production of *Puss In Boots* in 1818. The audience hated it – women allegedly began fighting in the audience as arguments broke out – and *Puss In Boots*'s opening night was also its last. Whether the show's reception alone knocked Grimaldi's confidence, or perhaps his failing health was already marring his abilities. Regardless, Grimaldi – the great Clown – began his slow decline. Never the most business-minded, he was repeatedly duped out of money by those he trusted and his relationship with JS deteriorated along with his own health. Struggling to grow up in the shadow of his famous father's reputation, JS had taken solace in both alcohol and snobbery, refusing to acknowledge his parents and only returning home each time he hit rock bottom. Taking advantage of his parents' desperation to keep the family together, while also developing a severe alcohol problem, JS eventually died in 1832. His now infirm parents decided to make a suicide pact – which failed to do anything other than make both Joseph and Mary extremely sick.

After Mary's death in 1834, Joseph himself became an alcoholic loner and saw no one except the other regulars at his favourite tavern, The Marquis of Cornwallis on Southampton Street in Pentonville (the inn has since been demolished and the streets renamed). On the morning of 1 June 1837, Grimaldi's housekeeper found him dead in bed, from what the coroner would later record as 'the visitation of God'. The Clown had taken his final bow.

* Grimaldi's memoirs were composed in collaboration with writer Thomas Egerton Wilks. Wilks continued to edit after Grimaldi's death and added remembered instances of his own – without distinguishing the difference – as well as converting it to third person narration. In addition, Charles Dickens was brought in to re-edit the manuscript before it was finally published in 1838. It is therefore difficult to separate the absolute truth from tales that may have been somewhat embroidered in the retelling.

Chapter 13

Some Kind of Monster

One day in May 1788, Mrs Maria Smyth was returning to her home in Johnson's Court, just off Fleet Street, London, when she realised she was being followed by a man who she would later describe as being 'thin and vulgar' and who apparently spoke to her in an offensive manner. According to the traumatised woman, the stranger had struck her as she attempted to enter her house, with what she believed to be some form of blade and she was lucky to have not suffered injury more serious than a small cut to the chest. This strange incident might have been lost to the mists of time, had it been a one-off. And for a while, it seemed as though it had been just that – a random assault in a city known for its hard living.

But over a year later, in September 1789, a Miss Mary Forster suffered an almost identical attack while walking on Dean Street in Soho. There were no witnesses, but Mary would later recognise her attacker as a fellow audience member at a performance at the Covent Garden Theatre. She attempted to get other theatregoers to detain him but nobody was keen to get involved and her alleged attacker left the theatre.

Late in the evening of 18 January 1790, sisters Sarah and Anne Porter were returning home from a ball held to celebrate Queen Charlotte's birthday, the official start of the London 'season'. As they returned to the family home, a hotel called Pero's Bagnio on St James's Street, a man appeared as if out of nowhere, hitting Sarah over the head and knocking her unconscious, before attacking Anne and cutting her with a blade, in the same way that Maria Smyth and Mary Forster had previously been assaulted. Again, the attacker made his escape before anything could be done to stop him. The girls' father reported the incident to the police at Bow Street and was informed that his daughters had, in fact, been only two of several victims of the same attacker that day. Details of the other attacks are sketchy (and may not even exist), but it was reported that a Miss Felton had been similarly attacked on nearby Dover Street. It was alleged that the attacker had managed to damage Miss Felton's clothing to the extent that an apple in her pocket was cut clean in half, yet the lady herself had somehow escaped injury.

In April 1790, women began reporting incidents in which a man – invariably a complete stranger – would approach them with a request that they smell a bunch of flowers that he was carrying. When they bent to do so, he would then cut their faces with a blade hidden within the flowers. It is uncertain just how many genuine victims there were – some accounts make it more than fifty – but certainly there were several documented attacks, some of them quite severe. The legend of the man the public was beginning to call 'the Monster' began to take on a life of its own as the press got hold of the story and stoked hysteria among the citizens of London. Some women took to wearing copper pans underneath their skirts, for fear of being stabbed by the Monster as they went about their daily chores.

Two years after she became the Monster's first victim, Maria Smyth thought she had spotted her attacker by chance, while attending a public auction with her husband. The couple followed the man home and identified him to the police as a Mr William Tuffing, who was brought before an array of victims in order for his guilt to be confirmed. Of all the women involved, Maria was the only one willing to attest that Tuffing was the Monster; in fact several of them proclaimed him to be a known local clothing salesman of good character. This didn't stop Tuffing being remanded into custody, but as the attacks continued while he was incarcerated, it was soon accepted that he couldn't, after all, be the person everyone was looking for.

Tuffing wasn't the only victim of mistaken accusations in the Monster case. After a woman was attacked in Arlington Street, a Dr Bush came to her aid, fending off her assailant with his walking cane and then setting off after him in the company of another witness. Unfortunately for the good doctor, as the pair got to the corner of Piccadilly, he was grabbed from behind by a man who declared Bush himself to be the Monster and a crowd rapidly gathered. The young lady who Bush had been valiantly attempting to assist caught up with the confusion and declared him to be her saviour rather than her attacker, saving him from what might well have turned into an ugly example of mob rule. In the midst of the confusion, the woman's attacker made his escape. Could the man who had grabbed Dr Bush and used him as a distraction for the crowd actually have been the Monster himself?

By now, society in general was becoming concerned about the Monster and began to clamour for his capture. Wealthy Russian banker and philanthropist John Julius Angerstein took a particularly keen interest in the case, collecting newspaper clippings and making his own notes about both the attacks and his theories thereof. It is sometimes alleged that Angerstein's motives may have been more to do with the number of fashionable young ladies with whom his investigations brought him into contact, but he was certainly dedicated to the cause, organising a fund of £100 to provide a reward for the capture and imprisonment of the London Monster. This gesture wasn't without its drawbacks – on at least one occasion the Bow Street Runners arrested a man with no evidence other than their own desire to pocket the reward. The press roundly mocked the police and questioned the usefulness of Angerstein's involvement.

Some men, concerned about the possibility of being falsely accused of this unusual crime, took to wearing lapel pins declaring they weren't the Monster. Of course, there would have been nothing stopping the real culprit donning such a decoration himself in a double bluff, but it is clear that excitement was building alongside the panic among the citizens of London. When all talk is about such an event, it is unlikely that it won't be exaggerated in some way. The alleged victims of the Monster now numbered in the dozens, but how many of those had actually been assaulted – and if they had, by whom – it is impossible to say.

A strange cachet had begun to develop around the attacks, the implication being that one must be of superior feminine qualities for the Monster to desire them enough to attack them. Indeed, when Elizabeth Davies, a washerwoman from Holborn, was attacked and badly injured in May 1790 after refusing to smell the man's proffered flowers on the basis that they looked artificial, it was noted that she was surprised and shocked as much by the fact that the Monster had chosen her as a suitable victim as by the assault itself. And reports weren't confined to the capital – on Wednesday 2 June, the *Hereford Journal* reported almost gleefully that the Monster had visited their city but had clearly changed his preference as to the sex he preferred, as the attack was on a man.

The MONSTER who has so long annoyed the females of the Metropolis, is said to have arrived in this city:– The ladies, however, are congratulated, that his singular passion is so essentially altered, that a gentleman only, and he one of the Quorum, had hitherto experienced the effects of his brutality.

(NB: A Quorum at the time was a group of Justices of the Peace, who oversaw legal activity in each county.)

By now, the Monster had become the subject of a sell-out theatre production at Astley's Theatre in Lambeth. *The Monster* set the dramatic and grisly tale to music and became hugely popular with audiences who cheered along to such songs as:

> When the Monster is taken in the fact,
> We'll have him tried by the Coventry Act,
> The Black Act,
> The Coventry Act!

(the 'Coventry Act' of 1671 had made assault involving personal mutilation a felony)

Men risked being the target of false accusations through sheer maliciousness, and petty thieves were not averse to shouting that they'd spotted the Monster in a crowd, in order to create havoc and make off with their ill-gotten gains in the ensuing melee. But who *was* the London Monster?

Rhynwick Williams's life wasn't an easy one. His father had brought the entire family to London from Wales, setting up as an apothecary on Broad Street in Carnaby Market (now Carnaby Street) and becoming a well respected druggist until his death in 1785. The apothecary business was left to Williams's older brother Thomas, who appears to have made it a success. His grandfather John, who was still alive and living in Radnorshire (now part of Powys, mid-Wales), was given a small yearly allowance from his son's estate. Williams, his mother and sisters, however, were not so lucky. It's not known why Thomas didn't support the entire family – perhaps he did to some extent, or possibly it was simply too much of a financial burden for one small shop – but Williams needed to find work. He took an apprenticeship at the King's Theatre, Haymarket (now known as Her Majesty's Theatre, as the name changes along with the monarch; the current building, which stands in the same spot, was built in 1897 and is the theatre's fourth iteration).

The owner of the King's Theatre at the time was Sir John Gallini. A native of Florence, Italy, Gallini wasn't in reality a 'sir' at all – the sobriquet came from his having received the Knighthood of the Golden Spur from the Pope in 1788. Gallini was struggling with debts left by previous owners and was running the theatre on such a shoestring that he was forced to use amateurs in his performances, a move which led to near-rioting by displeased audiences, and at least one occasion when both Gallini and his cast had to make a speedy exit while being pursued by unhappy punters. This is probably where the idea that William was a ballet dancer came from – he is often described as such in retellings of the story, but it is unlikely that he ever had any formal dance training.

Williams's fledging career in the theatre was put to an end sometime around 1786, however, when Gallini accused him of having stolen a pocket watch. There doesn't appear to be any real evidence that Williams had done such a thing, but he was dismissed nonetheless. This sudden lack of income didn't stop his social life, which according to contemporary report continued as before, presumably funded by the women to whom he attached himself. He found work alongside his sister in 1789, making artificial flowers for a French-owned company on Dover Street. Despite displaying a talent for floral creation, Williams managed to get himself fired for unknown reasons in June 1790, leaving him once again in financial difficulties. He took a room on Bury Street, not far from where the Christie's auction house now has its headquarters. In the late eighteenth century the area was not quite as salubrious as it is today and still sported dark back streets containing dingy boarding houses. One of these was The George, where Williams apparently saved money by sharing his room – and bed – with another man.

Around the same time that Williams was reduced to sharing a bed with strangers, Anne Porter had taken to walking out with an admirer, a young fishmonger called John Henry Coleman. While out in St James's Park with Coleman and their chaperones, Porter's mother and sisters, Porter suddenly shrieked and collapsed to the ground in shock, telling her companions that she had just seen the man who had assaulted her in January. Coleman saw his opportunity to make a good impression on Anne and set off after her supposed attacker. The young man wasn't much of a detective, merely wandering the streets at some distance from his target and eventually losing him in the crowds. By sheer luck, the defeated Coleman spotted Williams once again on St James's Street and somehow persuaded him to meet Anne Porter in person in order to clear the matter up once and for all. Anne and her family had returned home, so Coleman escorted Williams to Pero's Bagnio for identification. Upon seeing him, Anne cried out, 'Good God! That is the wretch!' and her mother grasped Williams so that he couldn't escape.

The fact that Williams claimed to have an alibi for the date on which he supposedly attacked Anne was conveniently ignored and he was taken into custody. His belongings were seized from the boarding house at which he was lodging, but no weapon was found. Nevertheless, Williams was sent for trial and the newspapers crowed that the Monster had finally been caught. Williams's sleeping arrangements at The George were commented on in reports of the Monster case, with some suggesting that he might have reasons other than penury for agreeing to share his bed with men he didn't know, and perhaps this was a factor in his supposed dislike of women. There was also his experience working in the fake flower industry, which could – in theory, at least – have given him the knowledge needed to create the nosegays with which the Monster supposedly tempted his victims. But despite the supposed evidence against him, only Anne Porter positively identified Williams as the culprit; the remainder of his supposed victims declaring that he did not resemble their attacker.

There was the added complication of there being no law against pricking someone with a pin. After much deliberation, during which Williams was held in jail, the judges found a statute dating back to 1721, which made it a crime to damage someone else's clothes. Williams was duly found guilty of assault with intent to damage clothing and sentenced to six years in Newgate. During his time in prison, Williams had a relationship and a child with fellow inmate Elizabeth Robins. To this day, there is no firm evidence that the 'London Monster' ever existed.

Chapter 14

There's Something About Mary

On a gloomy day in November 1795, those walking near the old Putney Bridge in West London might have spotted a young woman wandering around apparently aimlessly in the rain. It was only when her clothes were fully sodden that the lonely figure walked across the bridge itself, stopped in the middle and contemplated the cold water below. Climbing over the wooden railings, she jumped.

The young woman who threw herself into the Thames that cold day was an unmarried mother in a society that did not accept such transgression lightly. She was also – perhaps more intimidatingly for society at large – a woman in possession of both a strong intellect and even stronger opinions. Mary Wollstonecraft had made her name claiming equal rights for womankind, but the very lack of rights and equality in her own life had all but broken her. Having failed in a previous attempt at overdosing on laudanum, Mary had decided to take a more direct route to oblivion. But her plans were thwarted once again – this time by an off duty waterman called Mr May, who resuscitated the young woman and took her home to his wife until she recovered her senses.

Mary's life had been complicated from the start, her family leading so peripatetic a lifestyle that she would later express confusion as to precisely where she had been born. She supposedly told her husband, renowned philosophical anarchist William Godwin, that although she might have been born in London, the event could have just as likely take place on a farm near Epping Forest, where her father Edward was at the time making a doomed attempt at playing the country gentleman while his wife Elizabeth did her best to raise the children. The family certainly lived at the Epping Forest farm until Mary was around 5 years old, but records show that she was baptised in London in May 1759. Her birth is now believed to have taken place on 27 April 1759 at a house on Primrose Street in Spitalfields, an area of East London named after the twelfth-century hospital and priory, St Mary's Spittel. Now best known for its thriving markets in Brick Lane and Petticoat Lane, as well as Spitalfields Market itself, eighteenth-century Spitalfields was the often uneasy home to a cultural mix made up predominantly of Huguenot and Irish immigrants, all competing for a piece of the silk weaving trade. When Mary was 12 years old, the rebellious (and quite possibly falsely accused) weavers John Valloine and John Doyle had been publicly hanged outside the Salmon & Ball public house near to her home, as a warning from authority as to the dangers of demanding a wage rise (a newer incarnation of the Salmon & Ball now stands on the same site). Mary's father, himself a weaver by trade, was violent and erratic in his habits. The young girl sometimes slept outside her mother's bedroom door in a vain attempt to protect her from Edward's drunken rages, and took on a maternal role towards her sisters. In return, Mary received a strict upbringing from Elizabeth, who openly favoured Mary's older brother Edward, aka Ned. William Godwin would later say that Elizabeth eventually realised the damage her behaviour was causing and changed her attitude towards Mary's younger sisters, but not towards Mary herself. These early experiences of witnessing the unhappier side of some relationships clearly had an effect on Mary's view of marriage. Life was made all the more precarious for the Wollstonecraft family by Edward's habit of shifting them to various places across England and Wales in pursuit of various ill-fated projects. Although Edward had received a good-sized inheritance from his father, it was spent on his flights of fancy rather than being put towards the secure upkeep of his family.

Mary escaped her difficult family at the age of 19, when she left home to take up the position of lady's companion to a Sarah Dawson in Bath, Somerset. Mary possibly saw the post as a stepping stone to a more settled living as a governess, but Dawson, the widow of a wealthy London tradesman, was stern and demanding and made Mary's 'new life' almost as miserable as her old one. Life was made even harder by the enforced separation from her friend Fanny Blood, who had been Mary's closest confidante since the girls had first met at the age of 16. Mary returned to London in 1780 to care for her dying mother and, after Elizabeth's death, the Wollstonecraft family fragmented; one sister becoming housekeeper to Ned (by now a solicitor) and the other getting married to a Mr Bishop. Rather than returning to her employment in Bath, Mary chose instead to move in with Fanny and the rest of the Blood family.

The two years Mary spent living under the same roof as Fanny Blood disavowed her of any mutual feminist dreams she might once have had for herself and the friend to whom she was so deeply attached. Despite having previously been the main wage earner for her own family, after she was contracted to provide the illustrations for botanist William Curtis's *Flora Londinensis* series of books, Fanny was far more interested in traditionally feminine roles in life than Mary would ever be. Nevertheless, the two women set up a school in Islington together in 1783, which soon had twenty pupils and moved to larger premises at Newington Green. A year before the school opened, Mary had encouraged her sister Eliza to leave her miserable marriage and had helped her to flee, with her tiny baby in tow. This had been the only sensible decision Eliza could make, as far as Mary was concerned; becoming a wife did not, in her opinion, automatically make the woman a chattel of her husband, nor did it oblige her to stay in an abusive situation. Whether Eliza's marriage really was abusive or whether the new mother was suffering postnatal depression is debatable; what is certain is that, however ethically correct and well-meaning Mary's advice to her sister had been, she had failed to think through the ramifications for Eliza herself and thus condemned her sister to a life of ostracism and poverty. It's unsurprising, then, that Eliza took the opportunity to join Mary and Fanny's school, as it gave her both employment and somewhere to live.

Fanny's health began to fail in 1784, possibly due to the onset of consumption (pulmonary tuberculosis). She soon after became engaged to Hugh Skeys, an Irish merchant who had long coveted her and who was at the time living in Portugal. Fanny's eventual acceptance of his proposal was almost certainly in part at least in the hope that the move to warmer foreign climes would improve her health. Fanny married Skeys and left England for Portugal in February 1785, but her health deteriorated to the point that, by November, Mary was concerned enough to follow her beloved friend – who was now also heavily pregnant – in the hope of nursing her back to health. Fanny gave birth not long after her frantic friend arrived, only for mother and child to die soon afterwards. The loss of Fanny haunted Mary for the rest of her life – a decade later she would write,

When a warm heart has received strong impressions, they are not to be effaced. Emotions become sentiments; and the imagination renders even transient sensations permanent, by fondly retracing them. I cannot, without a thrill of delight, recollect views I have seen, which are not to be forgotten, nor looks I have felt in every nerve, which I shall never more meet. The grave has closed over a dear friend, the friend of my youth; still she is present with me, and I hear her soft voice warbling as I stray over the heath.

(From *Memoirs of the Author of the Vindication of the Rights of Women*, by William Godwin).

Returning back to England after a period of mourning with Skeys in Lisbon, a heartbroken Mary discovered that her school had not survived her absence well and it too was failing rapidly. In 1787, she took employment in Ireland as governess to the daughters of Robert King, 2nd Earl of Kingston. Life in Mitchelstown Castle in County Cork was not a happy one for Mary, reinforcing her beliefs that no one should be enslaved to others, regardless of the gentility of the situation. Lady Kingsborough did not take kindly to Mary's close relationship with the children in her care and Wollstonecraft was dismissed a year after she arrived. Kingsborough's daughter Margaret was deeply affected by her time with Mary and later, despite having become Lady Mount Cashell through marriage, adopted the name Mrs Mason, which she took from the only book Mary Wollstonecraft ever wrote for children, *Original Stories from Real Life*.

Her experiences in Ireland only reinforced Mary's determination that she should carve her own path in life regardless of the social consequences and she returned to London with the aim of making her name in the field of literature. Luckily, she rapidly became acquainted with the publisher Joseph Johnson, whose liberal-minded social network she took to with gusto. Clearly a force of nature in herself, the first time Mary met the man who would later become her husband, William Godwin, they took an instant dislike to each other. This is perhaps unsurprising when we read Godwin's own account of the meeting:

The interview was not fortunate. Mary and myself parted, mutually displeased with each other. I had not read her Rights of Woman. I

had barely looked into her Answer to Burke, and been displeased, as
literary men are apt to be, with a few offences, against grammar and
other minute points of composition.

Determined as she was to be a feminist force to reckoned with in the
literary world, it is unlikely that Mary would have taken kindly to a man
who had barely read her work, yet still felt entitled to allow his critique
of it to influence his opinion of her. By now living in George Street in
Blackfriars, Mary published both a novel, *Mary* and *Original Stories
from Real Life* by the end of 1788. The George Street house became a
sanctuary for her siblings and she often visited Johnson to ask his advice
on whichever drama a sister of brother was currently going through.

A Vindication of the Rights of Men was published in 1790, but the title
that Wollstonecraft is still best remembered for to this day is *A Vindication
of the Rights of Women: with Strictures on Political and Moral Subjects*,
published in 1792. Primarily focused on challenging the patriarchal
expectation that women should be subservient to men, in *Vindication*,
Mary – unsurprisingly – became a beacon for emerging feminism through
her belief that men and women should be treated as equals. She argued
vociferously that only a lack of education separated the abilities of the
sexes and – in a rather nifty sleight of hand – that women could only be
expected to behave 'reasonably' if they had an educated knowledge of
what 'reason' actually meant.

Mary's firm beliefs in the necessity of equality and fairness didn't
always translate into treating other people's relationships with respect.
Whatever the tragedies and failures she had already suffered in life, Mary
was still convinced that people should do what *she* considered sensible
and reasonable, whether or not society as a whole agreed. Around the
time that *Vindication* was published in 1792, Mary decided that *who* she
wanted was Henry Fuseli, a man in clear possession of artistic genius –
and a wife.

It seems likely that Fuseli did return her interest, at least to some extent.
He certainly found both her intellect and interest fascinating, especially
her seeming inability to be shocked by his intentionally crude references
in general conversation. The best part of two decades older than Mary,
Fuseli was already well known for his paintings of darkly supernatural
sexuality, the most famous of which was, and is, *The Nightmare* (1782).

Mary rapidly became obsessed with Fuseli, both professionally and personally, William Godwin later admitting, 'There is no reason to doubt that, if Mr Fuseli had been disengaged at the period of their acquaintance, he would have been the man of her choice.' The connection between them appears to have remained platonic, although whether that was entirely Mary's choice or more to do with the determination of Fuseli's wife Sophia (originally one of his models) to keep Wollstonecraft a safe distance from her man, isn't clear. Mary's straightforward approach to such matters of the heart was, however, the death knell for any potential relationship with Fuseli. She proposed a platonic living arrangement with the couple on the basis that if she only wanted Fuseli for his mind, then Sophia could have him for his physical and financial attributes and all three could live happily ever after. Sophia, perhaps unsurprisingly, was utterly horrified by this idea and Fuseli broke off contact.

It was at this point that Mary, according to Godwin's recollections, 'prudently resolved to retire into another country, far remote from the object who had unintentionally excited the tender passion in her breast'. He suggests that, despite her platonic intentions, Mary had secretly allowed herself to dream of a romantic future with Fuseli and, finding unrequited passion a difficult thing to live with while still in the presence of the object of her affections, decided that it would be prudent to leave him behind, both geographically and emotionally.

France at the end of 1792 was certainly distracting enough for even the most broken hearted. Arriving in Paris in December, Mary became an eyewitness to the Revolution and almost delighted in the intellectual fascination that came from observing events out of the window of her small bedroom which overlooked what is now the rue Meslay. On 26 December she watched as King Louis XVI was taken to plead his defence against the charge of high treason:

About nine o'clock this morning, the King passed by my window, moving silently along (excepting now and then a few strokes on the drum, which rendered the stillness more awful) through empty streets, surrounded by the national guards, who, clustering round the carriage, seemed to deserve their name. The inhabitants flocked to their windows, but the casements were all shut, not a voice was heard, nor did I see anything like an insulting gesture. For the first time since I entered France I bowed to the majesty of the people, and respected the propriety of behaviour so perfectly in unison with my own feelings. I can scarcely tell you why, but an association of ideas made the tears flow insensibly from my eyes, when I saw Louis sitting, with more dignity than I expected from his character, in a hackney coach, going to meet death, where so many of his race had triumphed. My fancy instantly brought Louis XIV before me, entering the capital with all his pomp, after one of his victories so flattering to his pride, only to see the sunshine of prosperity overshadowed by the sublime gloom of misery.…

Louis XVI went to the guillotine on 21 January 1793, at the Place de la Révolution (now known as Place de la Concorde, after being renamed in 1795). Life became very difficult for foreigners in newly republican France, involving more or less permanent surveillance and the constant risk of arrest. Mary had moved to Neuilly, now a city suburb but then still a small village on the outskirts of Paris. She spent her time in Neuilly writing her thoughts on the Revolution and walking in the woods near to her house, despite dire warnings from locals about the risk to her safety. Sometime around March 1793, Mary Wollstonecraft met Gilbert Imlay for the first time. An American trader, Imlay was so far from Mary's view of the ideal man that she disliked him at first sight – but, as had happened with Henry Fuseli, her strong feelings against Imlay rapidly changed course and she was very soon besotted with him. According to Godwin,

Her confidence was entire; her love was unbounded. Now, for the first time in her life, she gave a loose to all the sensibilities of her nature.… Her whole character seemed to change with a change of fortune. Her sorrows, the depression of her spirits, were forgotten, and she assumed all the simplicity and the vivacity of a youthful mind.… She was playful, full of confidence, kindness and sympathy. Her eyes assumed new lustre, and her cheeks new colour and smoothness. Her voice became cheerful; her temper overflowing with universal kindness: and that smile of bewitching tenderness from day to day illuminated her countenance, which all who knew her will so well recollect.

Mary and Imlay became an item by mid-April and their relationship was conducted almost entirely in secret for the next four months. Mary saw no reason to marry her lover – a view most unusual for the time – and considered their relationship all the more inviolable precisely *because* of its intense secrecy. However, as the Reign of Terror began to pick up its gruesome pace, life became even more precarious for an unmarried British women living in France. On 16 October, Marie Antoinette went to the guillotine. Several of Mary's friends followed on the 31st of the same month, their crime being membership of the opposing Girondin party. The French government decided that all British citizens should be imprisoned until such time as peace was declared and both Mary and Imlay realised that something would have to be done in order to avoid her being incarcerated. Imlay declared to the American Ambassador that he and Wollstonecraft had been married (they had not), thus gaining certification to 'prove' that she was, in fact, an American citizen. There was no longer any reason for the relationship to remain secret and the couple returned to Paris, where they moved in together to all intents and purposes as the husband and wife they were accepted to be.

Mary's mistake, perhaps, was to assume that she knew Imlay as well as she thought she did. He was certainly fascinated her and almost certainly loved her; however his was not as constant a love as she had imagined it would be. Mary soon found herself pregnant and although Imlay professed to be delighted at the prospect of a child, he immediately headed to Hâvre de Marat on business (the town's original name, Le Hâvre, had been changed in honour of Jean-Paul Marat in November 1793, but Marat's reputation declined and the old name was restored by January 1795), leaving his pregnant partner alone in Paris during the Revolution's most violent period. In January 1794, Mary, growing tired of waiting for Imlay to reappear and sick of bearing witness to Robespierre's violence, took herself to join him in Hâvre de Marat.

On 14 May 1794, Mary gave birth to a baby girl who she named Frances in memory of Fanny Blood. Writing to her sister later the same year, Mary said of little Fanny,

> I want you to see my little girl, who is more like a boy. She is ready to fly away with spirits, and has eloquent health in her cheeks and eyes. She does not promise to be a beauty, and though I am sure she has her father's quick temper and feelings, her good humour runs away with all the credit of my good nursing.

In September, Imlay left for London on business and as he was only due to be away for two months and violence was receding in Paris, Mary returned there with 4-month-old Fanny to await his return. By the time the two months were up it was clear that Imlay's ardour had cooled, his return delayed repeatedly with barely credible explanations. It was April 1795 before Imlay finally requested that Mary instead come to him in London, and when she arrived it was to discover that he was living with a young actress. He provided Mary and the baby with a furnished house in which to live separately from him, and for a time at least, Mary thought their relationship might still be saved. When it became clear that her erstwhile lover had no intention of being as devoted to her as she was to him, she decided to end her life – using logic and reason once again, are rather than hysterical passion. The details of this first suicide attempt have always been confused; it seems most likely that it involved an overdose of laudanum, but whether Mary actually drank it or not is unclear. Whatever the true details, she was somehow prevented from seeing her plan through by the intervention of Imlay himself. In an attempt at distracting her, Imlay asked Mary to take a business trip to Norway on his behalf, making much of the fact that he was trusting her as his business representative and confidante and describing her in documents of the time as, 'Mary Imlay, my best friend and wife.'

When Mary returned to England in October, it was with a sense of foreboding. Imlay had promised to meet her at Hamburg on her return journey so that they might take a trip to Switzerland together, but he had failed to materialise. When she arrived back in London, her worst fears were confirmed – Imlay was living with someone else. It was after hunting Imlay down and finding him in the house he had furnished for the other woman that Mary decided to drown herself. She had originally intended to jump from Battersea Bridge but had found it crowded with people, so walked on to Putney where she paced a sad track up and down until her clothes were heavy from the rain.

It's not hard to see why Wollstonecraft might have considered drowning herself to be the best available option. She certainly went about it with rational forethought, writing a letter for Imlay before heading out to the waiting Thames, in which she both reprimanded him for his behaviour and also set out arrangements for both her child and her personal belongings.

London, Nov. 1795

I write to you now on my knees; imploring you to send my child and the maid with ——, to Paris, to be consigned to the care of Madame ——, rue ——, section de ——.

Should they be removed, —— can give their direction. Let the maid have all my clothes, without distinction. Pray pay the cook her wages, and do not mention the confession which I forced from her—a little sooner or later is of no consequence. Nothing but my extreme stupidity could have rendered me blind so long. Yet, while you assured me that you had no attachment, I thought we might still have lived together.

I shall make no comments on your conduct; or any appeal to the world. Let my wrongs sleep with me! Soon, very soon shall I be at peace. When you receive this, my burning head will be cold. I would encounter a thousand deaths, rather than a night like the last. Your treatment has thrown my mind into a state of chaos; yet I am serene. I go to find comfort, and my only fear is, that my poor body will be insulted by an endeavour to recal my hated existence. But I shall plunge into the Thames where there is the least chance of my being snatched from the death I seek.

God bless you! May you never know by experience what you have made me endure. Should your sensibility ever awake, remorse will find its way to your heart; and, in the midst of business and sensual pleasure, I shall appear before you, the victim of your deviation from rectitude.

MARY.

In a second letter to Imlay shortly after the event (also dated 'London, Nov. 1795', but this time with the more intimate 'Sunday Morning' appended to it), Mary views her failed attempt at death with sharp pragmatism.

I have only to lament, that, when the bitterness of death was past, I was inhumanly brought back to life and misery. But a fixed determination is not to be baffled by disappointment; nor will I allow that to be a frantic attempt, which was one of the calmest acts of reason. In this respect, I am only accountable to myself. Did I care for what is termed reputation, it is by other circumstances that I should be dishonoured.

You say, 'that you know not how to extricate ourselves out of the wretchedness into which we have been plunged.' You are extricated long since.—But I forbear to comment.—If I am condemned to live longer, it is a living death.

It appears to me, that you lay much more stress on delicacy, than on principle; for I am unable to discover what sentiment of delicacy would have been violated, by your visiting a wretched friend— if indeed you have any friendship for me.—But since your new attachment is the only thing sacred in your eyes, I am silent—Be happy! My complaints shall never more damp your enjoyment— perhaps I am mistaken in supposing that even my death could, for more than a moment.—This is what you call magnanimity.—It is happy for yourself, that you possess this quality in the highest degree.

Your continually asserting, that you will do all in your power to contribute to my comfort (when you only allude to pecuniary assistance), appears to me a flagrant breach of delicacy.—I want not such vulgar comfort, nor will I accept it. I never wanted but your heart—That gone, you have nothing more to give. Had I only poverty to fear, I should not shrink from life.—Forgive me then, if I say, that I shall consider any direct or indirect attempt to supply my necessities, as an insult which I have not merited—and as rather done out of tenderness for your own reputation, than for me. Do not mistake me; I do not think that you value money (therefore I will not accept what you do not care for) though I do much less, because certain privations are not painful to me. When I am dead, respect for yourself will make you take care of the child.

I write with difficulty—probably I shall never write to you again.— Adieu!

God bless you!

MARY.

Mary eventually resumed her place in London literary society, aware that her writing talents were the only thing that might keep her and little Fanny from the workhouse. Back within Joseph Johnson's social circle, she met William Godwin again and by 1796 the pair were close friends. As the friendship developed into something more intimate, Mary and William decided to live together in the Polygon, a new form of multi-level housing complex in Somers Town which had become the destination of choice for literary types fleeing the French Revolution (Charles Dickens would also live in the Polygon for a short time in the 1820s). Their unmarried cohabitation was made even more unusual by William's conviction that a couple should never live together fully, or else risk ruining the relationship entirely. To this end, he kept his own rooms in Chalton Street, just a few doors away from the family home. Leaving his little family as soon as he woke in the morning and only returning at supper time seemed to work and the couple kept in touch during the intervening hours via notes querying what they would eat for dinner or simply asking how the other was getting on with their day.

Despite their jointly principled opposition to marriage, Mary Wollstonecraft and William Godwin were married at Old St Pancras Church on 29 March 1797. It's unlikely that the ceremony would ever have taken place had Mary not been pregnant with her second child and William's first – they may both have flouted convention but another illegitimate child was clearly a step too far. The wedding itself made public the fact that 'Mary Imlay' had actually never been married and was, in fact, still Mary Wollstonecraft, complete with bastard child. Not only did the couple lose those friends who could not cope with this level of unacceptable behaviour, it was said that some of William's more ardent female admirers collapsed in tearful heartbreak at the news of his betrothal to such an unsuitable woman. But despite the drama and although they were now legally united, the couple's day-to-day lives changed very little and they looked forward to the birth of what they both hoped would be a healthy son. Mary was so unconcerned at the prospect of imminent childbirth that she informed her husband that she planned to do no 'lying in' after the birth and was expecting to be sitting down to dinner as usual within twenty-four hours. She had, however, hired a Mrs Blenkinsop as her midwife and was careful to have met the woman several times in advance of the birth, so that both would feel comfortable in each other's company. In many ways, Mary Wollstonecraft approached the birth of her second child with the educated confidence of any well-read twenty-first-century mother-to-be.

Mary Godwin was born late on the evening of Wednesday, 30 August 1797, after a few hours of undramatic labour (the situation seemed so under control that William had even spent the day in his rooms on Chalton Street as usual). The baby turned out to be a girl rather than the longed-for boy, but the more immediate worry was that the placenta had ruptured during the birth and Mary was at risk of infection. A doctor was called in the early hours of Thursday morning and he endeavoured to deliver the retained tissue as well as he could. Despite losing huge amounts of blood, Mary informed her husband that she was determined not to leave him and therefore simply could not die. William even reported some amusement in the household when, Mary having been forbidden by the physician from breastfeeding the baby because of her own weakened state, puppies had been brought in to suckle from her in order to give her some relief by drawing off the milk. By the weekend, her condition had improved enough for William to feel safe in conducting some business in different parts of town. Mary's physician had been administering painkilling medication which worked enough for her to declare to her husband, 'Oh Godwin, I am in heaven!' Godwin's biographer, the nineteenth-century cleric and writer Charles Kegan Paul, would later claim that even on his wife's deathbed, William couldn't bring himself to agree with the notion of heaven, replying, 'You mean, my dear, that your physical sensations are somewhat easier.'

But the household's growing sense of hope was soon to be snuffed out. Mary's condition suddenly deteriorated and the mother of modern feminism died early in the morning of Sunday, 10 September, eleven days after the birth of the daughter who was to become a literary genius in her own right. Mary was buried at Old St Pancras – the same church in which she had so recently been married.

'This light was lent to me for a very short period, and is now extinguished forever.'

William Godwin

Chapter 15

The Godwin Girls

As the offspring of Mary Wollstonecraft and William Godwin, Mary Godwin was never likely to be ordinary. Wollstonecraft's death after Mary's birth left her with a lifelong sense of guilt that she might in some way have been personally responsible. William was devoted to both Mary and his stepdaughter Fanny, but had no plans to give up his career in order to care for them and regularly left them with friends while he travelled. Louisa Jones, a friend of the Godwin family, was briefly employed soon after Mary's birth in order to care for both the newborn and her older stepsister, but the situation became uncomfortable when she became emotionally attached to William. Her affection was unrequited and she soon left the household (although it's unclear which side of the arrangement decided to call a halt). William eventually remarried when Mary was 4 years old, to Mary Jane Clairmont, a neighbour of the Godwins in the Polygon. 'Mrs' Clairmont had two children of her own, both illegitimate – a son, Charles, fathered by a notable Swiss merchant and a daughter, Clara (known as Claire) from a brief relationship with John Lethridge (later to become Sir John Lethridge, MP for Minehead). As with Mary before her, Mary Jane was part of the London literary scene – fluent in French, she worked as both a translator and an editor. And like Mary, it was pregnancy that precipitated her marriage to William Godwin. The baby boy died soon after his birth in the late spring of 1802, but the couple went on to have another son, William Godwin Junior, born on 28 March 1803, who survived.

Although not particularly unkind, Mary Jane certainly favoured her own children among the five – of whom only little William was living with both of his parents – that the Godwins had combined into one household. Fanny, then aged 7, adapted to the situation more easily than 3-year-old Mary, who from the start clearly resented the woman she perceived to be an interloper in the Godwin household. William was both a loving father and also perhaps a slightly emotionally negligent – albeit progressive –

one. He allowed Mary to find her own way in life from a young age and expected all the children to read widely and be interesting and well mannered in company – a tall order when one considers the literary circle in which the Godwins lived.

It's said that Mary once hid behind a sofa in order to listen to Samuel Taylor Coleridge reciting his poem *The Rime of the Ancient Mariner* in the Godwin's living room. She certainly spent a lot of time alone reading, often next to her mother's grave at St Pancras Old Church (the bodies of Mary and William Godwin were moved to Bournemouth by their grandson Sir Percy Shelley in 1851, in order to reunite them with his mother in the family plot). Mary's sense of being an outsider was reinforced by the fact that she had a skin condition which led her family to treat her as though she was sickly or otherwise infirm. She was in fact no such thing – the most likely explanation is that she had a relatively minor issue such as eczema, but in the days before proper understanding of the condition, it was considered a general physical weakness and the sufferer was treated accordingly. Around the age of 15, Mary was sent to stay with the Baxters, friends of the family in Scotland, for several months. The extended visit was supposedly for the good of her health but also very likely in order to relieve some of the tension between the teenage girl and her stepmother. Although she initially felt rejected by her father and didn't want to leave the family home in order to make the trip, Mary came to love both the Baxters and Scotland, returning home with a habit of wearing plaid kilts as part of her daily dress.

Soon after Mary's return from a second visit to Scotland in 1814, she was introduced to a young man who had come to visit William, whom he had long admired. Percy Bysshe Shelley was, by all accounts, a rather fey and affected young man who resented greatly his own privileged upbringing and delighted in standing against it publicly whenever possible. Having been sent down from Oxford University after standing outside the college chapel handing out pamphlets exhorting the joys of atheism, he had written to Godwin several years previously, offering himself up as a devoted follower of the anarchist philosopher's work. William had replied suggesting that Percy would be better finishing his education and healing the rift with his family before he took on any more political agitation. By the time Percy finally met Godwin at the age of 22, he was already married with a child and another on the way. Percy Shelley appears to have had a penchant for 'rescuing' young women – he had sprung his wife, Harriet Westbrook, from a boarding school when she was only 16, after Percy had decided that she needed saving from its strict and old-fashioned ways. Regardless of his marital status, Percy's meeting with Mary is most often portrayed as a lightning bolt moment, with both sides falling in love all but instantaneously. Whatever the romantic truth of the matter, the young Mary was rapidly smitten and they famously had sex for the first time very soon after they first met – upon the grave of her mother, Mary Wollstonecraft.

Carried away with the romantic drama of their situation (and perhaps to escape the inevitable fallout from Percy's extramarital activities), the couple eloped for Europe, leaving a trail of overexcited gossip in their wake. They didn't travel alone, however. This was a triad rather than a duo, Percy and Mary having been joined on their journey by Mary's stepsister, Claire Clairmont. Claire was ostensibly asked to accompany them because she spoke French; however it is more likely that she went of her own accord, in the hope of catching the eye of Shelley's friend, Lord Byron.

Shelley is often described as being a keen proponent of 'free love', but although we usually associate the phrase with the sexual revolution of the 1960s, in the early 1800s it translated more as a dislike of the strictures of traditional relationships and/or marriage. This created some interesting intellectual juxtapositions – while one might laud Mary for living her life more freely than other women of her age, the proto-feminists of the time were surprisingly not keen at all. In an age when a woman still became the property of her husband upon marriage, her security had to be balanced against personal independence and many feminists of the time believed that marriage was a safety net, which women could not do without.

The trio walked across France – quite literally; although some sections of the journey were by horse and cart, the majority was undertaken on foot – towards Switzerland, which they had decided would be the perfect place for such free thinkers as themselves. Unfortunately they had limited funds, not least because both Godwin's and Shelley's families had expressed their disapproval of their activities by cutting off the lovers' financial support. Disheartened, the three plucky adventurers eventually headed back to England, having spent six weeks trekking across Europe.

George, Prince Regent and Prince of Wales; later George IV, by Thomas Lawrence. (*Public domain, via Wikimedia Commons*)

Caroline Amelia Elizabeth of Brunswick by Thomas Lawrence, 1804. (*Public Domain, via Wikimedia Commons*)

Lord Byron in Albanian Dress, by Thomas Phillips, 1835. (*Public Domain, via Wikimedia Commons* {*PD-US*})

The Rt. Hon. Lady Caroline Lamb. (Artist unknown, 1813)

Princess Charlotte Augusta of Wales, heiress presumptive of the British crown by George Dawe, c.1817. (*Public Domain, via Wikimedia Commons*)

What remains of Bethlem Hospital, now the Imperial War Museum, London. (*Public domain*)

William Norris restrained by chains at the neck and ankles in Bethlem hospital, London. Coloured etching by G. Arnald, 1815, after himself, 1814. (*Wellcome Collection. Attribution 4.0 International (CC BY 4.0)*)

An 1852 woodcut illustration of the *Lady Juliana* convict ship leaving Plymouth in 1789. (*Public domain, artist unknown*)

'Princess Caraboo' aka Mary Baker. Image originally appeared in the book *Devonshire Characters and Strange Events* by S. Baring-Gould, 1908. (*Nathan Cooper Branwhite, engraver, Public domain, via Wikimedia Commons*)

The Funeral of Shelley by Louis Édouard Fournier, 1889. (*Public domain, via Wikimedia Commons*)

John 'Mad Jack' Mytton, riding into dinner on his bear, Nell. Engraving by H. Alken & T.J. Rawlins from Nimrod's "Life of John Mytton".

Portrait of Sir Humphrey Davy, from *Famous Men of Science* by Sarah K. Bolton (New York, 1889). (*Public Domain, via Wikimedia Commons* {{*PD-US*}})

SIR HUMPHREY DAVY.

'*Thomas de Quincey, 1785–1859. Author and essayist*' by John Watson Gordon, 1846. (*Public domain, via Wikimedia Commons*)

M⁣ʳ J. S. GRIMALDI.

(as Scaramouch.)

Hand-coloured lithograph print of Joseph Grimaldi as Scaramouche, by Charles Chabot, c.1815. (*Public domain, via Wikimedia Commons*)

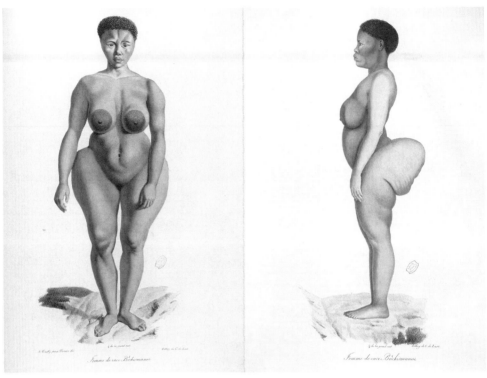

Saartjie 'Sarah' Baartman, 1815. (*Public domain, via Wikimedia Commons*)

New Covent Garden Theatre, 1809. (*Public domain, via Wikimedia Commons*)

Temperance Enjoying A Frugal Meal, by James Gillray. This depiction of King George and Queen Charlotte illustrates their perceived miserliness in the face of enormous wealth. (*British Museum, Public Domain, via Wikimedia Commons*)

A Voluptuary Under The Horrors of Digestion, James Gillray, 1792. A companion piece to *Temperance*, Gillray's cartoon illustrates the effect of uncontrolled self-indulgence on the heir to the British throne. (*Public domain, via the Met Museum Open Access policy*)

Dido in Despair, Gillray's caricature of Emma Hamilton watching Nelson sail away. (*J. Gillray, H. Humphrey; Public domain, via Wikimedia Commons*)

Portrait of James Gillray by Charles Turner.

Lady Hamilton as Circe, by George Romney, c.1782. (*Public Domain, via Wikimedia Commons* {{*PD–US*}})

The Ancient of Days Setting a Compass to the Earth, etching by William Blake, first printed 1794. (*Public Domain, via Wikimedia Commons* {{*PD–US*}})

Miniature of Beau Brummell, by John Cook, published by Richard Bentley.

Mary Shelley, wife of Percy Bysshe Shelley and author of *Frankenstein; or, the Modern Prometheus*. Painting by Richard Roswell, 1840. (*Public Domain, via Wikimedia Commons* {{*PD–US*}})

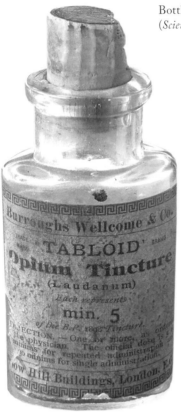

Bottle of opium tincture, more commonly known as laudanum. (*Science Museum, London. Attribution 4.0 International (CC BY 4.0)*)

Plas Newydd – home to the 'Ladies of Llangollen' and their maid, Mary Caryll. (*Winston Gomez*)

By the time they arrived in London, Mary was pregnant with Percy's child. Penniless and shunned by most of their respective families and much of their social circle, their predicament was complicated further by Percy's need to hide from creditors. Harriet had given birth to Percy's second child while the new couple were still the hottest gossip in town and by this time, Percy was also quite possibly having an affair with Claire, despite her stepsister being pregnant with his child. Mary gave birth to a daughter on 22 February 1815. Two months premature, Clara Evelina Shelley lived for only eight days. By the time Mary gave birth to her second child (and Percy's fourth) William (known as Willmouse to his family) in January 1816, Claire had finally become the on-off lover of Lord Byron, whose marriage to Annabella Milbanke was rapidly disintegrating. Mary, Percy, Claire and baby William travelled to Switzerland once again in the summer of 1816, but this time they had plans. They rented a house near to Lake Geneva, close to where Byron was staying at the Villa Diodati with his physician John Polidori. Byron had taken the trip in order to escape the endless gossip that was swirling around him in England at the time – gossip that is unsurprising when one considers that not only was his marriage on the rocks, Byron had allegedly fathered a daughter with his half-sister, Augusta Leigh (his only child with Annabella Milbanke was another daughter, Augusta 'Ada' Lovelace, now renowned for her work in the development of computer programming alongside Charles Babbage).

1816 is often called 'The Year Without A Summer', for very good reason. The catastrophic eruption of Mount Tambora on the island of Sumbawa in modern-day Indonesia in 1815 was the biggest in recorded human history. The clouds of ash that were created spread across the world, lowering average global temperature by more than half a degree centigrade. It's estimated that 100,000 people died of the effects of the eruption itself, while weather patterns were disrupted to such an extent that global crop failure and the consequences thereof killed millions worldwide. In order to keep themselves entertained, the group set themselves the task of each writing a ghost story and thus, the face of literature was changed forever. Byron achieved nothing more than a fragment of a story before giving it up as a lost cause (Polidori would later go on to take Byron's initial idea and run with it himself, resulting in *The Vampyre*, eventually published in 1819 and the absolute cornerstone of the vampire legends we know and love today). But Mary took it more seriously, taking an idea that she said had come to her in a dream and working on it over many days until it grew a life of its own.

While Mary was busy writing in her Swiss villa along with her friends, tragedy was beginning to unfold at home. On 9 October 1816, Fanny Imlay took a coach and travelled alone to Wales, taking a room at the Mackworth Arms on Wind Street, Swansea. The next morning she was found dead in her room by a maid, a note lying beside her.

> I have long determined that the best thing I could do was to put an end to the existence of a being whose birth was unfortunate, and whose life has only been a series of pain to those persons who have hurt their health in endeavouring to promote her welfare. Perhaps to hear of my death will give you pain, but you will soon have the blessing of forgetting that such creature ever existed as—

Here the note was torn off, as if to remove a signature. With no way of identifying the body, the nameless young woman was buried by the local parish. It's believed that Fanny died of a laudanum overdose, but we only have third-party recollections to attest to this, handed down over a century or more. The reasons behind her actions are equally unclear. Fanny certainly felt abandoned by Mary and Claire leaving for Europe without her, and was possibly envious of their freedom. Despite being the only child with no blood tie to either William or Mary Jane, she had ended up being the one left behind to support what family was left. Some interpretations of the family dynamics suggest that Fanny was treated cruelly by Mary Jane – cast in the age-old trope as the 'wicked stepmother' – but her own letters to Mary suggest this wasn't the case. Their relationship certainly wasn't a comfortable one, but the strange little family seemed to be rubbing along together reasonably well. Fanny had even written to Mary in defence of their stepmother, presumably in response to Mary's concerns over what was being said of her back home in London, after her elopement with Shelley: 'Mrs Godwin would never do either of you a deliberate injury. Mamma and I are not great friends, but always alive to her virtues, I am anxious to defend her from a charge so foreign to her character.'

The strangest thing about Fanny's tragic end was that torn note found with her body. Theories exist, but none can be proven absolutely. Perhaps

Fanny herself tore it, deciding in her last moments of life to make herself even more invisible than she already was. Perhaps the maid did it, not wanting anyone to have to bear the shame that at the time would be brought down on the family of a suicide victim. Or perhaps – just perhaps – it was Percy Shelley himself. He had arrived at the Mackworth Arms on 11 October, having received a letter from Fanny that she had sent from Bath – he had been worried enough by its contents to have tracked her down to Swansea (Mary Godwin also received a separate but similar letter). It wouldn't have been so unusual for him to have removed any identifying name from the note, given the social issues surrounding suicide at the time. For the same reasons, it's believed that Shelley refused to formally identify or claim Fanny's body, hence leaving her to the parish to take care, presumably via a pauper's grave.

William Godwin certainly believed that avoiding the tragic event altogether would be the best course of action. Having himself set out for Bath when news of Fanny's frantic letters had been made known to him, he had immediately turned around and headed back to London upon hearing of her death. He wrote to Shelley (or possibly to Mary; accounts differ),

Do nothing to destroy the obscurity she so much desired, that now rests upon the event. It was, as I said, her last wish. It was the motive that led her from London to Bristol & from Bristol to Swansea. Think what is the situation of my wife & myself, now deprived of all of our children but the youngest; & do not expose us to those idle questions, which to a mind in anguish is one of the severest of all trials.... We are at this moment in doubt whether during the first shock we shall not say she is gone to Ireland to her aunts, a thing that had been in contemplation. Do not take from us the power to exercise our own discretion.... What I have most of all in horror is the public papers; & I thank you for your caution as it might act on this. We have so conducted ourselves that not one person in our house has the smallest apprehension of the truth. Our feelings are less tumultuous than deep.

And thus Fanny Imlay fell from public record. Most theories behind Fanny's death converge on the idea that she had in some way felt let down by Percy Shelley. There is certainly suggestion that she was in love with him, but the extent to which her feelings were reciprocated are difficult to ascertain. Fanny had been the first of the Godwin sisters to meet Shelley and she was likely disappointed when he chose her younger sister over her. Her feelings were hurt further with the discovery that Mary and Percy had supposedly mocked her behind her back, a fact which had been reported to her by her own stepmother. In a letter to the Shelleys in May 1816, Fanny had written,

> Whatever faults I may have I am not sordid or vulgar. I love you for yourselves alone. I endeavour to be as frank to you as possible that you may understand my real character. I understand from Mamma that I am your laughing stock – and the constant beacon of your satire.

To be passed over in favour of her sister and have the same sister laugh at her in private, only to follow it up by taking her unrequited love *and* her only other sister away from her might be enough to break anyone, let alone a girl as lonely and depressive as Fanny Imlay. After losing her mother, her sisters and her secret love, perhaps Fanny saw oblivion as the only way out.

> Her voice did quiver as we parted,
> Yet knew I not that heart was broken
> From which it came, and I departed
> Heeding not the words then spoken.
> Misery—O Misery,
> This world is all too wide for thee.

> 'On Fanny Godwin', by Percy Bysshe Shelley

On 10 December 1816, just two months after Fanny Imlay's death in a rented Welsh room, the body of a young woman was pulled from the Serpentine in Hyde Park, London, after being spotted floating in the water by a pensioner of the nearby Chelsea Hospital. The body was identified as that of Harriet Smith, who had taken lodgings in Chelsea in the September of that year and stayed there until she left without warning on 9 November. Harriet 'Smith' left little behind other than a letter addressed to her husband – Percy Bysshe Shelley.

When you read this letr [*sic*] I shall be no more an inhabitant of this miserable world. do not regret the loss of one who could never be anything but a source of vexation & misery to you all belonging to me. ... My dear Bysshe ... if you had never left me I might have lived but as it is, I freely forgive you & may you enjoy that happiness which you have deprived me of ... so shall my spirit find rest & forgiveness. God bless you all is the last prayer of the unfortunate Harriet S—

Harriet, still only 22 years old, was heavily pregnant when she died – yet she and Shelley had separated two years previously. Percy used this fact to justify his unfaithfulness towards, and abandonment of, Harriet, alleging that she had 'descended into prostitution' and had been living with a groom named Smith. No evidence for this supposed extramarital relationship has ever been found, but his desperate attempts to salvage his reputation were picked up on by others and newspaper reports of the time were suitably disdainful in the tone of their reports on Harriet's tragic demise.

On Tuesday a respectable female, far advanced in pregnancy, was taken out of the Serpentine River, and brought home to her residence in Queen-street, Brompton, having been missing for nearly six weeks. She had a valuable ring on her finger. A want of honour in her own conduct is supposed to have led to this fatal catastrophe, her husband being abroad.

From *The Sun (London)*,
Wednesday, 11 December, 1816.

'A want of honour in her own conduct' – unfortunately for Harriet, society was never going to look kindly on a woman who found herself pregnant and alone, even if the situation was not of her doing. No one has ever managed to clarify with any certainty who the father of Harriet's unborn child might have been. There is a reasonable chance that it could actually have been Percy himself, as circumstances show that the couple would have had opportunity to meet in London around the time that conception must have occurred. What is known is that Harriet had returned to her father's home after Percy had left her for Mary Godwin, and that her children with Percy – Ianthe and Charles – were sent by the family to live with relatives in the countryside. Whether it was the loss of her children that tipped Harriet over the edge or simply the cold fact that even her own family were unlikely to be sympathetic when they discovered that she was once again pregnant, is unknown. Whatever the reason, Harriet left the family home and took the rooms in Hans Place, Knightsbridge from which she would eventually walk to her cold end in the Serpentine.

Mark Twain would later disembowel Shelley's reputation in his 1888 polemic, *In Defense of Harriet Shelley*. In it he skewers both Shelley's behaviour towards Harriet and the flowery language of Shelley's acclaimed biographer, Edward Dowden. Of Dowden's approach to his subject in his *Life of Shelley* (1886), Twain sniped gleefully,

> The ordinary forms of speech are absent from it. All the pages, all the paragraphs, walk by sedately, elegantly, not to say mincingly, in their Sunday-best, shiny and sleek, perfumed, and with boutonnieres in their button-holes; it is rare to find even a chance sentence that has forgotten to dress.

Twain also lambasted Shelley for his misogynistic treatment of Harriet both in life and in death, his scorn rippling off the page in waves of sarcastic vitriol:

> During these six years I have been living a life of peaceful ignorance. I was not aware that Shelley's first wife was unfaithful to him, and that that was why he deserted her and wiped the stain from his sensitive honor by entering into soiled relations with Godwin's young daughter. This was all new to me when I heard it lately, and was told that the proofs of it were in this book, and that this book's verdict is accepted in the girls' colleges of America and its view taught in their literary classes.

The social stigma of suicide in the nineteenth century meant that, like Fanny before her, Harriet was doomed to be swept under the carpet of Shelley's history, to preserve her family's, and her husband's literary, reputation.

As he appears to have been one of the few people prepared to be publicly sympathetic towards Harriet Shelley's predicament in the face of those determined to preserve the reputation of her erstwhile husband, albeit from a distance of several decades and an entire continent, the last word on this sad saga should go to Mark Twain:

> What excuse was there for raking up a parcel of foul rumours from malicious and discredited sources and flinging them at this dead girl's head? Her very defencelessness should have been her protection. The fact that all letters to her or about her, with almost every scrap of her own writing, had been diligently mislaid, leaving her case destitute of a voice, while every pen-stroke which could help her husband's side had been as diligently preserved, should have excused her from being brought to trial. Her witnesses have all disappeared, yet we see her summoned in her grave-clothes to plead for the life of her character, without the help of an advocate, before a disqualified judge and a packed jury.

While death and loss were haunting her family, Mary Godwin had continued working on the story she had started at the Villa Diodati back in the summer of 1816. *Frankenstein; or, a Modern Prometheus* is now viewed as one of the greatest of literary classics, beloved the world over. But in 1816 the world wasn't quite ready to accept that the first real work of modern science fiction might have come from the pen of a woman, and a young one at that; it was published anonymously on New Year's Day 1818.

The darkness that permeates *Frankenstein* is perhaps unsurprising when one considers Mary's life at the time. Little William died in June 1819 and Percy Florence – the only child of the Shelleys to survive to adulthood – was born a mere six months later. By this time, Mary had carried and given birth to four children, with only Percy Florence to show for it. Although Frankenstein had been written before William's death, the subconscious foreshadowing is notable in Mary having named Frankenstein's brother (who is killed by the monster) William, after her beloved son. Fanny's lonely death and the ghostly shadow of Harriet Shelley must also have been lurking around the family like a cloud and Mary, unsurprisingly, succumbed once again to depression. It's alleged that, rather than being sympathetic to his wife's plight, Percy instead accused her of being boring and decided that his wife's 'unreasonable' behaviour was justification for him once again taking up with other women.

But by the summer of 1822, Mary and Percy had settled in the bay of Lerici, northern Italy, where they lived with their young son in the Casa Magni, a rented villa with views over the sea. 29-year-old Percy was making the most of the villa's proximity to the coast by indulging his love of boats. The *Don Juan*, a heavy sailing boat whose design had been based on a scaled-down model of an American schooner, had been delivered to him in the May and was to be his plaything of choice for that summer. Although a keen river sailor, Percy Shelley had little experience of guiding a boat at sea. Regardless, he set sail in the *Don Juan* on 1 July 1822, against the wishes of his wife – Mary was going through a depressive phase at the time and didn't want him to leave her (unsurprisingly, as she had suffered a miscarriage only a month earlier and had become seriously ill as a result). The trip with his old friend Edward Williams and an English boat-boy, 18-year-old Charles Vivian, as well as boat designer Charles Roberts (who had recently refitted the *Don Juan* to make her faster), was intended to be a relatively short one. They were headed to Livorno, forty-five miles down the coast, in order to meet up with poet and essayist Leigh Hunt, who had travelled to Italy to discuss the potential launch of a new quarterly magazine. But on the return leg of the journey, Shelley's boat – this time carrying only the poet, Williams and Vivian – foundered in bad weather, some way out to sea off the coastline of Viareggio.

Mary, along with Williams's wife Jane, was left waiting at the Lerici villa for ten frantic days before all three bodies – identifiable only by the remains of their clothes – were washed up on the shore. Williams was still wearing his boots, and Shelley had somehow managed to shove a copy of Keats's poetry deep into his pockets before he went under – the remains were still in his jacket pocket when his battered body was recovered.

Louis Edouard Fournier's 1889 painting, *The Funeral of Shelley*, is perhaps the most well known account of the poet's final departure – it is, however, an almost entirely false depiction. The funeral pyre around which stand Trelawney, Hunt and Byron, with Mary Shelley in the background and all surrounded by terrible gloomy weather has only one correct image – that of the funeral pyre itself. In reality, the August day on which the pyre burned was recorded by those who attended as having been hot and sunny and Leigh Hunt wasn't present. Neither was Mary Shelley – at the time, women were not permitted to witness such occasions, for 'health' reasons. Lord Byron was indeed there, but was so overcome with emotion at the sight of Shelley's funeral pyre that he stripped off and swam out to sea, thus missing most of the strange, sad ceremony.

Percy's heart had failed to burn with the rest of his body (perhaps due to it being partly calcified after an earlier bout of tuberculosis) and Mary kept it in the drawer of her desk for the rest of her life, perhaps realising that it was the nearest she would ever get to truly owning it. Its presence wasn't discovered until a year after her death – it was eventually buried with their son (by then Sir Percy Florence Shelley, 3rd Baronet of Castle Goring, having inherited the baronetcy from his grandfather) when he died in 1889, at the age of 70.

Shelley was certainly a man of Genius and great feeling – but the effects of both were perverted by some unhappy fightings of mind that led him to cause much unhappiness to his connections.

Evelina Wollstonecraft

'He was soon borne away by the waves, and lost in darkness and distance'

From *Frankenstein; or, The Modern Prometheus*,
by Mary Shelley

Chapter 16

The Price of Fame

But words are things, and a small drop of ink,
Falling like dew, upon a thought, produces
That which makes thousands, perhaps millions, think;
'Tis strange, the shortest letter which man uses
Instead of speech, may form a lasting link
Of ages; to what straits old Time reduces
Frail man, when paper – even a rag like this – ,
Survives himself, his tomb, and all that's his.

From *Don Juan*, Lord Byron

'That beautiful pale face is my fate.'

Lady Caroline Lamb

One could argue that Lord George Gordon Byron was the first modern celebrity. As the poet himself would later describe it, 'I awoke one morning and found myself famous.' *Childe Harold's Pilgrimage*, first published in 1812, had become the bestseller of its time; not quite overnight, but certainly rapidly enough to take its author by surprise. Byron's newfound notoriety brought with it literary fame and sexual fortune, as endless society ladies all but threw themselves at the new golden boy of literature. Byron had been cultivating his 'untamed wild man' image for some time, holding court in his rooms at Trinity College, Cambridge, alongside the small bear which he had acquired on the basis that college rules only precluded students from keeping dogs. He loved his dog and had been furious to discover that it wouldn't be allowed to live with him, so had installed his furry friend as a form of revenge against the masters. The bear was tame enough to be walked around on a lead and Byron even attempted to register it as a fellow student (an attempt which failed, the university staff clearly having their limits).

Byron's family background certainly set him up for scandalous notoriety. His paternal grandfather was Vice Admiral John Byron, who set a world record for circumnavigating the globe and became known as 'Foul Weather Jack' due to how often he sailed in terrible weather (and having surviving a particularly difficult voyage during the American Revolution). His father (John Byron Jnr.) had a somewhat convoluted relationship history – having been caught in flagrante with Amelia, Marchioness of Carmarthen, by one of her husband's servants, the pair eloped and married as soon as the Marquis had divorced his unfaithful spouse, Amelia already eight months pregnant with Byron senior's daughter. After Amelia died at the age of 29, a year after the birth of the couple's third child, John rapidly remarried, this time to Catherine Gordon of the Gight estate in Aberdeenshire, Scotland. John's motives for the marriage were almost certainly financial and his treatment of his second wife was known to be dubious, to say the least. The future Lord Byron was the couple's only child and John soon abandoned both Catherine and son child, having first squandered her fortune.

When George was still only 10 years old he inherited the title of Baron Byron of Rochdale following the death his great uncle William, along with the family home of Newstead Abbey. Rather than living in the dilapidated ancestral home, Catherine instead chose to let it out and took lodgings in nearby Southwell with her son. Catherine and George had a difficult relationship – the young boy would take delight in running away from his overweight mother and openly mocked her heavy drinking habits, while Catherine in turn had no compunction in deriding George for being 'lame', due to the deformed right foot with which he had been born. In turns overindulgent and austere, Catherine nevertheless sacrificed her own comforts in order to make sure that George was given the best that money could buy. Educated first at Dulwich and then at Harrow (where he was badly bullied, leading to his obsession with boxing in order to be able to stand up for himself), Byron eventually went up to Trinity College, Cambridge.

While at Cambridge, Byron increasingly indulged his innate desire for passion, declaring himself deeply in love with both men and women at different times. Although it's unclear whether his professions of love for his male objects of desire translated into physical relationships, it's worth bearing in mind that to admit to such publicly would have been social death – and potentially a real one, homosexuality at the time being a crime punished by hanging (the last public hangings for homosexuality were not until 1835, when John Smith and James Pratt were put to death at Newgate Prison, having been convicted on the testimony of a third party who had spied on them through the keyhole to a private room).

Whatever his true sexual proclivities, Byron clearly loved fast and hard and he saw no reason to hide such passions, whether they be with other people or the written word. In 1806, when Byron was still only 18, he published *Fugitive Pieces*, a collection of his own poetry. The volume was recalled and burned on the advice of one Reverend Becher, a friend of Byron's, who was concerned about what he deemed to be explicit content in some of the works. Becher particularly had reservations about the poem *To Mary*; perhaps understandable when one contemplates a priest reading a teenager's ode 'to view each other panting, dying. In love's extatic posture lying [*sic*]'. Despite his reservations, Becher did, however, keep an original copy of *Fugitive Pieces*, his being one of only three intact copies that are known to still be in existence today.

At Cambridge, Byron and friends would swim at a weir hidden away in woodland near Grantchester. The fact that it is now known as Byron's Pool simply because a 20-something poet liked to take an occasional dip in it gives some idea of his influence, even across the centuries. He certainly enjoyed seducing people – less a sport, more perhaps proof to himself that he was, despite his parents' rejection and his distinct lack of physical perfection, capable of winning people over.

Byron was clearly hyper-sexualised, with wit and intelligence as his weapons. There has been many a hunt for the specific details of Byron's sexuality in the intervening years, but the simplest take is that, had he been alive today, he'd have quite possibly described himself as pansexual. While his most documented affairs were all with eligible women, at least some of the focus on these is due to the understandable avoidance of records of relationships that didn't fit the social 'norm'. To allow such social transgressions to be recorded for posterity would find one condemned, both socially and possibly also literally. Lack of evidence of Byron's relationships with other men certainly cannot be assumed to equate to a lack of passion for them. Byron had developed deep feelings for Lord Clare, four years his junior, while both had been students at Harrow. Years after they had been at school together, the two young men met again in 1822, on a dusty Italian road. Byron later said of those few moments he unexpectedly spent with Clare,

> It was a new and inexplicable feeling, like rising from the grave, to me. Clare, too, was much agitated – more in appearance than was myself; for I could feel his heart beat to his fingers' ends, unless, indeed, it was the pulse of my own which made me think so.

The poetry of the Romantics focused on intensity of thought, passion and art, a combination which played perfectly into Byron's all-or-nothing nature. His works developed what we now know as the 'Byronic' hero – pale, brooding, deep with passion and intellect – and people began to assume that the poet and his created character were one and the same. Despite his increasing fame and his aristocratic background, Byron was, at this point, still not notably wealthy – a status that was accentuated by his talent for making money and then spending it rapidly. *The Corsair* had sold thousands of copies on its first day of publication, but Byron was hobbled by the belief at the time that it was unbecoming for the aristocracy to actually work for a living. He could be seen to write for entertainment's sake, but not for commercial purposes. This was a time before royalties, when authors would be paid a set sum for their work and the publisher then got on with the happy job of selling as many copies as possible in order to line their own pockets.

Regardless of his financial status, Byron's public acclaim kept on growing. He received fan mail on an incredible scale, the like of which hadn't been seen before. The majority of these missives came from women who felt a connection between themselves and the words on the page, leading them to assume that Byron understood them in a way others didn't. Often, the letters didn't hold back when it came to flattery:

> My Lord, You cannot retire to any part of the civilized globe, where you will not be followed by the echoes of the world's applause. You must be satiated with the sound of public praise – but you may yet endure it in the still, small voice of a retired and nameless individual who has admired your splendid abilities from their very dawn.

Letter to Lord Byron from 'A Stranger', 17 April 1819
[National Library of Scotland]

Many of the letters attempted to use Byron's own style and expressed delight at the sheer thrill of writing to someone as excitingly intellectual as himself. Byron's wife Annabella Milbanke coined the phrase 'Byromaniacs' for those women who obsessed over her husband, centuries before Beatlemania kicked off the Swinging Sixties. But Lady Caroline Lamb surpassed any fan letter Byron may have previously received when, in 1812, she sent her own letter. Tucked into it was a unique token of her appreciation for Byron's work – a lock of her pubic hair. The note describes how Caroline 'cut too close' and therefore could only apologise for there being '…more blood than you need'.

Caroline Lamb is often portrayed as being some form of crazy – without any context as to where exactly that crazy might have come from – and stories such as that about the very personal fan letter only reinforce this. In reality, Caroline's unusual background had a lot to do with her behaviour in later life. Born to Harriet Spencer and Frederick Ponsonby, Caroline was ignored by her fighting parents to such an extent that she was barely parented at all, learning to scream and throw tantrums in order to get her own way. Her behaviour was such that her parents rapidly decided that they could not cope at all and shipped Caroline off to live with her aunt when she was still only 9 years old. Unfortunately for Caroline, said aunt was Georgiana Cavendish, Duchess of Devonshire, who had quite enough on her plate without the added stress of a badly behaved niece. The young girl was shipped off to boarding school and various medical solutions were tried to aid her fragile mental health, including dosing with laudanum. Caroline herself clearly realised something was amiss but didn't know quite what. While still a teenager she attempted to make sense of the confusion in her head through verse:

> I'm mad
> That's bad
> I'm sad
> That's bad
> I'm bad
> That's mad

Her family consulted a doctor, who declared Caroline to be far too sensitive for the confines of boarding school and the young girl was brought back home, her education ending before it had chance to begin. Home life for

Caroline had precious few boundaries and her erratic behaviour simply became part of who she was. Much has been made over the intervening years about her precarious mental health, but it has to be a possibility that psychological issues were merely a small part of her problematic behaviour. It's perhaps more like that ignorance and mis-management (or lack of any real management whatsoever) simply exacerbated pre-existing issues. Certainly, Caroline was considered all but uncontrollable – and she didn't do anything to disabuse people of the notion. Deciding to take matters into her own hands, she began to educate herself from the family library and took solace in increasingly strict religious beliefs. This obsession with religious doctrines hindered rather than helped Caroline in her adult life, the dissonance between how she felt and what the Bible said she should feel being at confusing odds with each other. At 20, she was married off to William Lamb, a family friend who was by all accounts generally kind and caring towards his sometimes fragile wife, but whose physical attentions confused Caroline greatly. Caroline was clearly deeply sensual in her nature, but her self-taught religious faith appears to have led her to believe that the sexual act itself (or at least, enjoying it) was a crime against God. In a letter to Lady Melbourne in 1805, Caroline said of her husband,

> He called me prudish – said I was strait-laced, – amused himself with instructing me in things I need never have heard or known – & the disgust that I at first felt for the world's wickedness I till then had never even heard of – in a very short time this gave way to a general laxity of principles which little by little unperceived of you all has been undermining the few virtues I ever possessed.

Perhaps she saw in Lord Byron an outlet for her tormented thoughts and emotions; a way of venting them without judgment or censure. Whatever the reasonings behind it, Caroline Lamb latched onto Byron like a drowning woman clutching at a lifeboat. Her passions burst forth and she launched herself into her passion like a woman possessed. If she had hoped that the poet would return her desires with equal fervour, she was mistaken; although he evidently found her to be exciting company initially, his ardour waned in the face of her continued obsession. If Byron was invited to parties where Caroline was not on the guest list, she would wait outside for him to leave, and on several occasions she donned disguises in order to walk in on him when he had left instructions that she was not to be allowed in.

Caroline's reaction to these perceived rejections was to become ever more dramatic, especially when she felt that Byron was showing more interest in other women than she was comfortable with. On one occasion, she became frustrated with her lover's lack of attention when they were both guests at a ball and, after pressing a knife into his hand and whispering to him that she 'meant to use it', she cut her own hand in view of other horrified guests. By now, Caroline's behaviour was becoming a hot topic in society circles and Byron told friends that he was 'haunted with hysterics'. It was certainly the beginning of the end for perhaps the most ill-advised love affair in literary history, but the pair would go on to bicker at each other through their written words, even after their physical connection had ended. Lamb's hugely successful novel *Glenarvon* (1816) was a very thinly veiled caricature both of their relationship and of notable names in society circles. Byron, in turn, was clearly referring to Lamb when in 1819 he included in *Don Juan II* the line, 'Some play the devil, and then write a novel.'

The events leading to Byron's eventual exile in Europe were dramatic, even by his high standards. Already notoriously louche, Byron had somehow managed to hold on to his reputation just enough to stay afloat in high society, but the breakdown of his marriage to Annabella put paid to that. Lady Byron had long known of her husband's infidelities; he talked freely to her about his 'women of the theatre'. Byron certainly seemed to find the reality of marriage very different to the ideals he had envisaged. He told friends of his desire to move out into rooms of his own, or to move abroad without his wife and their baby daughter.

Byron's increasing debts led to regular visits from bailiffs and his drinking increased exponentially. Concerned about her husband's increasingly erratic – and often aggressive – behaviour, Annabella eventually sought advice from Byron's solicitor, who suggested that she should take the baby and go to stay with her parents in Leicestershire.

Byron's beloved half-sister Augusta moved in with him on the departure of his wife and it was Augusta who intercepted a letter from Annabella's own solicitor, requesting a formal separation. Believing that her brother was a suicide risk if he heard of his wife's plans, Augusta returned the letter along with the suggestion that both parties could perhaps make efforts towards repairing the relationship. This clearly fell on deaf ears, as a second request in the same vein was sent shortly afterwards and this one reached its intended target.

Byron could not believe that his erstwhile wife might be serious in her desire to end their marriage and refused to countenance any kind of formal separation – which is when Annabella brought out her shocking trump cards. Byron's relationship with his sister Augusta was, according to Annabella, incestuous. Augusta had given birth to a daughter, Elizabeth, in April 1814, in theory fathered by her husband, George Leigh. In reality, however, it appears to have been speculated from the start that Elizabeth was actually the daughter of Lord Byron. This was a moral accusation rather than a potentially criminal one (incest not being illegal in Britain at the time), but it wasn't Annabella's only complaint.

In addition to having fathered a child with his own sister, Lady Byron accused her husband not only of sodomising her, but also of having homosexual relations with men. These last two were criminal offences and, fairly unsurprisingly, Byron suddenly changed his mind about trying to cling onto his marriage. Soon after the separation was formalised, Byron left for the Continent. His last years are well documented; he travelled with friends – most famously, the Shelleys – and laid waste to local womenfolk wherever he went. After the death of Percy Bysshe Shelley, Byron seemed at something of a loss as to what to do with his life. Clearly incapable of avoiding drama, in 1823 he was coaxed into becoming involved in the Greek War of Independence, as a supporter of revolutionaries opposed to the ruling Ottoman Empire. Rather than simply lending his name in support, Byron found himself involved in negotiations on a political level and also paid for a refit of the Greek fleet; he would eventually sell his English estate in order to fund an entire military brigade. His war efforts were not the only thing soaking up his cash – Byron had become deeply infatuated with his young Greek manservant and wrote endless poems about him, but it appears that the only affections the boy himself held were for his besotted master's money.

Byron fell ill in early 1824 while in Greece and was weakened further by repeated bloodletting. It was possibly a lack of hygiene in this bloodletting which led to him developing sepsis. Byron died in Missolonghi on 19 April 1824. His body was repatriated to Britain but the scandals that had dogged him for all his adult life led to Westminster Abbey refusing permission for him to be buried within their sacred walls due to his 'questionable morality'. His body instead lay in state for two days at a house on Great George Street, before finally being interred at the Church of St Mary Magdalene in Hucknall, Nottinghamshire.

It might be considered a suitable postscript – or a sad indictment of the near-hysteric Byromania which continues to this day – that when his coffin was opened in 1938 in order to check the condition of his remains, the most notable thing reported on by those present was that Byron's genitalia apparently showed 'quite abnormal development'.

Chapter 17

Prince Charming

Being born into royalty might have helped one's living conditions, but it didn't necessarily make someone's personal life any easier. In fact royalty was (much as it probably still is) quite the burden to bear when it came to one's romantic life. King George brought in the Royal Marriages Act 1772, which was intended to avoid regal power being diluted by politically inadvisable marriages and which made it a requirement for any member of the royal family under the age of 25 to request his approval of any potential marriage partner (although repealed in 2011, the first six royals in line to the British throne still, to this day, require the same monarchal permission to marry if they are not to forfeit their right to succession). Without the reigning monarch's permission, any such marriage was considered null and void. This had been prompted by the marriage in 1771 of George's brother Prince Henry, Duke of Cumberland and Strathearn, to Anne Luttrell, a young widow who, despite being from landed stock, was still a lower social class. Indeed, Anne's late husband, Christopher Horton, was a commoner (albeit a commoner who lived in Catton Hall, a large country house which still stands within its extensive grounds on the Derbyshire/Staffordshire border). George's conviction that this new requirement for permission was the right thing to do was reinforced when, some time after the introduction of the Royal Marriages Act, his younger brother Prince William Henry confessed to having married Maria, Countess Waldegrave, in 1766. The illegitimate daughter of Sir Edward Walpole and granddaughter of Sir Robert Walpole, Whig politician and first de facto Prime Minister of Great Britain (whose term of 20 years 314 days is the longest in British history), Maria was not only unapproved, she came from the family of George's political rival.

The Prince of Wales had no more inclination to follow the regal rules than did his errant uncles. In 1784, George met Maria Anne Fitzherbert at the opera. Born at Tong Castle in Shropshire in 1756, Maria was the granddaughter of a baronet and was educated at a convent in Paris. By the time she entered London society in 1784, Maria had already been married and widowed twice. Left destitute after her first husband died just weeks after their marriage – before he had signed his new will – Fitzherbert had no option but to find herself a replacement husband as soon as possible. Having then married Thomas Fitzherbert in 1778, Maria might have been forgiven for thinking her life had finally settled down. But it wasn't to be – although the couple had a child, he died in infancy and Thomas himself followed their son to the grave in May 1781, just three years after the wedding. Maria was at least provided for financially in her second foray into widowhood. Thomas left her an annuity of £1,000 per annum (some £150,000 in modern money), as well as the lease of a house at 62 Park Street, Mayfair – as desirable (and expensive) an area then as it is today.

With assistance from her uncle, Lord Sefton, Maria managed to jump straight into the highest levels of London society and it wasn't long before she came to the attention of the younger – and very eager – Prince of Wales. Six years Maria's junior, George was soon smitten with the newcomer and pursued her with dogged determination. It's possible that the object of his affections had rather more reservations about embarking on such an unlikely relationship, given that she had already been widowed twice and was in all likelihood looking for someone to marry, in the hope of finally achieving some level of permanent security. But finding herself pursued by the heir to the throne must have been flattering to a young, single woman such as Maria, as much as she knew the relationship would never be publicly accepted. And George was certainly the one doing the chasing. Having proposed to Maria several times and been consistently rebuffed, it is alleged that the young prince eventually threatened suicide if she didn't accept his gift of a ring. Possibly unnerved by this rather passive-aggressive form of courtship and certainly concerned about the ramifications of entering into an illegal marriage with the heir to the British throne, Maria left for the Continent in order to avoid the situation. Stories differ as to whether Maria had a change of heart or George hunted her down, but what's for certain is that she returned to British shores some time in 1785.

The wedding of George, Prince of Wales to Maria Fitzherbert took place in the drawing room of her Mayfair house on 15 December 1785 and was witnessed by the bride's brother and uncle. It was completely illegal, as both bride and groom knew very well – not only had George not sought the king's permission (which would never have been given anyway), Maria was both a divorcee and – worse still – a Catholic. The law stated that no 'Papist' could take the British throne – and if his wife couldn't be queen, then George would not be recognised as king. Even if by some miracle the king had given his approval, George would immediately have been removed from the line of succession and his position as heir apparent taken by his brother Frederick, Duke of York. It isn't unkind to assume that George himself considered losing his claim to the throne too high a price, regardless of the strength of his feelings for Maria. Unsurprisingly, priests willing to conduct such a ceremony were thin on the ground. The Reverend Robert Burt was one of the Prince's Chaplains in Ordinary and the third priest approached by George with his unusual request. Having racked up debts of over £500, the Rev. Burt had been languishing in the Fleet Prison for some time, unable to pay his creditors. Seeing his opportunity, Prince George offered to paid off Burt's debts in order that he be freed from the Fleet – the only payment he required in return was that Burt conduct the prince's marriage to his beloved Maria. This can't have been an easy deal for Burt to strike – not only did it go against the religious tenets of the country at the time, he also risked being charged with treason, should his part in the affair ever come to light. It would be nice to think that George perhaps had some sympathy with Burt's imprisoned plight, but one has to assume that the king-to-be had very limited options and only someone in the direst of circumstances would be willing to conduct the illicit ceremony.

The couple made a home for themselves in Brighton, but lived separately in order to keep up the illusion that, even if their relationship was an open secret, it was a harmless one. Maria moved into a modest house that has long been demolished, close to where the north gate of the Royal Pavilion now stands. The prince had been renting a small farmhouse that faced the Old Steine, then a grassy promenade on which fisherman would dry their nets until a growth in tourism led to the area becoming increasingly enclosed in the late 1700s. In 1787, George commissioned Henry Holland – who was already building Carlton House for the prince in London – to enlarge the farmhouse and create something more fitting for royalty.

The initial building created by Holland was a still relatively modest villa, known as the Marine Pavilion. Lavishly decorated with imported Chinese furniture and ornaments, along with hand-painted Chinese wallpapers, it might have been enough for some people – but not George. By 1808 the Pavilion had its own stabling complex big enough to house more than sixty horses, complete with enormous stained-glass domed roof and adjacent indoor riding arena complete with royal viewing box. Its opulence wasn't lost even on George's closest friends, one of whom is alleged to have described the new build as, 'a most superb edifice, indeed quite unnecessarily so'. There was also a tunnel that connected the Pavilion to the stables, in order for the prince to get between the two without being seen by the public (local rumour had it that the tunnel led from the Pavilion to Fitzherbert's house, but this is – rather disappointingly – incorrect). When George was later established as Regent in 1811, he decided that Marine Pavilion was still not extravagant enough for an almost-monarch and commissioned John Nash to transform it into the spectacular building that still sits in Brighton today. Nash extended the original Pavilion building by installing a cast iron framework over and around it, which he then used to support endless rooms, galleries and turrets, all decorated with similar gilded taste as in the original building.

Although undoubtedly built with breathtaking extravagance at a time when so much of the population was living in poverty, the Royal Pavilion had a very positive influence on Brighton as a town, even if the benefits were localised. The sheer scale of the project meant employment opportunities for any number of local builders and craftsmen and the relocation of the heir to the throne to what had previously been a fairly unassuming seaside town led to many society figures following him and boosting the town's image in the public eye.

Although Maria continued the pretence of living separately with her own household, she and George socialised openly as a couple and were sometimes referred to as such without any drama in the local newspapers. However shocking their relationship might have been to formal society at large, Brighton clearly accepted them just as they were without making a song and dance about it.

But back to the early days of their illicit union and the first Regency Crisis of 1788 appears to have taken its toll on the couple's relationship. The formerly besotted George, already familiar with to the perils of overindulgence, began drinking heavily after his father's recovery stymied his attempt to become Regent. To add to Maria's woes, George took Lady Jersey as his new mistress, the adage of 'when a mistress becomes a wife, she leaves a vacancy' clearly being an old and very true one. Frances Villiers, Countess of Jersey, was the granddaughter of Sir William Twysden, 5th Baronet of Roysden Hall and the daughter of the baronet's youngest son, the Right Reverend Philip Twysden. George was 31 years old when he embarked on his affair with Frances Villiers. He had clearly not lost his penchant for older women because not only was Frances nine years older than him, she was also a mother of ten children and a grandmother to boot. He also ramped up his gambling habit and the debts began to mount to historic proportions, despite Parliament having agreed to increase his allowance (the king commented at the time that it was 'a shameful squandering of public money to gratify the passions of an ill-advised young man'). The exact figures are unclear, but by 1795, George certainly owed at least £600,000 (equivalent to more than a frankly heart-stopping £72 million today). King George III finally had the leverage he needed in order to bring his errant son back under regal control. Prince George was offered help to clear his debts, on one condition – he had to marry a cousin he'd never even met.

Caroline of Brunswick was the daughter of Charles, Duke of Brunswick, and his wife Princess Augusta, King George III's older sister. Brought up in what must have been an uncomfortable household – her father openly flaunted his mistress, Baroness von Hertefeld – she was raised in a competitive atmosphere from the start, as all German princesses were hoping to marry Prince George. Under constant supervision from a succession of governesses and so closeted away from the world that she was dissuaded from standing close to windows or even being alone with her own close male relatives, Caroline was perhaps the least likely potential royal candidate of them all. Despite this, there was certainly a spark of independence in the cloistered princess.

When the claustrophobic lifestyle finally got too much for the teenage Caroline, after yet again being refused permission to attend a ball, she pulled a dramatic stunt. Feigning illness so extreme that her parents were called back from said ball to see her, Caroline claimed to be suffering the agonies of childbirth. Despite her apparently never having been alone with a man in her entire life, the princess insisted that it was true and demanded that her parents call a midwife. Which, duly panicked, they did – only for their daughter to stop her writhing the instant the nurse walked into the room, turn to her mother and coolly announce, 'Now, Madam, will you keep me another time from a ball?'

Rumours circulated that Caroline really had become pregnant around this time, but whether there was ever a kernel of truth in them, or whether they started from the incident with the midwife is difficult to know. Although she was hidden away from the world for most of the time, Caroline was occasionally allowed to go out horse riding into the nearest town under far less supervision than she usually endured. This may be the source of the most persistent rumour, that she had become pregnant by a young man whom she loved, but whom her parents refused to accept because he wasn't royal. Whatever the truth of the matter, Princess Caroline was still unmarried at a far later age than most princesses of the time. The British royal family clearly saw a potential solution for both country's regal problems.

Deeply unpopular at the time, having 'lost' America and happily spending money while their country sank deeper into debt and civil unrest, the monarchy needed a steady hand at the tiller in order to salvage their situation. Prince George was possibly the least steady hand anyone would be able to find, with his spendthrift ways, illicit wife and aristocratic mistress; nevertheless, the future of the royal family rested on his shoulders. Princess Caroline was to be his salvation – a 'good' marriage to a princess of solid royal stock, who was said to be reasonably attractive in both looks and personality and who was definitely in need of a husband. Neither bride nor groom were enthusiastic about their union. Caroline is quoted as having said to a friend 'I am indifferent to my marriage … I think I shall be happy, but I fear my joy will not be enthusiastic … I resign myself to my destiny.'

Lord Malmesbury, a favoured and successful diplomat, was sent to Brunswick in order to secure the details of the marriage and escort the future bride back to England. Malmesbury's reservations were palpable from the start. Writing in his diary after his arrival in Brunswick, he notes Princess Caroline's attributes as if she were a beast being inspected at market (which, to all intents and purposes, is exactly what she was),

the Princess Caroline (Princess of Wales) much embarrassed on my first being presented to her—pretty face—not expressive of softness—her figure not graceful—fine eyes—good hand—tolerable teeth, but going—fair hair and light eyebrows, good bust—short, with what the French call 'des epaules impertinentes'.

The French that Malmesbury quotes best translates as 'sassiness' – which Caroline had in spades. Her claustrophobic upbringing had left her all but unsocialised and she refused to behave in a way that aristocratic households of the time would expect. Some of Caroline's behaviour may have been caused by mental health issues, three of her siblings having been born with significant learning disabilities. Whatever the reasons behind it, the young Caroline of Brunswick was utterly unsuitable for life as a British royal wife, a situation which Malmesbury had to do his best to rectify in the short time available to him before he would be expected to present the somewhat feral princess to her waiting husband. The diplomat clearly felt kindly enough towards the naive princess that he endeavoured to coach her in the ways of British royal life and certainly took his instruction seriously, his diary entry for Sunday, 7 December 1794 including the following:

> Sat next Princess Caroline at supper; I advise her to avoid familiarity, to have no confidantes, to avoid giving any opinion; to approve, but not to admire excessively; to be perfectly silent on politics and party; to be very attentive and respectful to the Queen; to endeavour, at all events, to be well with her. She takes all this well; she was at times in tears, but on account of having taken leave of some of her old acquaintance.

One cannot help but assume that some of Caroline's tears were for her carefully proscribed future, as well as the temporary absence of friends. She did, however, take to Malmesbury enough to ask him to be her Lord Chamberlain, a request which he turned down with a politeness sharpened by years in the diplomatic service – 'I told her any situation which placed me near her would be flattering to me, but that these situations were sought for by many persons who had better claims that myself.' His time with Caroline's family also taught him something of the Brunswick's attitude towards marriage and children, with Caroline's mother telling him during an apparently light-hearted conversation about ugly children taking after their fathers in looks, on the contrary, when a wife has done a wrong thing, and she is afraid of her husband, and if she sees him when she is breeding, she takes fright, and the child is marked with the husband, as it would with a spider, or cat, or anything she saw which frightened her during her pregnancy.

Malmesbury didn't shy away from appraising Caroline of the realities of her regal destiny.

I felt I had done what I wished, and set her mind on thinking of the drawbacks of her situation, as well as of it's 'agrémens,' and impressed it with the idea that, in the order of society, those of a very high rank have a price to pay for it, and that the life of a Princess of Wales is not to be one of all pleasure, dissipation, and enjoyment; that the great and conspicuous advantages belonging to it must necessarily be purchased by considerable sacrifices, and can only be preserved and kept up by a continual repetition of these sacrifices.

Finally having to face up to his royal destiny, George wrote to Maria Fitzherbert in June 1794, formally ending their relationship. That he was evidently more careful with Maria's feelings than with those of almost anyone else involved in his life perhaps gives credence to some of the long-held rumours that George and Maria had become parents while living in Brighton. Several of their friends, including the Duke of Gloucester, certainly believed that Mrs Fitzherbert may have become pregnant soon after the couple moved to the south coast, but it was never verified. After King George IV's death in 1830, one of his executors, Lord Stourton, asked Maria to sign a declaration on the back of their marriage certificate, confirming that they had never produced children, but later said that she, 'smilingly objected on the score of delicacy'.

Many people have claimed to be descended from Maria and George over the intervening centuries, but only two stand up to any real scrutiny. Maria had taken on the guardianship of Mary 'Minney' Seymour in 1798 and went on to adopt her as her daughter in 1804. Although Minney was supposedly the daughter of George's old friend Admiral Lord Hugh Seymour and his wife, Lady Anna Horatia Waldegrave (whose family fought a lengthy court battle against Maria adopting Minney permanently, the child eventually being awarded to Maria with the help of testimony from George), Maria and George acted as her de facto parents for the rest of their lives. George funded her education and provided the dowry for her marriage to Conservative politician Colonel George Dawson-Damer in 1825. Minney and George corresponded regularly, with Minney addressing her letters to 'My dear Prinny'. Of course, George's paternal input certainly doesn't mean that Minney was actually his daughter. But it's tempting to wonder if the court battle with the Seymours could have been due to Maria reneging on an agreement for them to adopt *her* child, who she then fought to keep. Perhaps Minney *was* the biological child of the Catholic widow and the prince after all?

But one of the most intriguing stories is that of James Ord, who was born in Britain somewhere between 1786 and 1789. Having never known his own parents, James was sent to Bilbao in Spain to live with a sailor called James Ord (the baby took the same name on arrival) who was supposedly his uncle. James's 'uncle' seemed to lead a charmed life after taking the young boy under his wing and was promoted to superintendent of the royal dockyards by the British Ambassador (allegedly a cousin of Maria Fitzherbert) despite having neither the rank nor experience generally required for such a post. James Jr was led to believe that he was the son of James's sister Mary and her husband Ralph, who had died before the boy was old enough to know him. James Snr, Mary and James Jr emigrated to America in 1790 and settled in Norfolk, Virginia. After Mary's death in 1796, James Snr took full responsibility for his nephew and the pair moved to Charles County, Maryland, for a while, before moving into a rented farm known as 'Non Such', near to the city of Washington DC. Their landlord on the farm was Rev. Notley Young, a Catholic priest of huge wealth who owned most of South Washington (he was also the third largest slaveholder in Maryland). James Ord Jnr enrolled as a student of Georgetown University in April 1800, his fees paid by the Rev. Young.

Ord would later recount his uncle once saying to him, 'if you had your rights in England you would be something great. God forgive those who have wronged you.' James Snr also, while on his deathbed, apparently told his nephew that he had 'something of the greatest importance' to tell him, but unfortunately he lost consciousness before he could continue with his confession. It's alleged that King William IV then offered James Ord Jr the choice of either the title Duke of Malta or a cash payment –

James took the money and the paperwork that went with it was locked away in the royal family's vaults within Coutt's Bank in London (the folders that supposedly contain all remaining paperwork connected to Mrs Fitzherbert are now in the Royal Archives). James Ord Jr married and had children of his own, it becoming family tradition for the eldest son to always be names James Ord and to always be told the story of how they would be the rightful heirs to the British throne, were it not for the monarchy's difficulties with Catholicism. At the time of writing, the current James Ord lives with his husband and four stepchildren in Salt Lake City, Utah.

When his (legal) bride to be finally arrived at court, the prince was less than enthusiastic. On the occasion of their first meeting, he greeted her politely before turning to Malmesbury and muttering, 'Harris, I am not well; pray get me a glass of brandy.' The patient diplomat suggested it might be more circumspect to take a glass of water, at which point the prince stalked from the room. It's said that Maria Fitzherbert watched him riding restlessly up and down within view of her rented house in Twickenham on the eve of his marriage, clearly struggling with the prospect of marrying his arranged bride. For her part, Caroline was equally disappointed, confiding in Malmesbury – who must have been wondering by this point what he could have done to deserve such a difficult post – in French that George was 'very fat and nothing like as handsome as his portrait'. Malmesbury notes in his diary that the princess seemed inclined to continue her criticism of her new and disappointing husband, but he was lucky enough to be called away.

The wedding of Prince George and Princess Caroline of Brunswick went ahead on 8 April 1795, regardless of the qualms of the two main participants. Neither had a choice in the matter – George knew it was his only opportunity to settle his debts and hopefully scrape back some popularity with the British public, and Caroline was a princess trapped in a strange new land with no option but to make the best of the situation. The small yet suitably grand affair took place in the Chapel Royal in St James's Palace and was attended only by the immediate family (and Caroline's four bridesmaids, none of whom she actually knew). There was some disapproval of Caroline's wedding dress, which was variously criticised for being too overdressed while also attracting attention for its very low décolletage. Any issues with the bride's clothing were, however, the responsibility of Queen Charlotte, whose letters to her son regarding arrangements for his bride's trousseau are still kept in the Royal Archives.

According to newspaper reports, Caroline 'seemed a little flustered upon her first entering the chapel, but perfectly regained her composure before the commencement of the ceremony'. Prince George, on the other hand, 'displayed much sensibility, and seemed so affected at one time as to be scarcely able to repeat the necessary part of the ceremony after the Archbishop'. George's problem was caused less by nerves and more by alcohol, having reportedly kept himself in a gentle state of drunkenness for the entire period of time between first meeting Caroline and then formally marrying her. George only got more drunk as the happy day wore on, presumably in an attempt to take his mind of the imminent wedding night – he had already confessed to Malmesbury that not only did he find Caroline unattractive and lacking in personal hygiene, he also suspected her of not being entirely virginal. Of course George himself was anything *but* a virgin, but sexual purity was considered a rigid requirement for royal princesses, if not their husbands. Mutual repulsion notwithstanding, George and Caroline did manage to do their duty and consummate the marriage, only for George to fall drunkenly into the fireplace after the deed was done. Caroline said afterwards that he 'passed the greatest part of his bridal night under the grate, where he fell, and I left him'. George would later claim that he and Caroline only had sex three times during their marriage – twice on their wedding night (which is impressive if true, given how much he had drunk) and once the night after. His determination to 'do his duty' in impregnating his new bride was successful, if unromantic; their daughter, Princess Charlotte of Wales, was born nine months later.

Despite having endured Malmesbury's crash course in etiquette before being escorted to Britain and her waiting husband, Caroline paid little attention to the niceties expected of a hostess at the very top of aristocratic society and rarely bothered to tone down her comments about other people, even when they were present. Lady Frances Villiers, who had encouraged George's reluctant choice of wife on the basis that she (correctly) believed they would be utterly incompatible, had been given the role of Caroline's First Lady of the Bedchamber. It didn't take long for the new royal wife to realise that her maid was sleeping with her husband and she took to insulting Frances in front of Prince George, knowing very well his attachment to her. The royal couple's open disdain for each other rapidly became obvious to anyone who saw them. No one involved in the sorry tale conducted themselves with decorum. Three days after Caroline gave birth to Princess Charlotte, her husband changed his will, leaving 'all the land in or about the pavilion at Brighton, all the property and furniture in the Pavilion and in the next house to it', to Maria Fitzherbert, whom he declared to be, 'the wife of my heart and soul. Although in the laws of this country she could not avail herself publicly of that name, still such she is in the eyes of Heaven, was, is and ever will be such in mine.' Caroline was to be left one single shilling.

George also took control over the life of Princess Charlotte. He didn't want to raise his daughter himself – she was handed into the care of a succession of governesses – but he wanted Caroline's input even less. In April 1796, Caroline received a letter from her husband which read in part, 'we have unfortunately been oblig'd to acknowledge to each other that we cannot find happiness in our union. Circumstances of character & education, … render that impossible.' Subsequently forced to leave court and move out to Charlton in south-east London, Caroline was isolated from her own child as well as from court itself. But she had a not-so-secret weapon – the British public. They *adored* her and saw her as in need of protection from the manipulative ways of the money-grabbing monarchy. With gossip being fanned by the expanding reach of what we would now call tabloids, Caroline rapidly became seen as the underdog behind whom public support began to gather apace. Unpopular at the best of times, the Royal family were an easy target for newspapers that were just getting the hang of information manipulation. Editors made the most of the situation, running stories alleging that Lady Jersey was intercepting Caroline's mail and telling tales of how badly the princess was being treated by, well, just about everyone.

Although she still saw her daughter often, Caroline clearly missed the closeness of the maternal relationship, because it was around this time that the she began adopting young children from poor backgrounds in her local area. She usually fostered them immediately out to suitable homes, but William Austin was different. Adopted by Caroline in 1802, when he was 3 months old, little William was the only one of the children to be taken into Caroline's own home and raised by the princess herself. After a falling-out with her neighbours Sir John and Lady Douglas –

who claimed that Caroline had been sending them threatening and obscene letters – Lady Douglas accused Caroline of covering up the fact that William Austin was, in fact, her biological son. There was certainly plenty of circumstantial evidence that made such a claim possible, at least in theory. Still only in her early thirties, Caroline had made the most of her unexpected and unwanted freedom from court, throwing parties and having all the fun she'd missed during her the cloistered years of her childhood and doomed marriage. Reports went so far as to suggest that Caroline was in the habit of dancing with her guests while stripped naked to the waist. Entertaining whichever men she so desired without a thought for outside opinion, Caroline threw to the winds the social correctness in which she had been so closely tutored by Lord Malmesbury.

Whatever the veracity of the stories told about her, Princess Caroline's behaviour did not meet the standards expected by royalty and Prince George decided that his only option was to find a reason to justify divorcing his unwanted wife. What became known as the 'Delicate Investigation' began in 1806, when George set up a commission to investigate Caroline's supposed biological connection to William Austin. Had she been found to be the child's true mother, George could prove her infidelity and thus gain the divorce he craved, while also blackening Caroline's name in the hope of lessening her public support. Unfortunately for him, Caroline really had adopted William and her servants testified that he had first been brought to her household by his biological mother, Sophia Austin. Sophia's husband had lost his job and she was hoping that the sight of her with a small child might soften Caroline towards using her influence to find him new employment. After being questioned by Caroline's servants, Sophia and William were taken to meet her. Rather than offering the support Sophia had hoped for, Caroline asked directly if she might buy the child – a not uncommon practice at the time – and the two women agreed on the price of one pound. Sophia had other children to feed as well as William and given the Austin's lack of family income, adopting William out to a household which could afford to give him everything in life that they could not would have seemed like a sensible decision. Young William Austin wanted for nothing except perhaps some well-placed boundaries in life. Caroline spoiled him to such an extent that he soon became all but unmanageable, saying, doing and helping himself to whatever took his fancy. The exiled princess's household rapidly became a sea of chaos as William, refused nothing by his indulgent adoptive mother, ran riot. Had they continued without further intrigue, mother and son might have continued being happily disruptive in their luxurious yet semi-feral solitude for many years. Caroline, however, continued to create scandal, even claiming at one point that William was the son of Louis Ferdinand of Prussia, whom she declared as having been her true love all along.

The investigators had to accept that William was not, after all, Caroline's child. But the scandal managed to achieve what George had wanted all along – her popularity with the British public was finally on the wane. Regardless of the investigation's outcome, it was followed by Caroline's visits with Charlotte being restricted to only one carefully scheduled meeting a week and then only if supervised by Caroline's widowed mother, the Dowager Duchess of Brunswick. When, in 1811, it was finally accepted that King George III no longer had capacity to reign and the prince was finally made Regent, he decided that his daughter also needed to be kept in check. Charlotte was informed that she was to be confined to Cranbourne Lodge, Windsor, with no visitors allowed except for her grandmother, the queen. The young princess ran out of the house onto the streets of St James, where she was helped to find a hackney cab – having never used public transport in her life – by a man who had seen her distress from the window of a neighbouring house. The cab took Charlotte to her mother's house, where members of her family and several Whig politicians gathered to advise her on the best course of action. One of the family members present was the Duke of York, who – unbeknownst to Charlotte – carried a warrant giving him the legal right to return the princess to her father by force, if necessary. The duke wasn't, in the end, required to use the law – after taking advice from politicians and spending a night cooling off under Caroline's roof, Charlotte returned home to Prince George the next day.

By now, the terrible state of the royal marriage was common knowledge across the country. Writing to her close friend Martha Lloyd in 1813, the author Jane Austen declared herself to be on the side of the princess, albeit with some reservation:

Poor woman, I shall support her as long as I can, because she is a Woman, & because I hate her Husband -- but I can hardly forgive her for calling herself 'attached & affectionate' to a Man whom she must detest -- & the intimacy said to subsist between her & Lady Oxford is bad -- I do not know what to do about it; but if I must give up the Princess, I am resolved at least always to think that she would have been respectable, if the Prince had behaved only tolerably by her at first.

Even Lord Byron felt obliged to give his opinion on the matter – although he took a different view to that of Jane Austen – writing to his publisher about his beliefs that Caroline was, indeed, an adulterer. Byron's views are less surprising when one remembers that he and Prince George moved in the same social circles and indeed were fellow members of certain upmarket gentlemen's clubs of very ill repute. Regardless, the storm created by the press was getting too much even for George. Clearly realising that things had more chance of settling down if his erstwhile wife was out of the picture entirely, he eventually arranged with the Foreign Secretary that Caroline should be offered an annuity of £35,000 (in the region of £2 million a year today, although inflation is difficult to calculate accurately), in order to leave the country.

George was also under pressure from elsewhere around this time. Maria Fitzherbert had taken to periodically reminding him of financial promises he had made to her early in their relationship. She wasn't above making veiled threats implying that she might not always be so quietly understanding, should her needs not me met. In 1813, she wrote:

The load of public business, which your Royal Highness must have had to occupy your time, has rendered me unwilling to press myself on your recollection; and the hope that I should find you remembering me without my having the pain of requesting you to do so, has with withheld me from writing sooner; but now that business is considerably over, permit me to urge the promise, when you are still in town, to recall to Your Highness's recollection myself and my situation.

Placed by you, Sir, when the memorable event of our Union took place in the year '85, under circumstances which rendered you the only person in this world, while life endured, that I could ever look up to for protection and support.... You were at that period pleased to settle me £10,000 per ann., as the income befitting the situation you placed me in…. Your difficulties in money matters put it out of your power to fulfil the settlement or give me more than £3,000 per ann. I was frequently distressed, but I do not complain.

Maria spent the rest of her life in Brighton, where she was treated with respect and affection by both local residents and visiting royalty.

In August 1814 Princess Caroline left Britain for Europe. Travelling to Italy via Switzerland, on her arrival in Milan, she engaged an ex-soldier by the name of Bartolomeo Pergami as the head servant of her new household. Despite Pergami being married with children, the pair became travelling companions, touring the Mediterranean as far as Turkey and Israel. Caroline clearly made the most of her newfound freedom, on one occasion apparently riding into Jerusalem on a donkey among a convoy of camels. Her adventures were still being reported in the British newspapers, who made the most of public antipathy towards George by casting a positive light on his not-yet-ex-wife's new life abroad.

In 1817, things began to fall apart. The warring couple's daughter Princess Charlotte had married Prince Leopold of Saxe-Coburg-Saalfeld the previous year. Theirs was a marriage based on deep affection, in great contrast to Charlotte's own parents – Leopold had been her own choice and she had had to fight her father for the right to marry him. Determined that Charlotte should marry William, Hereditary Prince of Orange, George had forced his daughter into his plan to such an extent that she – knowing it was almost inevitable and not entirely hating the idea of William as a prospective husband, this being the best that British princesses could hope for at the time – got as far as signing the marriage contract in June 1814. But in the meantime, Charlotte had become acquainted with Prince Leopold. Immediately taken with the prince when they first met at a party in London, Charlotte began to rethink the idea of marrying the Prince of Orange. Princess Caroline had been against the match from the start, and the public support she enjoyed at the time lent weight to her influence. Charlotte used the situation to her advantage, declaring that she would only agree to marry William if he agreed to Caroline being welcome in their home – something that she was well aware the Prince Regent would never allow. When William could not agree to her condition, Charlotte used it as reason to break off their engagement. It was a narrow escape, whether or not she realised it at the time – William would go on to become embroiled in blackmail after having homosexual relations with several of his male servants, who then used his secrets against him.

Things hadn't gone smoothly for Charlotte even then – having originally had her sights fixed on a Prussian prince, her hopes were dashed in December 1814, when she discovered that the object of her affections had become romantically attached elsewhere. Her thoughts returned to Leopold, whom she described to a friend as 'the next best thing'. Leopold indicated that he might be interested in such a connection, but was at the time on the Continent, fighting with his regiment in the Napoleonic wars. In fact Leopold didn't make very much effort to show his appreciation for Charlotte's interest in him at all – even when peace was declared he failed to return to Britain with as much eagerness as she might have liked. Eventually, it was the Prince Regent himself who summoned Leopold to visit the royal household, having finally given in to Charlotte's wishes. When the heir to the throne finally met his daughter's choice of husband he was pleasantly surprised, and gave the couple his blessing.

The wedding of Princess Charlotte of Wales and Prince Leopold of Saxe-Coburg-Saalfeld took place on 2 May 1816. It was a popular match and crowds lined the London streets in the hope of catching a glimpse of the wedding party. Arriving at Clarence House for a pre-wedding dinner (the ceremony itself was held at 9 o'clock in the evening), Leopold himself was very nearly crushed by the eager crowds. When he got into his carriage to travel to Carlton House for the ceremony, excitement was so high that some members of the crowd attempted to unharness the horses in order that they might pull his carriage themselves. The country as a whole saw Charlotte and Leopold as a potential shining light with which to guide the country out of the depressing years of war, poverty and a monarchy who were out of touch. Despite the fact that Britain was, at the time, in great financial difficulty, no expense was spared. Charlotte's dress alone cost the equivalent of more than half-a-million pounds in today's money and was made of the finest silver silk and Brussels lace. Leopold had been made a general in the British Army prior to the wedding in order to elevate his status and was dressed as such; this didn't stop Charlotte allegedly giggling during the service at her new husband's solemn promise to endow her with all of his worldly goods, of which she was well aware he had barely any. Princess Caroline did not attend the ceremony and neither did King George, who was in the middle of one of his episodes of poor mental health.

The newly married couple honeymooned at Oatlands Palace in Weybridge (home of the Duke of York), before returning to London for the social season. They then took up residence at Claremont, a large mansion in 350 acres of land near Esher, Surrey, which had been bought by an Act of Parliament in order to be given to the couple as a wedding gift from the nation. Keen to support those less well off than themselves, the happy couple made a point of employing the poorest of labourers to undertake the renovation work that Claremont was desperately in need of. Even old and infirm workers were employed and directed towards the less arduous tasks such as weeding and tidying up of the many 'walks' through the mansion's park. Charlotte and Leopold were devoted to each other and preferred to spend their time quietly at Claremont when not in London. After falling ill at the opera in late 1816 it had been declared that Charlotte had suffered a miscarriage, so when it was declared that the she was pregnant again the next spring, all eyes were on the princess and her unborn child.

Public interest was hugely invested in Charlotte and the baby, who would together be the future of the British monarchy. Prince George's popularity was still markedly less than that of his daughter and there was an air of waiting for the dawning of a new era when Charlotte would finally take to the throne. Bookmakers starting taking bets on what sex the child would be and newspapers regularly reported solicitously upon their wellbeing. Interest was global, with the tiniest of news updates syndicated in newspapers across the Empire. From the *Royal Gazette of Jamaica*, 4 October 1817 – 'The Princess Charlotte and Prince Leopold are living in the most retired and domestic manner at Claremont, truly happy in themselves.' Despite the outside excitement, Charlotte had kept her daily life quiet for much of the duration of her pregnancy in order to keep herself and the baby as safe as possible.

Most women would rely on female midwives to support them during childbirth, but royalty required a man. Charlotte's official prenatal care came from Sir Richard Croft, who did at least have more obstetric training than many physicians of the time. With nothing much to do except sit around at home and eat, the princess had gained a considerable amount of weight during the course of her pregnancy. As she got closer to the end stages of her pregnancy, Croft and his team decided to put the princess on a diet, in the hope that it would prevent the baby from growing too big for her to deliver safely. They were almost certainly concerned that she was showing signs of developing preeclampsia, a pregnancy disorder commonly known as 'toxaemia' at the time, and which was often fatal. She was also 'bled' on several occasions, which was standard medical practice at the time. With hindsight, it is easy to see that this treatment can only have further weakened Charlotte's physical strength, but at the time it was believed to be helpful in cases of toxaemia as it was thought to help lower blood pressure. She was forty-two weeks pregnant by the time she went into labour on 3 November 1817. When Charlotte had struggled for twenty-six hours through the early stages, Croft sent for support in the form of Dr John Sims, but the princess had been labouring for over thirty hours by the time he arrived. Croft had realised by this time that Charlotte's baby was lying in the transverse position – sideways across the womb, rather than with its head pointing downwards – and his options were limited. Transverse babies are sometimes manually moved by careful external manipulation even in the present day, but in the majority of cases the safest option for both mother and child is to perform a caesarean section. In the early 1800s, the mortality rate for a mother undergoing a caesarean section was something over 85 per cent, a figure that made it an impossible option for the increasingly worried Croft. Sims professed a desire to attempt a forceps delivery, but Croft refused; a decision that is often used to illustrate his supposed negligence of Charlotte's care. But what Croft knew was that the use of forceps was, at the time, as dangerous as going without them; bringing with it the risk of damaging both the mother and child to a potentially fatal extent. It's believed that Croft did eventually manage to manipulate the baby into the correct position for delivery, but by this time Princess Charlotte had been in labour for almost two days and was utterly exhausted.

Somewhere towards 9pm on the 5 November 1817, Princess Charlotte of Wales gave birth to a 9lb baby boy who had clearly, to the deep distress of all those present, been dead for some hours before his arrival. Leopold – who had been present throughout, showing a husbandly devotion to duty that was most uncommon at the time – was given an opiate to help him sleep off the shock, while Charlotte was allowed to rest. Croft had been concerned by the princess's condition throughout, and her physical state immediately post-birth didn't reassure him – the placenta broke apart as it was expelled and a portion of it stayed behind, Croft having to manually remove it in order to save Charlotte haemorrhaging. Once the immediate tragic panic was over, Croft too retired to rest after his exertions, leaving Charlotte – who appeared to be as well as could be expected, under the circumstance – in the care of nurses.

Sometime in the early hours of the next morning, Charlotte began vomiting and complaining of severe pains in her abdomen. Her nurses called Croft back into the room and he found her bleeding badly and struggling to breath. Croft called Leopold's private physician Christian Stockmar and asked him to get Leopold back into the room urgently. He struggled to raise the prince – who was still under the effects of the opiates he had been given – and went back to look in on Charlotte before turning to once again try to rouse her husband. As Stockmar left the room, Charlotte is said to have called after him, 'Stocky, Stocky!' In the few seconds it took Stockmar to return to his patient, Charlotte had died.

The sudden death of the young princess and her baby sent shockwaves across the country. Henry Brougham, Princess Caroline's legal advisor, said of the tragedy, 'It really was as though every household throughout Great Britain had lost a favourite child.' Leopold was understandably devastated, having gone in a matter of hours from being an excited and expectant father to a widower with a dead son. Writing to Sir Thomas Lawrence, a renowned portrait painter who was closely connected to the royal family, he said, 'Two generations gone. Gone in a moment! My Charlotte is gone from the country – it has lost her ... she was an admirable woman. None could know my Charlotte as I did know her!'

Indicative of the poor state of relations in the royal family at the time, no one bothered to inform Princess Caroline of her daughter's death. The erstwhile princess was in Rome at the time along with Bartolomeo and found out the tragic news more or less accidentally, when the courier that Prince George had sent to inform the Pope realised they were in the area and passed the information on.

The impact of the princess's death was felt worldwide. Lord Byron, never one for understatement, was alleged to have 'screamed in anguish' upon hearing the news while travelling in Venice, later writing to a friend,

'The death of the Princess Charlotte has been a shock even here and must have been an earthquake at home.' Percy Shelley published a pamphlet titled, *An Address to the People on the Death of the Princess Charlotte*, which was part tribute and part polemic against both the government and the monarchy. When Shelly wrote, 'Mourn then People of England. Clothe yourselves in solemn black. Let the bells be tolled,' he was speaking of liberty itself as much as he was of Charlotte. The princess and her mother were still hugely popular among the general public, but anti-establishment feelings were also on the rise. Prince George knew this only too well and was by now desperate to divorce Caroline, in the hope that he might still be able to remarry and produce an heir to the throne.

In September 1818, the 'Milan Commission' began. A team of investigators were dispatched by the Prime Minister, Lord Liverpool, to find out whether anything in Caroline's behaviour could be declared grounds for divorce. The government were well aware, however, of Caroline's continued popularity with the British people, at a time when King George was gravely ill and both Parliament and the Prince Regent were deeply unpopular. It was therefore decided that what evidence they had should be used as a bargaining tool in order to persuade Caroline that a permanent separation was the only sensible option and that she should stay on the Continent. Before any agreement could be reached, however, the inevitable happened. King George III died on 29 January 1820, making his warring son and daughter-in-law king and queen of Great Britain and Ireland.

The new king was by now absolutely determined that his estranged wife should not take her place on the throne and began to publicly push her out. From February 1820, churches across the country – who by religious tradition said prayers for the Royal Family every Sunday – were instructed to omit Caroline from their liturgies. This did not go unnoticed by a public already stirring against authority after the Peterloo Massacre of 1819 and the oppressive 'Six Acts' against radical rebellion which had been passed through Parliament in its wake. Caroline's return to British shores on 5 June was marked by riots breaking out in support, her treatment by the king and his government having made her an unlikely figurehead for those who would rebel against authority. Despite increasing hostility from his own people – the guards of the King's Mews mutinied in support of Caroline on 15 June, although the uprising was contained – the new King George was determined to get the divorce he so craved. On 27 June Parliament relented and agreed to appoint a secret committee to investigate the contents of the bags of evidence that had arisen from the Milan Commission. Although details of the information inspected by the committee were not divulged, they declared it to include information that 'deeply affect the honour of the Queen, charging Her Majesty with an adulterous connection with a foreigner'. The foreigner referred to in the report was, of course, Caroline's favourite travel companion, Bartolomeo Pergami.

On 5 July 1820, the 'Bill of Pains and Penalties for an Act to Deprive Caroline of the Rights and Title Queen Consort and to Dissolve her Marriage to George' made its first appearance in the House of Lords. Rather than passing through Parliament in the normal process, the second reading of this particular Bill was staged as a trial, complete with witnesses. Although Caroline attended the hearing, she wasn't permitted to speak in her own defence and had to rely on a legal team headed by Henry Brougham. George had clearly decided that Caroline should be made an example of in order that he be proven correct in his accusations of adultery, because the entire trial – unlike previous investigations into his wife's behaviour – was conducted as publicly as possible. All peers were obliged to attend throughout the proceedings and additional galleries were built in the Chamber in order to accommodate one of the largest gatherings the House had ever seen. The crux of the accusations against Caroline was that 'a most unbecoming and degrading Intimacy commenced between Bartolomeo Pergami and Her said Royal Highness'. Witnesses for the prosecution claimed to have seen the queen and Pergami in various intimate situations, including bathing together and kissing. In return, the defence claimed that witnesses had been offered bribes in order to stand against Caroline. Brougham argued that George's previous proposal of a formal separation all but gave Caroline licence to do as she pleased, so long as it was away from British shores. Although the Bill passed its second reading, by the time it reached the third, the government had come to the conclusion that the royal drama was not worth the amount of bad feeling it was stirring up among a population who were clearly prepared to support Caroline – a privileged foreign aristocrat – purely because she was the underdog against an establishment that was already deeply unpopular with its own people. On 10 November

1820, Prime Minister Lord Liverpool moved to formally withdraw the Bill, declaring that he 'could not be ignorant of the state of public feeling with regard to this measure'.

In addition, the claims against the queen had put the spotlight on the double standards suffered by women in such cases – while adultery on the part of a wife was considered grounds for divorce, adultery by a husband was not. The prosecution doubled down on this view when questioned by Brougham, stating that 'The counsel for the Queen seemed to think that there was no difference between adultery committed by a man and by a woman. This was a most extraordinary proposition, whether considered legally or with reference to its effects upon society.' This focus on women's rights (or lack thereof) was welcomed by those who supported radical change and Caroline found herself the unwitting figurehead of an early women's movement, with female-friendly societies in the north naming themselves after her. One motion of support from 'the married ladies of London' had upwards of 17,000 signatures. Caroline made the most of this, declaring, 'A government cannot stop the march of intellect any more than they can arrest the motion of the tides or the course of the planets', and 'All classes will ever find in me a sincere friend to their liberties, and a zealous advocate of their rights.'

Caroline's friendship with 'all classes' clearly had its price, however. That price turned out to be the £50,000 a year with no conditions, presented to her by the government as their full and final offer. Caroline accepted, and her career as a radical figurehead came to an end. She was still, however, held in great affection by much of the country and was thus determined to at least be formally crowned as queen. Early on the morning of 19 July 1821, Caroline arrived at Westminster Abbey for the coronation ceremony later that day, only to be refused entrance. George had given firm instructions that his wife was not to be admitted under any circumstances and she was refused admission at both the East and West Cloisters. She then tried to enter through Westminster Hall, but the door was slammed in her face by an embarrassed guard. In desperation, she tried the entrance at Poet's Corner, but was rebuffed and finally persuaded to return to her carriage. Reports of the time declare there to have been a crowd chanting 'Shame, shame!' as the unwanted queen was carried away, but it is unclear as to whether it was in sympathy with Caroline's treatment or mocking her plight.

While her husband was celebrating his first official night as king, Caroline became unwell. Her condition worsened over the next three weeks and, realising she was nearing the end, she began to make arrangements. Her new will requested that she be buried in her home town of Brunswick, in a tomb that was to bear the inscription 'Here lies Caroline, the Injured Queen of England.' Caroline died on the evening of 7 August 1821. The cause of death has never been definitively specified; it was thought at the time to have been caused by some form of intestinal obstruction, but could have been cancer. Some, aware of the desperation with which Caroline's husband wished to be rid of her, suggested she may have been poisoned.

Caroline's burial took place in her home town of Brunswick on 25 August 1821, with a funeral procession beginning on 18 August in London. Wary of potential unrest from supporters of the late queen if the cortege travelled through central London, Lord Liverpool instructed that it should instead skirt the north of the city and travel straight to Harwich en route for Brunswick. The gathered crowds were incensed at the realisation they were going to be prevented from saying their goodbyes. The *Manchester Guardian* reported on the violent and confusing events of the day:

Before six o'clock a crowd assembled at Hyde Park Corner. The anxiety of the people as to the course the funeral procession would take was here most strikingly displayed. The crowd were unwilling to depart from a place where there was a favourable chance of joining or viewing the procession; but there was the greatest agitation and alarm lest it should pass another way.

The procession reached Kensington at half past nine. It was after eleven that it moved on into Hyde Park, and an attempt was made to pass, but this failed, for the people, apprehensive that the hearse would not pass through the City, shut the gates.

About twelve o'clock the procession entered the Park, and during its passage through it a scene of confusion and outrage ensued of which the annals of this or any other Christian country can present few parallels. Vast numbers of persons on foot and on horseback passed with great speed along Park Lane. Their object was suspected by the Guards to be to reach that gate before them, with the view of meeting the procession, and forcing it to turn back. To prevent this, the Guards galloped through the Park to gain Cumberland Gate before them. The procession moved at a very quick pace through the Park. Suddenly, it halted, and it was understood that the people had closed the gates. It became necessary to force a way for the procession through whatever impediments might present themselves. The people were equally bent on turning the procession, and forcing it into the route of the city. Here a contest arose, and here, we deeply regret to say, blood was shed!

Some stones and mud were thrown at the military, and a magistrate being present, the soldiers were sanctioned in firing their pistols and carbines at the unarmed crowd. Screams of terror were heard in every direction. The number of shots fired was not less than forty or fifty. So completely did the soldiery appear at this period to have lost the good temper and forbearance they previously evinced, that they fired shots in the direction in which the procession was moving. Immediately upon the cessation of the firing, the latter part of the procession joined the rest of the funeral train. The rain, which had lately abated, again poured in torrents, as the procession advanced.

Two were killed and many injured in the melee. The man who made the decision to send the cortege through the city after all, Chief Metropolitan Magistrate Sir Robert Baker, was fired for doing so, despite having taken such action because he felt it was the safest option. And the drama still wasn't over quite yet. Parliament had refused to honour Caroline's request for the (admittedly rather acerbic) inscription that she favoured, yet when the English delegation stopped at the church in Colchester where Caroline's coffin was being kept overnight on its way to sail from Harwich, they discovered that the requested 'Here lies Caroline, the Injured Queen of England' had already been fixed onto the coffin by her close supporters. Argument broke out in the church as the opposing sides stood around the coffin of the dead queen until the Mayor of Colchester sent a party of local militia in to break up what newspapers reported as 'the sacreligious disputants'. The argument must have carried on elsewhere, because eventually the original plaque was removed and replaced with the Latin version preferred by Parliament and the king, an approximate translation of which is as follows:

Here lies the body of the most Serene Princess Carolina Amelia Elizabeth, by the Grace of God Queen Consort of the most August and Powerful Monarch George IV, by the Grace of God King of the Britains, Defender of the Faith, King of Hanover, and Duke of Brunswick and Lüneberg. She died on the 7th of the month of August, Year of Our Lord 1821, at the age of 54.

The monarchy had won their hollow victory.

*   *   *

However life separated George and Maria Fitzherbert, theirs was a bond that was clearly never quite broken. In 2017, London auction house Christies sold a diamond-set pendant that was thought to have belonged to Maria and which had been passed down through the family via her adopted daughter, Minney Seymour. Described by Christies as, 'a gold locket, set with 24 rose-cut diamonds. It contains a tiny portrait of George and boasts another larger, completely transparent diamond — known as a portrait diamond — as its cover', it was thought to have been commissioned as one half of a pair by London jewellers and silversmiths, Rundell, Bridge & Rundell, in approximately 1800. George had allegedly worn the twin locket – which contained a portrait of Maria, both images having been painted by royal miniature artist Richard Cosway – under the lapel of his coat throughout his life. Knowing that he was near death, the king placed a recent letter from Maria under his pillow, before requesting that his own locket be placed around his neck and buried with him when the time came. Some years later, the Duke of Wellington (who had been the executor of King George's will) was dining with Minney Seymour. He recognised a pendant in her possession that contained a portrait of George as being the pair to the one he had seen on the king's deathbed and relayed the story to Minney. Upon informing her mother of what the duke had told her, Maria apparently shed tears at the knowledge that she hadn't, despite everything the couple had been through, been forgotten at all.

*   *   *

William Austin, the little boy adopted by Princess Caroline, struggled to adapt to life outside the realm of royal privilege. Caroline did leave him money in her will, but nothing like as much as he might have expected, as the adopted son of a princess. He disappears from the history books for a while, but reappears in newspaper reports twenty-five years after the death of his adoptive mother, this time for the saddest of reasons. On 13 March 1845, the *Morning Post* reported:

COMMISSION OF LUNACY ON WILLIAM AUSTIN – THE ADOPTED SON OF THE LATE QUEEN CAROLINE.

Yesterday a commission *de Lunatico Inquirendo* was opened before Mr Commissioner Winslow and a Special Jury, at the Sheriff's Court, Red Lion-square, to inquire into the state of mind of William Austin, late of the city of Milan, but now residing at Blackland House, Chelsea, gentleman.... His name was William Austin, a gentleman of about forty years of age, but of limited means, his property consisting of about 4,000l invested in the funds. He had been brought recently from Milan, and the present proceedings had been adopted under the authority of Sir Thomas Wilde and Dr Lushington, who acted for Mr Austin as guardian. Mr Austin when first attacked with this infirmity, was resting in Milan, and it was thought advisable to place him in one of the asylums in that city. The time when he was first afflicted with loss of mind occurred as far back as the year 1830, but he [the Learned Counsel] was afraid, owing to the great trouble and expense in obtaining witnesses, that he should not be able to go further back than the year 1841, at which period Mr Austin was an inmate of the Hospice de Santé, at Milan. The unfortunate gentleman became completely imbecile, and his imbecility was so absolute as to amount almost to idiotcy [*sic*]. The guardians thought it advisable that he should be brought to England, and in the month of February last he left Milan in the care of a keeper, and on the 6th of the present month arrived in England. He was ... removed to Dr. Sutherland's establishment, Blackland House.

Louis Balbi, who was examined through the medium of an interpreter, said he was a keeper at the Hospice de Santé, at Milan. Under his care was a person named Austin, who was an inmate of the asylum about three years. He was there when witness first went, on the 15th of September, 1841, and was in the same state of mind then as at present. He would eat, drink and sleep, but never spoke. During the three years he never spoke once. When spoken to he never answered, and was incapable of doing anything. He was very much attached to a piece of stick, which never leaves his possession night or day. He never gave any reason for his attachment to the stick.... When he drank he would sing, but was never violent. He has not spoken once since he has been there, although witness has spoken to him frequently. He has not expressed his wants at all.

Dr Chowne, MD, said he saw Mr Austin on the 6th of March, and found him apparently imbecile. He saw him again on the 10th ... and he should say his incompetency of mind had been of long duration. There is no probability of his recovering. It was a bare possibility. He appeared to comprehend some things said to him but not others. Mr E. Duke Moore, surgeon, corroborated Dr Chowne's evidence, and ... and it would be a miracle for him to recover. Dr Sutherland concurred.... It was a case of chronic unsoundness of mind, had been of long duration, and beyond cure.

The unfortunate gentleman was brought into Court. He was attired in a long rifle-green great coat, thick trimmed with fur, with a cap en suite, red and black cross-bar trousers, and a similar waistcoat. In height he is about five feet six inches, and rather stoutly made. He is a good-looking man, with an intellectual countenance, and a remarkably high forehead. In his hand he held a small piece of grape-vine stick, which he kept twirling round, apparently totally unconscious of all that was passing.... On the Commissioner giving the order for him to withdraw, he followed the keeper out. It was a most painful sight.

The Jury immediately returned a verdict, 'That William Austin was of unsound mind, and incapable of managing his affairs, and had been so since the 15th of September, 1841.'

William stayed in the Blackland House asylum and died there in February 1857, at the age of 54. He is buried in Brompton Cemetery, Kensington, London.

* * *

Sir Richard Croft, the obstetrician in charge of Princess Charlotte's doomed final pregnancy, never forgave himself for what had happened. On 13 February 1818, while attending a Mrs Thackeray, who was struggling in labour with similar issues to those suffered by the late princess, Croft became visibly stressed and was sent to get some rest in a spare room. He was found dead by one of the servants in the early hours, having shot himself in the head. A copy of Shakespeare's *Loves Labour's Lost* was found on the hearth in the room where Croft lay, as if it had been dropped there by whoever had been reading it. According to a report in *The Times*, the book lay open at the line, 'Good God! Where's the Princess?'

Chapter 18

The Princess Diaries

It wasn't just the boys in King George III's family who could be a worry to their often ailing father – his daughters each had private stories of their own. Some of the king's children would go on to lead traditional royal lives, marrying into European royalty and generally taking care of family business, but others? Not so much.

Princess Sophia Matilda was the second youngest of King George III's surviving children and the fifth of his six daughters. The girls were doted on by their father but cowered in fear of their stern mother, so it was rather unfortunate that Queen Charlotte did most of the parenting due to George's bouts of mental ill health. Brought up in a home environment that she and her sisters called 'the nunnery', one would have perhaps expected the girls to be all but invisible in royal history – but most girls turn out to have a mind of their own, and being royal didn't change that.

Much of Sophia's life took place behind firmly closed doors, but those snippets of gossip that did make it out into the public domain read as if they were part of some fairy story come to life. According to an article published in the *Kentish Chronicle* on 31 March 1829, it was a very mysterious event indeed (the newspaper went on to note that 'some of the facts occurred, not twenty-seven, but twenty-nine years ago', a change of date which proves to be important):

In the summer season, about seven and twenty years ago, when his late Majesty was about to make his usual migration from Windsor to Weymouth, the Princess Sophia, then about 25 years of age, was in very indifferent health, insomuch that it became necessary for the party which left the Castle the first day, and which consisted of the Princesses Mary, Elizabeth and Sophia, attended by the late Generals Gwynne and Goldsworthy, and General Garth, to rest at Andover for the night, instead of making the journey in a single day, as was usual with Royal parties on such occasions; and when they arrived at the Royal residence at Weymouth, one Lady was so exhausted, that it became necessary for her to be carried upstairs in the arms of one of her attendants.

Soon after this, it happened that the wife of a tailor, named Sherland, living on the Esplanade at Weymouth, was one day delivered of a son, and was doing well after her travail, under the care of a Mr Beaver, an accoucher [midwife] of the same place; but about 3 o'clock the next morning, that gentleman returned to the tailor's house with another fine boy in his arms, and soon afterwards the nurse was called and informed that her mistress had made her husband doubly happy by presenting him with a second son, twin to the first.

On the morning after this strange affair occurred at the house of the tailor, it was announced to the Queen by Lady Cathcart and Lady Charlotte Bruce, who had been in attendance upon the Princess Sophia, that a great change had take place in the state of her Royal Highness, and that the medical attendant had declared that there was now every prospect that her Royal Highness would be completely restored to health after a short period of rest and quiet retirement.

The arrival of this mystery baby might have stayed a secret, had the tailor himself not become somewhat carried away with the potential importance of his unexpected young charge. Newspapers reported him as being 'raised so much above his level in the scale of importance' that he took to telling anyone who would listen all about the great responsibility with which he had been trusted. The tailor eventually visited General Thomas Garth – who had not only been present at Princess Sophia's strange weekend in Weymouth, but who was also facilitating regular payments towards the child's upkeep – and requested details of the boy's biological parents, in order that he might consult with them as to his welfare and upbringing. This move on the part of the tailor was deemed unbecoming – the child was removed from the family's care and was instead fostered by the wife of a sergeant in the Royal Scots Greys, who lived with the boy in the general's own household. The boy's name was changed to Tommy Garth and the general would tell him that he himself was the boy's 'papa'. When little Tommy questioned who then was his mother, the general would allegedly bring out a miniature from inside his jacket pocket and suggest that Tommy kiss the image of his 'mama'.

Given the confusion and upheaval surrounding both his parentage and upbringing, it's little wonder that Tommy Garth junior went somewhat off the rails. He only learned of his true parentage when Garth senior was thought to be on his deathbed and confessed all to his son. The Garth family were deep in debt at the time, and young Tommy realised that he potentially had the perfect blackmail opportunity. He approached representatives of the Royal Family with evidence that he was, in fact, the son of Princess Sophia. Sophia had never married, remaining at court until her mother died and then moving into Kensington Palace, taking rooms next to her niece – and future queen – Princess Victoria. When Tommy took a box of evidence to the royal family, they allegedly offered him a substantial sum of money for it, only to refuse to pay up when the box was safely in their possession. Having run out of options, Tommy then took his story to the newspapers, who duly reported the whole sorry tale. The difference, however, was that while investigating Tommy's story, the press discovered another rumour – that Tommy's father wasn't General Garth at all, but rather Sophia's older brother Ernest, the Duke of Cumberland. The media's fascination with the princess and the child with unknown parentage would follow Sophia around for the rest of her life.

After Queen Charlotte's death, Sophia moved out of the royal household and into Kensington Palace with her widowed sister-in-law Princess Victoria, Duchess of Kent, and her daughter, Princess Alexandrina Victoria. The house was run by Sir John Conroy, the duchess's comptroller (a person who takes charge of business and/or finance for another), who rapidly sucked Sophia into his unhealthy web. Disliked by her sister-in-law and distrusted by the young future queen, Sophia came increasingly under Conroy's control, acting as his spy. Conroy was also allowed to squander most of Sophia's wealth – on her death it was discovered that, despite her familial wealth and social standing, she had almost no money at all to her name.

So, was Tommy Garth really the secret son of a Royal princess? Various theories have been put forward over the years, but the evidence does stack up in favour of Tommy having been the offspring of an illicit affair between Sophia and General Garth. An improbable pairing on the surface – Garth was more than three decades older than the princess, had a large purple birthmark on his face and was once described by the diarist Charles Greville as a 'hideous old devil' – but according to a lady-in-waiting, the princess was 'so violently in love with him'. Sophia had been closeted away from the outside world for so long that perhaps an older member of her own social circles felt like a safe haven.

Sophia's older sisters had equally secretive private lives, not least because keeping secrets was the only way they were likely to be allowed a personal life at all. Princess Augusta, the king's sixth child and second daughter, was so affected by the cloistered upbringing of her youth that she was terrified of being out in public and stammered when nervous. In contrast, she was said to be lively and boisterous within the confines of her home and considered by her few friends to be both intelligent and amusingly entertaining. Both Prince Frederick of Sweden and the Crown Prince of Denmark put forward marriage proposals (although the Denmark proposal was rather impersonal – the Prince simply wished to marry any of the British princesses and didn't much care which one), but King George refused to give permission for either. One would like to think that the King was being careful with whom he allowed his daughters to consort, but in reality it was much more to do with his increasing desire to keep his children at home with himself and Queen Charlotte.

Augusta became acquainted with Irish soldier, Lieutenant General Sir Brent Spencer around 1800. Eight years the princess's senior, Spencer had fought in the American War of Independence and would go on to see action at the Battle of Alexandria. By 1803, Spencer and Princess Augusta were romantically entwined, but kept their relationship tightly under wraps. Not only would their connection be frowned upon because of their differing social status, the princess was concerned that if her father found out about it, it might trigger another episode of his mental health problems. They clearly succeeded in keeping their secret, as Spencer was employed by the unwitting king as an equerry in 1805. By 1812, Augusta's beloved brother George was installed as Prince Regent and she saw her opportunity to grab a more formal connection with her long-term secret lover. In a long and personal letter to George, Augusta begged his permission to marry Spencer in private, promising the utmost discretion if her wish was granted. Queen Charlotte discovered Augusta's request and, outraged by what she perceived as her daughter's betrayal of the ailing king, absolutely forbade any marriage taking place (although the queen's permission was not, in fact, a formal requirement). Regardless, although there are no records to show that the marriage took place, there are equally no records to prove that it *didn't* and nor would there be. Whatever the couple's legal standing, they remained devotedly together until Spencer's death in 1828.

Princess Elizabeth, the king's third daughter, born in 1770, was only two years younger than Augusta and the closest to Queen Charlotte of all the royal princesses. As such, the Queen was reluctant to let her daughter marry for fear of losing her, but Elizabeth knew that a proposal was her only potential means of escape from the suffocating atmosphere of Buckingham House.

There have long been rumours of Elizabeth having contracted a secret marriage of her own, to George Ramus, the son of a royal page and two decades Elizabeth's senior. No evidence exists for this union, but that hasn't stopped people speculating that this unlikely couple not only managed to keep a wedding entirely secret, but that they had a daughter, Eliza, in 1788. In addition, court records show Princess Elizabeth as being present at social events throughout the time she would have been pregnant with any illegitimate child – one cannot imagine the entirety of high society keeping such a secret.

An Elizabeth Ramus certainly existed, as George Romney painted a portrait of her – but he undertook the commission in 1777, when Princess Elizabeth was still only 7 years old. Given that the painting depicts a young adult woman, it's safe to assume that the sitter was neither the princess nor her alleged daughter.

A much more likely dalliance is that suggested to have occurred between Princess Elizabeth and Alleyne Fitzherbert, 1st Baronet of St Helens. Seventeen years older than the princess, Fitzherbert shared many beliefs about the royal court system (they both considered it outdated and stuffy). Elizabeth wrote to Lady Harcourt, 'There is no man I love so well and his tenderness to me has never varied.' Elizabeth commissioned a portrait of Fitzherbert from the renowned miniaturist Henry Pierce

Bone in 1810 and he in turn commissioned an enamelled miniature of the princess that he carried with him.

Fitzherbert remained childless and unmarried for the rest of his life, but Elizabeth was more pragmatic. She had already desired to accept a proposal from the Duke of Orleans in 1808, but had been made to refuse on the grounds of his Catholicism. In 1814, the princess spotted Prince Frederick of Hesse-Homburg at a ball and allegedly declared, 'If he is single, I will marry him.' It took four years for Frederick to become inclined to ask for Elizabeth's hand – and when he did, Queen Charlotte tried to dissuade her daughter – but the pair were finally married in 1818. It was far from a tale of true love, but the couple got on well enough and each benefited from the arrangement – Frederick could claim connection to the British royal family and Elizabeth escaped the cloistered courts for the relative freedom of Germany. Not for the first time in royal affairs, pragmatism had won out.

Princess Amelia was the youngest child of King George III and Queen Charlotte, and allegedly her father's clear favourite. She would also be the child who finally brought her father to full mental health crisis, after her death at the age of 27. Almost six years younger than Sophia, their intervening brothers Octavius and Alfred had both died after illness caused by the smallpox vaccine. Amelia's arrival was seen as a shining beacon of hope and she became the king's firm favourite. His worries about losing his daughters to marriage were so extreme that even as the princesses grew older, Queen Charlotte avoided contemplating potential suitors for them, for fear of triggering yet another of the king's bouts of insanity. In addition, Amelia had been a sickly child from the start and this delicacy of health made her parents even more protective. In 1801, at the age of 18, Amelia was sent to stay at the seaside resort of Weymouth in the hope that the sea air would improve her ongoing ill-health, the symptoms of which would eventually turn out to be tuberculosis. The group of courtiers sent with her included the Hon. Charles Fitzroy, equerry to the king and twenty-one years Amelia's senior. As was rapidly becoming a habit with the young royals, neither the gap in age or social standing prevented the pair becoming close. Their relationship was so overt that a servant took it upon themselves to inform Queen Charlotte, but for once the queen decided to turn a blind eye to her daughter's extra curricular behaviour. Such tolerance was unusual for the queen, but perhaps she felt more lenient towards Amelia because she was in ill health. The queen certainly knew that hearing of his favourite daughter's indiscretions risked tipping the king into another bout of mental illness, so Princess Amelia and Charles Fitzroy were, in effect, left to get on with their relationship in a peace that was not afforded to any of her siblings. Amelia certainly planned to marry Fitzroy whenever she could make it happen and took the initials A.F.R. (Amelia Fitzroy). But it wasn't to be. In 1808, the already-frail Amelia suffered a severe attack of measles and was again sent to the seaside in the hope of recovery, accompanied by her older sister, Princess Mary. Although Amelia's condition improved marginally, it was to be a temporary respite. In October 1810 Amelia developed a severe case of erysipelas, a streptococcal bacterial infection that causes a form of cellulitis. In the days before antibiotics, such afflictions could easily turn out to be fatal, and so it was with Amelia.

King George's youngest princess died on 2 November 1810, at the age of 27. She had a mourning ring made up in advance for her father, who burst into tears when it was given to him. Other than this one item, the entirety of Amelia's possessions were left to Charles Fitzroy.

Chapter 19

Love For Sale

I shall not say why and how I became, at the age of fifteen, the mistress of the Earl of Craven. Whether it was love, or the severity of my father, the depravity of my own heart, or the winning arts of the noble lord, which induced me to leave my paternal roof and place myself under his protection, does not now much signify; or, if it does, I am not in the humour to gratify curiosity in this matter.

Harriette Wilson, *The Memoirs of Harriette Wilson,*
Written By Herself, 1825

The Dubochet family lived at 2 Carrington Street, Mayfair, London. Parents John and Amelia ran a small shop while also raising fifteen children. Few formal records of the family business exist, but it's believed that John Dubochet was a clockmaker of Swiss extraction. For reasons that are unclear, he changed the family name to Wilson somewhere around 1801. Amy Dubochet was the first of the siblings to realise that selling her body might be more profitable than joining the family business. Three of Amy's sisters – Harriette, Fanny and Sophia – followed her into her chosen profession, although the youngest, Sophia, would be the only one to 'get her man' – she became the Rt. Hon. Lady Berwick upon her marriage to Thomas Hill, 2nd Baron Berwick, in 1812.

Harriette initially blamed Amy for leading the rest of them astray, but soon became competitive in her conquests and was mistress to the Earl of Craven by the age of 15. She certainly set her ambitions high, writing to the Prince of Wales (while still living with Craven),

I am told that I am very beautiful, so perhaps you would like to see me … this is all very dull work, Sir, and worse even than being at home with my father: so, if you pity me, and believe you could make me in love with you, write to me…

She received a rapid response written in the third person, requesting her attendance at an 'interview' with the target of her commercial affections, but this wasn't enough for Harriette. She responded in turn, making it very clear who was to be the grateful party in any potential coupling.

> SIR,—To travel fifty-two miles this bad weather, merely to see a man, with only the given number of legs, arms, fingers, &c., would, you must admit, be madness in a girl like myself, surrounded by humble admirers who are ever ready to travel any distance for the honour of kissing the tip of her little finger; but, if you can prove to me that you are one bit better than any man who may be ready to attend my bidding, I'll e'en start for London directly. So, if you can do anything better in the way of pleasing a lady than ordinary men, write directly: if not, adieu, Monsieur le Prince.

There is no evidence of Harriette ever having bedded the prince, so one can only assume that he decided against 'proving' himself. She did, however, consort with others of Lord Craven's acquaintance and did so with such little discretion that he soon found out and cast her adrift. Harriette worked her way through many other noted men of high society, most of whom proved all too susceptible to her charms while failing to offer quite the passion or lifestyle the young girl was looking for. Her 'failures' were few, but notable. The Prince of Wales might have been politely transactional in his brief correspondence, but Lord Byron took the time to go into detail about why he should not consort with the enthusiastic young lady.

Harriette had developed something of a crush on Byron – 'sentimentally in love' with him, as she recalls in her memoirs – and wrote to the famous poet, asking that, '[...] you will honour me with a little of your friendship'. When she received no reply, Harriette wrote to Byron again, this time in indignation:

> I was furious, and wrote again to tell him that he was a mere pedant; that my common sense was a match for his fine rhymes; [...] Was he really so superior, and would he crush the poor worms which dared not aspire to his perceptions? Or was he but a mere upstart man, of extraordinary genius, without strength of mind to know what

he would be at? Could he not, at least, have declined the honour I wanted to confer on him, civilly?

Perhaps thinking she still hadn't got her point across *quite* forcefully enough, Harriette ended her missive, 'you be hang'd!'

There was, however, method to this seemingly outspoken madness – Harriette was firmly of the opinion that provoking an argument was almost as good as winning one – in either case, she got the attention she craved. She was also savvy enough to know that many men could not resist the challenge of an angry woman. Unfortunately for Harriette, Byron was not one of them – he replied to her outburst with a tactfully written rejection:

> I am not unacquainted with your name or your beauty, and I have heard much of your talents; but I am not the person whom you would like, either as a lover or a friend… I am not of a nature to be loved, and so far, luckily for myself, I have no wish to be so…. You tell me that you wished to know me better; because you liked my writing. I think you must be aware that a writer is in general very different from his productions, and always disappoints those who expect to find in him qualities more agreeable than those of others…. I will not risk your good opinion by inflicting my acquaintance upon you.

Harriette's list of known conquests is a long one and includes many famous writers and politicians of the time. Arthur Wellesby, 1st Duke of Wellington, might have led Britain to victory over Napoleon, but he was clearly weak in the face of Harriette's intimate talents. He is accepted to have been one of the men with whom she had an ongoing financial arrangement in order to fund the lifestyle to which she became accustomed.

The shelf life of a courtesan has always been limited, such women generally being discarded by their 'patrons' as they age. Having embarked on her illustrious career in her teens, Harriette must have been well aware of the clock ticking increasingly loudly as she headed towards her thirties. Despite her extensive cv, she had yet to find any man willing to marry her and her options were becoming ever more limited. Ever the savvy businesswoman, Harriette knew that her survival as an older society lady was reliant on the goodwill of the men of her intimate acquaintance. She also knew very well that said goodwill generally waned as a woman aged and, unless she was lucky enough to marry one of her consorts, she was likely to be left to fend for herself. When it became clear that Harriette's own coterie of gentlemen did not include any who might be devoted enough to take care of her in her dotage, she took matters into her own hands.

The Memoirs of Harriette Wilson, Written By Herself, were first published in 1825 as serialised paper editions, by John Joseph Stockdale, a publisher based in the Royal Parade, Pall Mall. Stockdale already had a reputation for being somewhat louche with regards to what he was prepared to print, including some works considered to be on the margins of pornography. The publisher and the courtesan were a perfect match – equally savvy in their determination to make as much money as possible from their potential victims, they consulted the long list of establishment names in her little black book and contacted each in turn, offering to take their details out before publication, in return for a suitable payment. This blackmailing attempt worked on some better than others; while some men, including Henry Brougham MP (later to become Lord Chancellor), paid up in order to save their reputations, the Duke of Wellington famously retorted, 'Publish and be damned!', a saying which has long been recognised as a classic of the English language. The fact that he almost certainly never said it is ignored in favour of a good story.

Harriette's memoirs – which she herself described as 'a desperate effort to live by my wits' – were an immediate sell-out, with demand for her salacious gossip and intrigue being so great that it's said that Stockdale had to install a barrier inside his shop in order to control the crowds who flooded in. Some of those who made an appearance in Harriette's memoirs did decide to take recourse in law, despite the potentially embarrassing publicity that such action would almost certainly cause. *Baldwin's London Weekly Journal* dated Saturday, 9 July 1825, includes a report on the case of Blore vs Stockdale, a libel claim brought against Stockdale in his role as publisher of the memoirs. In her recollections Harriette had related a letter from her younger sister Fanny, who had allegedly turned down a marriage proposal from a local stonemason.

The case against Stockdale was brought by Blore, the stonemason mentioned in Harriet's memoirs, who claimed that that not only did he have no connection to Fanny, as a married man with a family, the comments in Harriette's memoirs were damaging to both his personal life and wider reputation. Stockdale, reading from notes, claimed that the case had been brought simply to 'crush' him in order to save embarrassment for those mentioned intimately in Harriette's memoirs. He argued that, as the stonemason had a brother of the same name, it couldn't be claimed that he had targeted any specific person. Said brother was brought before the court to assure those present that not only had he never made Fanny an offer of marriage, he had in fact never even met her. Despite there apparently being no balance of proof on either side, Stockdale was ordered to pay damages of £300 (the equivalent of £28,000 as of 2019)

A caricature dated 1 July 1825, titled 'SCARLET FEVER versus YELLOW JAUNDICE, or, The LIBEL PUBLISHER CUT UP' (now in the ownership of the British Museum), shows Stockdale as a weaselly character standing trial before a demonic version of Scarlett, the plaintiff's lawyer. A masked stonemason in the background carves the amount of damages into a tombstone while muttering curses in the direction of a portrait of Harriette herself, sitting brazen and blousy, writing at a desk in a dilapidated room. Harriette's revelations were such that Sir Walter Scott commented on them in his journal, late in 1825,

> Some one asked Lord A—y .... if Harriette Wilson had been pretty correct on the whole. 'Why faith', he replied, 'I believe so ... I once supped in her company more than twenty years since.... She was far from beautiful ... but a smart saucy girl, with good eyes and dark hair, and the manners of a wild schoolboy.'

Harriette did marry once and, perhaps surprisingly, it appears to have been the one major misjudgement of her life. There are few records to be found of her time with William Rochfort and it is unlikely that the couple ever legally married, although Harriette took his name as her own. Whatever the legalities, the relationship eventually broke down. Harriette died in 1845 at the age of 59 and is buried at Brompton Cemetery, West London. Her last recorded address was 3 Draycott Place, Chelsea, indicating that whatever her personal circumstances, she had maintained her standards right until the very end. Organised enough to have pre-booked her own funeral, she also left a note for her old friend Henry Brougham, asking that he and other men of her acquaintance should perhaps see their way to paying her final bill in her memory. The undertaker's bill was, indeed, paid.

Chapter 20

The (not so Grand) old Duke of York

> Oh, the grand old Duke of York,
> He had ten thousand men;
> He marched them up to the top of the hill,
> And he marched them down again.
>
> When they were up, they were up,
> And when they were down, they were down,
> And when they were only halfway up,
> They were neither up nor down.

Although there are versions of the well known nursery rhyme dating back to 1642, by far the most well known is the one that supposedly refers to Prince Frederick, Duke of York and Albany. The younger brother of the Prince Regent and the favourite son of King George III, Frederick was thrust into military service by his father in November 1780, at the age of 17. With no experience, yet indulgently garnished with the rank of colonel from the start, it really shouldn't have been much of a surprise to anyone that Frederick was utterly out of his depth. He did his best, however, and was appointed colonel of the Coldstream Guards by 1784, when he was still only 21. Frederick's lack of experience betrayed him on many occasions, including notable losses during the Flanders Campaign in the early stages of the French Revolutionary Wars. Nevertheless, he found himself Commander-in-Chief of the British Army by 1795. Military organisation was something Frederick really *was* good at, and his reforms of the army system were mostly seen in a positive light. His was an ethos strong on discipline and proper training, bringing in structured practising of both field and drill manoeuvres. In a surprisingly egalitarian move, he also took some of the responsibility of clothing the troops away from their individual colonels, by ensuring that greatcoats – one of the most important items of a soldier's uniform, for its protective aspect – were supplied with public funds. His administrative talents – including the development of a system for sending confidential reports to central office – were key in the defeat of Napoleon's plans to invade Britain in 1803.

In 1791, Frederick married Princess Frederica Charlotte of Prussia. A very carefully arranged union between cousins, the pairing was possibly encouraged by the Prince Regent, whose secret marriage to Maria Fitzherbert was threatening to stymie his chances of becoming king. It's possible that Prince George was hoping that Frederick and his princess would produce children and therefore be viewed as far better prospects as heirs to the British throne, presumably taking the heat off both himself and his illicit consort. Unfortunately for George, Frederick and Frederica were not as well matched as their names might suggest. Despite apparently liking each other well enough as people, there was to be no romance in the air for these newlyweds and they instead quickly settled into living amicable but almost entirely separate lives. Frederica settled at Oatlands Palace, the couple's royal residence in the village of Oatlands, near Weybridge in Surrey. There she oversaw support for the poor and needy of the nearby villages, as well as amassing a large collection of animals. It was reported at the time that the Duchess of York was often to be seen roaming the grounds of Oatlands with upwards of thirty dogs keeping her company. Frederica also kept monkeys and parrots in quite some number, and eventually created a small cemetery in the grounds in which to bury them when they eventually died. Writing in his *Select Illustrations of the County of Surrey*, published in 1828, George Frederick Prosser claims to have seen some seventy grave markers, each for one of the duchess's late beloved dogs. That of 'Pepper' stands out as evidence that Frederica possibly preferred animals to people:

> Pepper, near this silent grotto
> Thy fair virtues lie confest;
> Fidelity they leading motto,
> Warmth of friendship speak the rest.

Prosser also notes the remains of Frederica's beloved grotto with its ornate fishpond and tumbling ivies, for which she collected shells with a passion, and the building of which cost many thousands of pounds. It seems to have been well known among their friends that the couple lived in an almost entirely platonic relationship and they enjoyed a lively social life – although not everyone was impressed with the care (or lack of) that guests received. Diarist Charles Greville wrote of one visit,

> I went to Oatlands. There was a very large party ... we played whist till four in the morning. On Sunday we amused ourselves by eating fruit in the garden and shooting at a mark with pistols and playing with the Monkeys. I bathed in the cold bath in the grotto which is as clear as crystal and as cold as ice. Oatlands is the worst managed establishment in England; there are a great many servants, and nobody waits on you, a vast number of horses and none to ride or drive.

While his wife busied herself with her community work and the animals, Frederick concentrated on the military. In 1800, he founded and trained the Rifle Brigade – initially known as the Experimental Corps of Riflemen – who were the first British regiment to carry rifles (the 'Baker' flintlock), rather than muskets. He also changed their military uniform from the romantically decorative red so often depicted in paintings of the time to a less easily spotted green, in order to give his men a level of camouflage that had never seemingly been considered before. The duke's determination to ensure that officers were promoted on merit rather than through nepotism led to him throwing his support behind the establishment of the Royal Military College at Sandhurst in 1802. Frederick was, in his own way, a great success in life, despite his rocky start and sexless marriage. Then in 1803, the Commander-in-Chief met Mrs Clarke. Born Mary Anne Thompson in April 1776 (some records note her as being born in 1772), Mrs Clarke was not, as might otherwise be assumed, a widow. Rather, she had left her husband Joseph not long after marrying him, having discovered rather too late he was both a heavy drinker and a bankrupt. Still only around 18 years of age, Mary Anne determined to use her personal assets to the full and entered the world of the London courtesans. Clearly talented at her art, Mary Anne had brief but profitable attachments to several high-ranking members of the aristocracy, including Sir Charles Milner and Sir James Brudenell, before meeting Frederick, Duke of York sometime around 1802–03.

Mary Anne was forever sketchy about the exact circumstances of her first meeting with His Royal Highness, including whether it was he who funded her move into a house on Tavistock Place somewhere around 1803. Regardless of the precise dates, she was certainly firmly established as Frederick's mistress by the early part of 1804, when the courtesan from a humble background moved into a grand house at 18 Gloucester Place in London. When Mary Anne moved in, she must have felt as though she really had made it in the world. Taking to the high life with gusto, Mary Anne established herself as a society hostess, her royal consort by her side.

Mary Anne and Frederick were so closely entwined that she often helped him with his admin duties. It was common practice in the British Army at the time for commissions up to the level of colonel to be bought as a straight transaction by those rich enough to do so. Thus, the sons of the wealthy began their military careers at a far higher rank than their experience would otherwise allow. This benefited both sides – the newly commissioned officer was given a rank above those soldiers who were lower than him in the social order and the army could be certain of not diluting its class hierarchies. Not only did paid commissions bring in much needed money towards military campaigns, it also – in theory, at least – kept the higher ranks for those wealthy enough to be trusted not to feel the need to loot and pillage while out on campaigns. And of course, the wealthy were unlikely to want to change the system in favour of the men further down the military food chain. Frederick was responsible for the approval and signing off of these purchased commissions and Mary Anne helped him by organising and writing out his lists. Whether Frederick was lazy, naive or simply in on the scam is uncertain to this day, but what is certain is that Mary Anne was able to add names to the list without their veracity being fully checked. Thus, she could offer favoured contacts huge discounts on commissions without anyone questioning it and, of course, a payment of thanks would be dropped into her own silken pockets. The extra money would have been extremely welcome as, despite having installed Mary Anne in the Gloucester Place house, the duke of York had failed to provide her with enough of an income to enable her to fund the lavish lifestyle that went with it.

The duke tired of Mary Anne and left her in 1805, buying her silence by providing her with an annual pension. Perhaps Frederick thought his rejected consort would eventually disappear, or perhaps he simply grew tired of making payments to someone with whom he was no longer intimate, but whatever the reasoning behind it, he cancelled her pension entirely in 1808. This was something Mary Anne was neither able to afford, nor prepared to accept. Rumours conveniently began to circulate within London society that the Duke of York had, with the encouragement of his mistress, been accepting bribes in return for army commissions. Not only was Frederick being publicly accused of corruption, he was also clearly an adulterer – each being equally distasteful in the public's view.

The rumours gained currency when, in January 1808, the following title was published by J.M. Richardson of Cornhill, in the City of London:

An
APPEAL TO THE PUBLIC,
and a
FAREWELL ADDRESS
to the
ARMY
by
BREVET-MAJOR HOGAN,
Late a captain in the thirty-second Regiment
of Infantry—in which he resigned his
commission, in consequence of the
treatment he experienced
from the
DUKE OF YORK,
and the system that prevails in the Army
respecting promotions.

The major (the 'brevet' prefix denotes an unpaid promotion in rank usually conferred as an honour) adds the acerbic subtitle, 'Let others tamely suffer if they will—I'll state my wrongs, and tell them to the world.' In his lengthy missive, Major Hogan wrote of his attempts to gain what he believed to be a justifiable promotion, only to be stymied by the Duke of York. According to the *Edinburgh Register,* Hogan resigned his post in protest and expected to be refunded the cost of such commissions for which he had previously paid, as was the custom of the time. Finding himself short-changed by the not inconsiderable sum of £400, Hogan published his 'Appeal' in 1808. He was allegedly visited very soon afterwards by a lady who left a letter at the door of his lodgings which contained the missing money, along with a note. In it, the writer explained,

> I hope this will prevent the publication of your intended pamphlet; and if it does, you may rely upon a better situation than the one you had. When I find that you have given up all ideas of opening your secrets to public view, (which would hurt you with all the royal family,) I shall make myself known to you, and shall be happy in your future acquaintance and friendship, by which, I promise you, you will reap much benefit. If you will recall the advertisement, you shall hear from me, and your claims shall be rewarded as they deserve.

The implication of nefarious activities by the Duke of York and/or his accomplices was clear to anyone who read Hogan's claims and as a result, his pamphlet sold in the thousands. However it wasn't long before people were questioning how an army major had the courage – or indeed, the foolishness – to speak of the Duke of York in such a way. It was also queried as to whether there was any proof that Hogan hadn't simply set up the supposed financial delivery himself, in order to fake the evidence he needed. It was too late to question the major – when no response came to demands that he provide proof of the validity of his claims, it was discovered that he had in fact sailed for America before the pamphlet was even published.

The Duke of York took this opportunity for revenge against a hostile press. Peter Finnerty, the hapless editor of Hogan's pamphlet, was prosecuted, alongside twenty-six printers and publishers who had quoted from Hogan's writings or otherwise publicly recommended them. But on 27 January 1809, public attention was diverted elsewhere. Gwyllym Lloyd Wardle, MP, alongside Sir Francis Burdett, put forward a motion against the Duke of York on the grounds that his desperate attempt to silence the press was, in fact, being done in order to prevent news of the duke's relationship with Mary Anne Clarke – and her illicit sideline in selling commissions – becoming public knowledge.

The way in which Wardle had claimed to come about his knowledge of the duke's financial dealings was, in itself, entertainingly unlikely. According to Welsh diarist Captain Rees Gronow's version of events published in his *Reminiscences and Recollections* of 1862, Wardle had discovered the intrigue while making a clandestine visit of his own to the delightful Mrs Clarke:

> A carriage with the royal livery drove up to the door, and the gallant officer was compelled to take refuge under the sofa; but instead of the royal duke, there appeared one of his aide-de-camps, who entered into conversation in so mysterious a manner as to excite the attention of the gentleman under the sofa, and led him to believe that the sale of a commission was authorised by the Commander-in-Chief; though it afterwards appeared that it was a private arrangement of the unwelcome visitor. At the Horse-Guards, it had often been suspected that there was a mystery connected with commissions that could not be fathomed; as it frequently happened that the list of promotions agreed on was surreptitiously increased by the addition of new names. This was the crafty handiwork of the accomplished dame; the duke having employed her as his amanuensis, and being accustomed to sign her autograph lists without examination.

On 1 February 1809, Mary Anne Clarke stood before the House to answer questions about the alleged selling of commissions. Wardle himself led the questioning, during which Mary Anne answered openly and guilelessly that she had indeed been taking payment for commissions and that the Duke of York had been fully aware of this. Hansard records of her questioning certainly don't include much in the way of denial:

(Mr Wardle.)

...

Did you at the same time state to the Commander, in Chief, that you were to have any pecuniary advantage, provided the exchange took place? *His royal highness asked me if I knew the parties, and I said I did not, that they would make me a compliment.*

Did you state the amount of the compliment you were to have? *I am not certain that I did.*

Are you certain that you mentioned to the Commander in Chief, that you were to have any pecuniary compliment? *I told HRH that I did not know the men at all, and certainly they would make me some sort of compliment; I did not know them then.*

...

Do you recollect afterwards receiving any pecuniary consideration? *Yes, I do.*

How much? *A 200l. bank note was sent me.* [allowing for inflation, the £200 Mary Anne was paid would equate to approximately £16,500 in 2020]

After receiving the 200l. do you recollect at any time making that circumstance known to the Commander in Chief? *Yes, I do.*

When did you mention it to him? *The same day.*

What passed upon the subject? *I only merely said that they had kept their promise.*

Did the Commander in Chief know from you the amount of the money you had received? *He knew the amount, because I shewed him the note; and I think that I got one of his servants to get it exchanged for me through HRH*

Gronow notes in his memoirs that Clarke had indeed been installed in an expensive society house by the duke with no legitimate way of funding its upkeep; he certainly doesn't seem surprised that she chose the solution she did. He is also amused by Clarke's lack of discretion with regards to the secret lives of the royal family:

She regarded the Duke of York as a big baby, not out of his leading-strings, and the Prince of Wales as an idle sensualist, with just enough of brains to be guided by any laughing, well-bred individual who would listen to stale jokes and impudent ribaldry. Of Queen Charlotte she used to speak with the utmost disrespect, attributing to her a love of domination and a hatred of every one who would not bow down before any idol that she chose to set up.... In short, Mary Anne Clarke had been so intimately let into every secret of the life of the royal family that, had she not been tied down, her revelations would have astonished the world.

The duke wrote directly to the Speaker of the House protesting his innocence – while acknowledging and publicly regretting his adultery – but Wardle determinedly moved for the duke's dismissal from the post of Commander-in-Chief. Wardle lost the vote, but the minority who agreed with him were of a large enough number that the duke resigned his commission anyway. Mary Anne Clarke was paid £7,000 plus a healthy annuity (thought to be in the region of £400pa) in return for handing over all letters from the Duke of York and destroying the draft copies of her memoirs.

And there the drama might have ended, had Clarke not had cause to force Wardle's own manipulations into the spotlight. In June 1809, an upholsterer by the name of Francis Wright sued Wardle at Mary Anne's behest, after he had refused to pay the bill for furniture Wright had prepared for her home. The court found in Wright's favour and it was realised that Wardle had almost certainly agreed to fund Mary Anne's home decor in return for her testimony against the duke. Wardle immediately returned fire by suing Wright, Clarke and Wright's brother for conspiracy – a case which he again lost.

Wardle's last vote in the Houses of Parliament was in 1811, against a motion to reinstate the Duke of York as Commander in Chief of the Armed Forces. The motion was passed, Wardle gradually faded from political view and by 1815 he had fled abroad to evade his creditors. Mary Anne continued her writing career, sailing even closer to the slanderous wind with her next collection of memoirs, *The Rival Princes*, in which she gaily exposed the relationship and rivalries between the Dukes of York and Kent, based on her own personal knowledge of both men. It wasn't royalty who finally felled Mary Anne's pen, however – despite the risks she had taken with the royal family, she was finally (and almost inevitably) imprisoned for libel against a politician and spent nine months in prison, supposedly mostly in solitary confinement.

After her release, Mary Anne moved to Boulogne-sur-Mer in France, where she lived out the rest of her life very comfortably, thanks to the remuneration she received in return for not publishing the duke's letters (and she certainly had a good deal – the annuity even transferred to her daughter Ellen after Mary Anne's death). Generations later, a fictionalised version of Clarke's life was published by her great-great-granddaughter, acclaimed author Daphne Du Maurier. Mary Anne is perhaps, of all courtesans, the one who was most successful in keeping both her lifestyle *and* her legacy intact.

Chapter 21

Turning A Blind Eye

As all school history lessons remind us, Vice Admiral Lord Horatio Nelson died a hero's death on his ship the *Victory* at the Battle of Trafalgar, on 21 October 1805. Although he did indeed utter the phrase 'Kiss me, Hardy' (a request directed at his flag captain, Vice Admiral Sir Thomas Masterman Hardy, who duly bent and kissed him on the cheek and forehead), Nelson's actual last words were, according to the *Victory*'s chaplain, Alexander Scott, 'Thank God I have done my duty.' The prequel to Lord Nelson's famous last words, according Robert Southey's 1813 biography, *The Life of Horatio, Lord Viscount Nelson* is perhaps even more interesting – 'Take care of my dear Lady Hamilton, Hardy. Take care of poor Lady Hamilton.' Southey also makes reference to other requests Nelson made with regard to Mrs Hamilton before he died, including, 'Let my dear Lady Hamilton have my hair, and all other things belonging to me.' According to records held by the Royal Museums Greenwich, the 'undress' coat that Nelson had been wearing when he died was returned to Lady Hamilton after his death, as per his wishes; however, his other requests were ignored. The coat was to be Emma Hamilton's only memento of her lost lover.

Emma Hamilton's life began far from the social circles in which it would end; she was born Amy Lyon on 26 April 1765, near Neston in Cheshire. Amy is sometimes written as 'Emy', possibly from the difference in pronunciation of certain vowels in a Wirral accent, as Amy's birth records were transcribed by a parish clerk from that area. Amy's blacksmith father died when she was 2 months old and her mother, Mary, took the baby girl with her to live with her own mother Sarah in Hawarden, a small village in Flintshire, North Wales. The trio apparently settled quite happily for some time, but for reasons unknown, Mary left the home she shared with her mother and daughter in 1777 and moved to London. Although Amy found work as a housemaid in order to help keep herself and her grandmother, it didn't last long and she found herself unemployed within a few months. Clearly having inherited her mother's wanderlust, Amy left North Wales towards the end of 1777, while still only 12 or 13 years old, and moved to London herself. Having found domestic work with a family in Blackfriars, Amy was befriended by another maid in the household, who introduced the young girl to the world of the West End theatre. Amy somehow managed to rapidly find herself employment as a maid at the Drury Lane Theatre, assisting actresses in their dressing rooms.

Perhaps desiring a larger share of the limelight, Amy moved on to a rather more outré appointment around 1780, as a model for James Graham at his 'Temple of Health' in Aldwych. Often described as a 'quack' medic, in reality Graham was possibly one of the first modern sexologists. As well as offering advice on 'marital relations', Graham invented the 'Celestial Bed', which he claimed could improve a couple's chances of conception. This canopied bed was enormous, measuring around three metres wide by four metres in length. The physical exertions of the bed's occupants would prompt music to play at gradually increasing tempo through built-in organ pipes. The end of the bed was raised post-coitally, in order to keep the female partner's feet elevated (a method of aiding conception which is often still recommended to this day). Girls such as Amy were hired to pose nude in front of paying customers, as examples of physical perfection. The same year that Amy worked at Graham's Temple – when she was still only 15 – she met Sir Harry Fetherstonhaugh. A great friend of the Prince of Wales, Fetherstonhaugh was eleven years her senior and already the bearer of a fearsome reputation for disreputable behaviour. It is an illustration of how louche Fetherstonhaugh's social circle was that the playboy politician hired the teenager to act as both hostess and entertainer for a bachelor party he was hosting at his country estate, Uppark on the South Downs. This upmarket 'stag do' went on for months. Amy was in attendance as Fetherstonhaugh's mistress, but her entertainment duties included dancing nude on the tables. She developed a close friendship with one of the quieter of Fetherstonhaugh's friends. Charles Greville was the younger son of the Earl of Warwick and, despite allegedly being rather staid and straight-laced, rapidly became very fond of the young girl. Which was lucky for Amy, because she threw herself on Greville's mercy when, in the latter half of 1781, she discovered she was pregnant with Fetherstonhaugh's child. Despite having paid for Amy's extended and intimate company, Fetherstonhaugh had no intention of also paying for any child that might result from that intimacy. Greville was more pragmatic – he offered to take 16-year-old Amy in as his own mistress, on the condition that her child was fostered out elsewhere as soon as he or she was born. There were other conditions – Amy was to dress modestly at all times, not go out socially and to accept Greville's polishing of her accent and general manners. Greville also insisted on changing Amy's name to something more suited to his station in life.

Thus, Emma Hart was born. Greville planned to make the most of Emma's beauty and commissioned renowned portrait artist George Romney to paint her portrait, probably with a view of selling the resultant paintings. Romney was smitten from the start, seeing in Emma his perception of idealised beauty, with classical features and Rubenesque flowing hair. She also had an engaging and enthusiastic personality, along with an ability to hold poses that had probably been honed during her time in the Temple of Health. Romney believed her to be the greatest of muses and rapidly became obsessed, eschewing more mundane commissions in favour of painting his favourite model over and over again. Between 1782 and 1786, it's believed that Emma sat for Romney more than 100 times. He wasn't the only artist to see the potential in the young woman; many other artists – including the great Joshua Reynolds – painted Emma's portrait in the 1780s. The most interesting thing about Emma's popularity as an artist's model is that she was almost always portrayed in the guise of something or someone else. Very few portraits show her simply as 'Emma Hart'; instead she is depicted as characters from Shakespearian tragedies, or Greek myths. There are notable outliers – Romney's 1784–5 portrait titled 'The Spinstress' is thought to have been painted in Emma's own home on the Edgeware Road, possibly the first time she had been portrayed in her own surroundings. In it, she is dressed in white and seated demurely at a spinning wheel, the billowing white scarf draped around her head and shoulders reinforcing an air of domestic purity. This was almost certainly an intentional move, in the hope of softening Emma's somewhat tainted reputation as Greville's mistress. Other than in occasional portraits such as 'The Spinstress,' Emma Hart was invariably displayed for viewing with the male gaze absolutely at the forefront of the artist's (or more likely, the person commissioning the painting's) mind. Her success in life – and that of her mother and children – relied entirely on Emma's ability to stay beautiful and amenable and to ride out the storms of male possession. And a possession she surely was. Charles Greville was tiring of his mistress and knew that in any case her background made her thoroughly unsuitable to ever be the wife of an aristocrat. He had become acquainted with Henrietta Willoughby, who – being both well bred *and* a wealthy heiress – was a far more pragmatic choice of life partner. With this in mind, Greville made plans to move Emma on.

Sir William Hamilton was British Envoy to Naples, where he had lived since 1764. Cultured and urbane, Hamilton and his wife Catherine (née Barlow, the daughter of the MP for Pembroke) held musical evenings during which they played the violin and pianoforte for assembled guests – including, on one presumably memorable occasion, the young Wolfgang Amadeus Mozart (who was apparently very taken with Catherine's musical abilities). Catherine died in 1782 and William returned to Britain in August 1783 in order to repatriate her remains to the Barlow family vault at their estate in Slebech, Pembrokeshire. During his stay in Britain, William regularly socialised with his nephew, Charles Greville, often with Emma as company. Her entertaining presence clearly intrigued the much older man, who nicknamed her 'the fair tea maker of Edgeware Row'. Said to have compared her appearance and presence to that of a Greek goddess, Hamilton commissioned Reynolds to paint her portrait as 'bacchante', one of the maenads who performed frenzied, orgiastic dances while possessed by the god Dionysus. Hamilton returned to Naples in late 1783, taking Emma's portrait with him.

Two years later, Greville was in trouble. His finances were not matching up to his lifestyle and he needed to marry a suitable prospect who would fit the required template of the society wife while also bringing enough money to the family coffers to shore up Greville's embarrassing lack in the matter. Emma – with her background as an erotic dancer and courtesan, not to mention a distinct lack of independent financial means – was wholly unsuitable for the position of wife. In a neat sleight of hand, Greville offered Emma to his uncle as a potential mistress, in the hope of both neatly disposing of her and also distracting Hamilton (whose marriage to Catherine had been childless) enough that he might not decide to marry elsewhere, thus protecting Greville's own inheritance. Hamilton was presumably not averse to this proposition – being widowed after a long and happy marriage had left him missing the companionship of a woman, and he could be confident that Emma was an adept enough hostess to pass muster on the social scene of foreign politics. And he did, of course, have a reputation for collecting beautiful works of art.

Emma was informed that she was to leave for Naples for an extended visit with Hamilton, but was wholly unaware of the real reason for the trip. George Romney did not take news of her planned departure well and had her sit for him on at least fourteen occasions before she left Britain, desperate to capture her for himself as many times as possible before he potentially lost her forever. Some of these portraits clearly illustrate Romney's sense of impending loss, executed in a faster and looser style than he had previously used. George Romney was patently in love with Emma Hamilton, although the relationship was never a physical one. He did in fact have a wife and children of his own living in Cumbria but, despite supporting them financially, rarely visited. He demonstrated his adoration of his vibrant young muse with brush strokes, depicting her as the many different characters whose personalities she could put on like a costume. The perfect artist's model, Emma was enthusiastic about Romney's ideas and could hold any pose he suggested like the professional she was. Emma's mother Mary had suffered a stroke and Greville used that as another reason to persuade her to travel to Naples, suggesting that an extended vacation would be good for both women. They travelled overland, setting off from London in early March 1786 and arriving in Naples on 26 April – Emma's 21st birthday – with Emma still blissfully unaware that she, in fact, was the gift.

Indeed, it would take Emma a surprisingly long time to realise the truth of the situation. Perhaps she was just incredibly naive, or it might quite possibly simply not have occurred to her that Greville would do such a thing. There is certainly no evidence to suggest that Hamilton was anything other than a genial host towards Emma, pleased to have company and perhaps hoping she would develop a fondness for him without being pressured into it. Whatever the truth of the matter, it took her at least three months to recognise that Greville had perhaps not been entirely truthful about the reason for her extended stay with Hamilton. As she finally began to understand the situation she was in, she wrote pleadingly to Greville:

I am poor, helpless & forlorn. I have lived with you 5 years & you have sent me to a strange place … me thinking you was coming to me; instead of which I was told I was to live … with Sir W. No. I respect him, but no, never shall he perhaps live with me for a little while like you & send me to England, then what am I to do, what is to become of me.

Emma became William Hamilton's mistress within six months of arriving in Naples. Perhaps surprisingly, it wasn't entirely against her will; despite still mourning both Greville and his uncaring behaviour, Emma was flattered by William's determined attempts to woo her, along with his evident appreciation of her intellect as well as her more obvious physical charms. Her fears of being taken for a temporary mistress were unfounded; William became so enamoured of her that he forgot she was supposed to be a casual arrangement and began to include her more intimately in the workings of his life. She moved into his living quarters and began attending events as his official consort, despite the consternation of those in the ambassador's social circle.

Five years after Emma Hart arrived in Naples for what she thought was a holiday, she married her host William Hamilton. She was 26 years old, he was 61. They returned to London for the occasion, marrying at Marylebone Parish Church on 6 September 1791. The bride signed the register under her true name of Amy Lyon, however marriage to Sir William gave her the automatic title of Lady Hamilton; a name she would use for the rest of her life. Hamilton clearly loved his young bride with genuine fervour and she grew deeply fond of him in return.

George Romney had been stirred into great creativity upon Emma's return to British shores and crammed in as many sittings as possible while she was available, excitedly writing ahead of time to a friend, 'The greatest part of this summer I shall be engaged on painting pictures from the divine lady.' Again, he produced endless rough sketches and worked at breakneck speed, the brush strokes and movement in the resultant paintings a visible record of his passion. The newlyweds left for Naples once again shortly after their wedding, but not before Romney painted what would be his last portrayal of Emma from life, *The Ambassadress*. Once the painting was finished and Emma was no longer around to inspire him, Romney sank into a deep depression. In 1799 he finally returned home a sick and broken man to Cumbria, where – despite having been away from her for thirty-seven years – he was nursed by his wife, Mary, until he died on 15 November 1802.

Returning to Naples with both a husband and a title, Emma Hamilton wasted no time in getting acquainted with the uppermost echelons of society. She became close to Queen Maria Carolina, sister of Marie Antoinette and wife of Ferdinand I, King of the Two Sicilies. A quick learner, Emma rapidly became proficient in speaking both French and Italian, and developed her singing talents to such a level that she was allegedly offered a paid season's engagement with the Madrid Royal Opera, but turned it down. She also developed what became known as her 'Attitudes', a form of performance art in which she held a range of poses wearing matching costumes that depicted various Greco-Roman figures that her audience would have to guess. The drapery-style clothing she wore for these events led to an upsurge in Grecian-influenced fashion right across Europe.

In August 1793, the ship *The Agammemnon* docked in the Bay of Naples in order to gather reinforcements for its fight against the French. Its captain, Vice Admiral Lord Horatio Nelson had good reason to desire an audience with Emma Hamilton; not only was she the wife of the British ambassador, it was widely believed that it had been her close friendship with Queen Maria that had aided Sir William's negotiations for an Anglo-Neapolitan treaty. This alliance had persuaded the Kingdom of Naples that it would be in their best interests to declare allegiance to Britain during the war with France, rather than staying neutral (which had been the king's favoured approach). This brief connection would be their only meeting until 1798. In the meantime, much had changed for the Hamiltons and their Neapolitan friends. Sir William had long been fascinated by Mount Vesuvius and had climbed it many times in order to take rock samples and make notes on its geological changes; in 1794, one of the biggest eruptions of Vesuvius since the destruction of Pompeii in AD 79, buried the nearby town of Torre del Greco (nowadays part of the city of Naples itself) under a layer of lava ten metres deep. Incredibly, only fifteen of the town's 18,000 residents died in the disaster, according to reports sent back to the Royal Society by Sir William himself.*

In October 1793, the French Revolution had seen Queen Maria's sister Marie Antoinette sent to the guillotine, reinforcing Neapolitan animosity towards the French. Sir William's health declined and although Emma continued to perform for selected audiences, she became depressed, her comfortable lifestyle enabling her to overindulge to the point that she was notably obese. When Nelson finally made arrangements to visit the Hamiltons for a second time in 1798, he was fresh from his victory over the French at Aboukir Bay. He hadn't escaped unscathed – his adventures in battle had left him with the sightless eye and partially missing right arm for which he is so famous. Nelson was concerned enough about the reaction his damaged physique might evoke that he wrote ahead in order to warn his hosts. 'I trust my mutilations will not cause me to be less welcome.' The heroic Vice Admiral's injuries certainly didn't put off Emma, who supposedly threw her by now heavily upholstered self upon him as soon as he appeared, crying out 'Oh god, is it possible?' In turn, Nelson was so enamoured of Emma and her visible adoration of him that he rather tactlessly wrote at length to his long-suffering wife Fanny, extolling Lady Hamilton's many supposed virtues. The Hamiltons took Nelson into their home and Emma determinedly nursed him while he recovered from his wounds. The peace was to be short lived. The French advanced and on 23 December 1798, the Hamiltons – along with Queen Maria and King Ferdinand – escaped for the safety of Palermo on Nelson's ship HMS *Vanguard*, leaving utter chaos behind them as they sailed away into the sunset.

It was in Palermo that both Emma's drinking habits and her indiscretion when around Nelson began to concern Sir William. He was well aware that he was perhaps too old for his young and vibrant wife; he was also possibly infertile, Emma having tried and failed to get pregnant for several years. But while he could tolerate some level of affection between his wife and the sea captain, society was beginning to talk – and worse still, it was beginning to mock. In 1801, celebrated caricaturist James Gillray produced a piece titled *Dido in Despair*, in which Emma is portrayed in her nightclothes, overweight and wailing at the sight of Nelson's fleet sailing off into the distance. In the dim background, a weak and elderly Sir William is obliviously sleeping through the drama in the marital bed. The caption underneath the image reads, 'Ah, where, & ah where, is my gallant Sailor gone? – He's gone to Fight the Frenchmen, for George upon the Throne, He's gone to Fight ye Frenchmen, t'loose t'other Arm & Eye, And left me with the old Antiques, to lay me down, & cry.' While society mocked Emma for her weight gain, what they didn't know was that there was good reason for it – Lady Hamilton was pregnant with Nelson's child.

Naples was recaptured from the French in the summer of 1799 and King Ferdinand regained his throne. The Hamiltons remained in Palermo, as did Nelson. Sir William, by now in failing health, had requested to be allowed to return to British shores and in early 1800 his wish was granted – Sir Arthur Paget was sent out to Naples as Hamilton's replacement. Sir William and Emma made the homeward journey overland and had a third traveller with them – Horatio Nelson. The trio set out on 8 June 1800 and were met by cheering crowds in many of the towns that they passed through. The enthusiastic reception was not, however, for the men – public appreciation was being shown to Emma herself. While the great and good of the Neapolitan court had found safety on Sicily, those on the nearby island of Malta had not been so lucky. The French invasion had initially been welcomed by the Maltese, as it brought to an end the long-standing feudal system which had been overseen by the Knights Hospitaller Order of St John of Jerusalem for the previous 250 years. Maltese citizens were relieved to be free of the yoke of slavery, but their relief was to be short-lived. The French began looting Maltese churches, a step too far for such a deeply religious country and the Maltese fought back, forcing the French to retreat into the country's capital, Valletta. What the islanders hadn't considered, however, was that the Malta's stocks of grain were also stored safely behind Valetta's fortified walls. The French simply settled in, knowing that they had enough supplies to wait it out until the beleaguered Maltese either gave in or starved. A joint British and Portuguese blockade of the island had the intended effect of preventing French supplies getting through, but of course the French didn't need anything – it was the islanders themselves who were suffering. Pleas were sent to King Ferdinand – Sicily at that time held sovereignty over Malta – but were ignored, even when Nelson attempted to intercede on their behalf.

Enter Emma Hamilton. Using her close friendship with Queen Maria to its full advantage, Emma managed to arrange for supplies of both money and corn to be sent to the beleaguered islanders. The extent of her contribution to Malta's salvation has been contested over the centuries, but such criticism appears to have little foundation other than an ingrained societal disrespect towards a woman who was not of the 'right' background. Writing in 1888, author John Cordy Jeaffresson declared savagely:

> It is needful to look into this matter, because a few years later, when she had talked herself into believing strange and unreal things of her doings in Italy, Lady Hamilton put forward her great munificence to the starving Maltese as one of the reasons why she ought to have a national pension,

He continues along the same theme:

> The story … was either one of those egregious exaggerations or one of those mere fictions, of which Lady Hamilton was so often guilty in her later time, when talking about her services to ungrateful England.

In fact much of Jeaffresson's book *Lady Hamilton and Lord Nelson* appears to be dedicated to denigrating anything and everything Emma ever achieved. His argument challenges whether or not Emma actually contributed financially towards the crisis as she claimed; while it is difficult to prove in either direction, what is not up for debate is that Emma's intervention unquestionably saved countless Maltese lives. She was, in return, awarded the Maltese Cross by order of Tsar Paul, Emperor of Russia, who had recently become Grand Master of the Knights Hospitaller. As well as being the first Englishwoman to be awarded the Cross of Malta, the receipt of such also automatically made her a Dame – her first independent title. Although already a Lady through her marriage to William, her correct title for that was Emma, Lady Hamilton, as the honour belonged to her married name rather than Emma personally. Now she was Dame Emma Hamilton – and the title belonged to her alone.

The fly in this particular ointment was that the title meant nothing outside Malta – it would only be recognised at home in Britain if King George III gave his personal permission for her to wear it. The king refused. The Hamiltons and Lord Nelson travelled home with praise for Emma ringing in their ears, but once back in Britain she would again be treated as nothing more than a mistress with ideas above her station.

There is only one recorded portrait of Emma wearing her Maltese Cross, painted by Johann Heinrich Schmidt of Dresden in 1800. Said to be Nelson's favourite painting of Emma, it went on to be hung in his cabin on board the *Victory*.

The Hamiltons and Vice Admiral Nelson arrived back on British shores on 6 November 1800, Nelson being afforded a hero's welcome when they finally landed in Yarmouth after stretching their journey out for as long as possible. Incredibly, both Lady Nelson and her father went to meet the returned travellers – which must have been an uncomfortable meeting, as by then Emma was clearly pregnant – and there was no attempt to disguise the father's identity.

Nelson's treatment of his wife Fanny may not have been as entirely selfish and cruel as it might appear, as there is no denying that he had been somewhat duped when he met her. In the days when a marital partner's financial situation was an important part of the deal, Fanny and her uncle (with whom she lived after being widowed at the age of 23) had implied that she had a far greater dowry on offer than was actually the case. Additionally, Fanny was infertile – another personal fact she decided to keep from her new husband. Having offered Nelson a large payment in return for an engagement to his niece, Fanny's uncle John Herbert then reneged on the deal after the betrothal had been announced, handing over far less than had been originally agreed. Unable to face the dishonour of breaking off an engagement, Nelson had been cornered into going through with the marriage. But regardless of the Nelson's true feelings towards one other, Fanny was now being publicly humiliated by her husband's open attachment to another man's wife.

William, however, was more tolerant; the Hamiltons by this point seemingly having developed a deep affection for each other that was perhaps more platonic than passionate. The couples each took rented houses in central London and somehow managed to get along together reasonably civilly, despite the growing complication of Emma's pregnancy. At the beginning of January 1801 Nelson returned to sea, having been promoted to vice admiral. Before her husband left for his ship, Fanny Nelson finally decided she had had enough of the situation and asked Nelson to choose between her and his pregnant mistress. He chose Emma, and never saw Fanny again.

Horatia Nelson Thompson was born on 29 January 1801 in the house that Sir William had rented for himself and Emma at 23 Piccadilly, London, while her father was onboard the HMS *Elephant*, waiting to set sail for the Battle of Copenhagen. The new parents covered up the true circumstances of Horatia's birth, presumably with Sir William's full knowledge and acceptance (considering that he must have also been at the house when Emma gave birth, it is highly unlikely he didn't know exactly what was going on). Mrs Gibson, the wet nurse to whom Horatia was immediately passed to for care, was told that her small charge was at least five weeks older than she really was, in order to provide Emma with an alibi (she had been in Vienna on the date of birth that the family gave to the nurse). Gibson was led to believe that the baby was the orphaned offspring of Vice Admiral Charles Thompson, who had died in early 1799 (one can only assume that Gibson was unaware of the purported father's actual date of death). Sir William's devotion to Emma and his complicity in her relationship with Nelson was made remarkably clear when the future King George IV, then Prince of Wales, became infatuated with her soon after Horatia's birth. Realising the jealousy that the prince's attentions was stirring in Lord Nelson, then away at sea, Hamilton took the surprisingly generous step of writing to him in order to offer reassurance that Hamilton's own wife was being true and faithful to the absent sea captain. Nelson's own family were well aware of his connection to both Emma and Horatia and seem to have been accepting of it; his brother's wife stayed with the Hamiltons in both Margate and Deal during 1801.

Later that same year, Nelson bought Merton Place near Wimbledon – the only home he ever bought or owned – as a base for himself, Emma *and* Sir William. The three of them appear to have lived in very congenial domesticity. Long since demolished, its ghost can be seen in the names of the streets which spread across the original parkland during the late 1800s – long rows of Victorian housing bearing the names Hardy, Nelson, Victory and, most touchingly, Hamilton. It was only after moving to Merton that Emma finally confessed to Nelson that she already had a daughter before Horatia's arrival; he appears to have taken the news in his stride and Emma Carew was soon brought to visit her new and unusual family.

Nelson left active service in 1802, but a year later tensions once again began to grow with France. On 6 April 1803 Sir William collapsed and died in Emma's arms. On the surface this might have been Emma's opportunity to finally devote herself solely to her beloved Nelson; in reality her husband's death was the first toppled domino in the cascade of disaster that her life was about to become. Sir William's executor was Emma's erstwhile lover Charles Greville – and he wanted Emma out. Social standards of the time meant that it was inconceivable that she should live openly as a couple with Nelson, so she had to rent another house nearby on Clarges Street. Greville had by now realised just how far beyond their means the Hamiltons had been living and, presumably furious at the reduction in his inheritance, refused to help Emma any further.

To make matters worse, Nelson had been offered the position of Commander in Chief of the Mediterranean Fleet and was due to leave for Malta and then on to the ongoing blockade of Toulon, France, on his new ship, the *Victory*. Their daughter Horatia was hurriedly baptised before her father's departure, with Emma and Horatio listed as her godparents. What neither Emma or Nelson knew as he left to join his ship was that Emma was pregnant with their second child. Born sometime in early 1804, the baby was another girl, who died at six weeks old. Emma hid both the baby's existence from the press – there is no record of her burial – and her ensuing deepening depression from Nelson's family. Instead, she focused on helping them wherever she could and also decorated Merton Place ever more extravagantly, running up increasing debt in the process. There were rumours of marriage proposals from several influential and wealthy men during this period, despite Emma's decline in both looks and mental state, suggesting that she was still capable of using her charm to seductive effect. But however tempting financial security must have been, Mrs Hamilton stayed devoted to her seafaring lover. She would see him only once more, when he came home briefly in August 1805 before heading back to his ship and the looming battle of Trafalgar.

On 19 October 1805, Nelson wrote to his daughter from the *Victory*.

My dearest Angel … I rejoice to hear that you are so very good a girl, and love my dear Lady Hamilton, who most dearly loves you. Give her a kiss for me. The Combined Fleets of the Enemy are now reported to be coming out of Cadiz; and therefore I answer your letter, my dearest Horatia, to mark to you that you are ever uppermost in my thoughts. I shall be sure of your prayers for my safety, conquest, and speedy return to dear Merton, and our dearest good Lady Hamilton. Be a good girl, mind what Miss Connor says to you. Receive, my dearest Horatia, the affectionate parental blessing of your Father.

The eighth codicil to Nelson's will was dated 21 October 1805. In it he requested that the British government should support Emma in the event of his death, as reward for his long and ongoing service:

October the twenty-first, one thousand eight hundred and five, then in sight of the Combined Fleets of France and Spain, distant about ten miles. Whereas the eminent services of Emma Hamilton, widow of the Right Honourable Sir William Hamilton, have been of the very greatest service to our King and Country to my knowledge, without her receiving any reward from either our King or Country … I leave Emma Hamilton therefore a legacy to my King and Country, that they will give her an ample provision to maintain her rank in life. I also leave to the beneficence of my Country my adopted daughter Horatia Nelson Thompson, and I desire she will use in future the name of Nelson only. These are the only favour I ask of my King and Country at this moment, when I am going to fight their Battle. May God bless my King and Country and all those who I hold dear.

Signed 'NELSON AND BRONTE', this request for ongoing support for Nelson's beloved Emma must have been almost the last thing he ever wrote. Having had the enemy fleets in sight since dawn that morning, Nelson knew he had to outwit them fast, before they were all hit by an oncoming storm. His intention was to go in fast and hard and simply annihilate them, with the aim of removing Napoleon's main threat to Britain's security. The story of the Battle of Trafalgar is well known – *Victory* severely damaged the French flagship, the *Bucentaure*, only to become blocked by the *Redoutable*, rapidly finding herself trapped on three sides by enemy fire. Nevertheless, Nelson's fleet waged determined war against the Franco-Spanish opposition and slowly managed to break down their defences. Pacing the *Victory* with his flag captain Sir Thomas Hardy, Nelson was hit by a 0.69 inch diameter lead musket ball. It ripped through an artery to his lungs and lodged in his spine, knocking him to the deck. It was evident to anyone who saw him that his injuries were mortal and he was carried below to where Surgeon William Beatty was desperately working on a growing multitude of casualties. As Nelson lay below decks, the crew of the *Redoutable* repeatedly attempted to board the *Victory*, but were driven back by heavy fire from Nelson's men. Vice Admiral Pierre-Charles Villeneuve, captain of the enemy fleet, officially surrendered at 2.15pm.** At 3.30pm Hardy went below decks to inform Nelson that his fleet had indeed been victorious. The dying man was by now struggling to speak, but managed to remind Hardy of his desire to keep Emma Hamilton safe. 'Take care of my dear Lady Hamilton, Hardy … take care of poor Lady Hamilton. Kiss me, Hardy.' As Hardy bent to kiss him on the cheek and forehead, Nelson continued, 'Now I am satisfied. Thank God I have done my duty.'

Admiral Horatio Nelson died just before 4.30pm on Monday 21 October 1805, at the age of 47. The Admiralty sent word to Emma Hamilton at Merton Place, where she and Lord Nelson had finally found such happiness. But as soon as her lover was gone, Emma's life began to crumble around her. She – along with several of Nelson's relatives – had been spending money lavishly on the assumption that he would bring riches home with him, but on his death what wealth he had was inherited by his brother and nephew. Nelson had made it clear that should he die before her, he wished for Emma to sing at his funeral. Not only did this not happen, Emma was prevented from even attending. She spent the day of Nelson's funeral at home with the female members of their combined families, while the men attended the grand funeral procession and the lavish ceremony at St Paul's Cathedral which followed. Admiral Lord Nelson was laid to rest in the crypt of St Paul's in front of an audience of thousands – but not the woman who loved him.

The British government decided to ignore the last requests of the hero of Trafalgar. Nelson's older brother William inherited everything that Nelson left behind, apart from the estate at Merton. William was also created Earl Nelson and made Viscount Merton, in honour of his younger brother's service to the country, and awarded a pension of £5,000 a year. Emma Hamilton received £2,000 and the Merton estate as per Nelson's will, plus a £500 annuity from the Bronte estate. The government itself decided to give nothing to either Emma or Horatia, despite the instructions in the codicil that Nelson had written on the last day of his life. Such a reduced income wasn't enough to maintain Merton itself, let alone keep Emma in anything like the manner to which she had become accustomed. In addition she had built up debts on the assumption that Nelson would be coming home with enough financial wherewithal to settle everything.

Merton Place was sold in 1810, but the profits were sucked up by Emma's creditors who by now were circling like sharks. She still had some wealthy benefactors who were prepared to prop her up financially, but these all either died, or developed financial problems of their own which had to take precedence. Prosecuted in 1813 for the debts she could not pay, Emma Hamilton was sent to the King's Bench debtor's prison in Southwark, South London. At that time it was possible for prisoners of a higher rank to purchase the right to live within the 'Rules' – an area of approximately three square miles around the prison in which prisoners could live fairly freely so long as they didn't travel further than the boundary line. Emma took this option and moved into the Rules with Horatia, gradually selling off those mementoes of her life with Nelson she still owned, in order to survive. In 1814, James Harrison published his biography of Lord Nelson in which he quoted from letters between Nelson and Emma, in which the Admiral had described the Prince Regent as both a villain and an 'unprincipled liar'. Although Emma vociferously denied having anything to do with the publication of Harrison's book, very few believed her. Regardless of the injury to her personal pride, the public airing of the war hero's comments about Britain's own Prince Regent put paid to any last hope Emma might have been clinging to that Prince George might one day give in and award her the income she so clearly felt she deserved.

In April 1814, the Treaty of Fontainebleau forced Napoleon to abdicate the French throne after his failed attempt at invading Russia and banished him into exile on the Mediterranean island of Elba. Newly peaceful France was suddenly a much more appealing prospect than Southwark debtors' prison. With the help of those friends she still had, Emma managed to scrape together enough money to escape the Rules and she and Horatia left for France in June 1814. Living in a cheap rented room in Calais, Emma's already poor health deteriorated rapidly. Quite possibly suffering from severe jaundice caused by heavy drinking, Emma Hamilton died with 13-year-old Horatia by her side on 15 January 1815. She was 49 years old.

* * *

The *Victory* was used as a prison hulk between 1813 and 1817 while moored near Gosport at the mouth of Plymouth harbour (see chapter 5).

*   Sir William Hamilton's report to the Royal Society regarding the eruption of Mount Vesuvius included the following anecdote, which is interesting enough to be worth relaying here:

> Five or six old nuns were taken out of a convent in this manner on the 16th of June, and carried over the red hot lava, as I was informed by the friar who assisted them; and who told me, that their stupidity was such as not to have been the least alarmed or sensible of their danger; he found one upwards of 90 years of age, actually warming herself at a point of red hot lava, which touched the window of her cell, and which she said was very comfortable; and though now apprised of their danger, they were still very unwilling to leave the convent in which they had been shut up almost from their infancy; their ideas being as limited as the space they inhabited.
>
> Having desired them to pack up whatever they had that was most valuable, they all loaded themselves with biscuits and sweetmeats; and it was but by accident that the friar discovered that they had left a sum of money behind them, which he recovered for them; and these nuns are now in a convent in Naples.

** The wonderfully named Pierre-Charles-Jean-Baptiste-Silvestre de Villeneuve, Admiral of the French Navy and Commander of the Franco-Spanish fleet at the Battle of Trafalgar was taken prisoner after his surrender and brought back to Britain on the *Euryalus*. Released on parole, he lived for some time in Bishop's Waltham, Hampshire, along with approximately 200 of his men, who were billeted in local houses. It is often said that Villeneuve attended Nelson's funeral, but however fascinating a story that might make, there is no evidence to back it up.

Freed in 1806, Villeneuve returned to France where his request to rejoin the military efforts was rejected. On 22 April 1806 he was found dead in a hotel bedroom in Rennes, where he had been waiting to find out just how displeased the French Emperor was with him. The cause of death was recorded as suicide, which implies that, considering that Villeneuve had been stabbed several times, he was either very determined, or Napoleon had decided to exact his revenge from a distance. British newspapers of the time described Villeneuve's death as almost certainly having occurred 'par ordre' (by order), with the *Stamford Mercury* going so far as to state, 'there is much reason to suppose that he [...] fell by the order of Bonaparte.'

Chapter 22

The Ladies Of The Vale

A large woman so as to waddle in walking but, tho', not taller than myself. In a blue, shortish waisted cloth habit, the jacket unbuttoned shewing a plain plaited frilled habit shirt – a thick white cravat, rather loosely put on – hair powdered, parted, I think, down the middle in front, cut a moderate length all round & hanging straight, tolerably thick. The remains of a very fine face. Coarsish white cotton stockings. Ladies slipper shoes cut low down, the foot hanging a little over. Altogether a very odd figure…. Mild & gentle, certainly not masculine & yet there was a je-ne-sais-quoi striking.

> Anne Lister's description of Sarah Ponsonby, written in her diary some time after her visit to Llangollen in 1822

Plas Newydd (the name translates as 'New Hall' or 'New Mansion') is a large house set in impressive gardens in the town of Llangollen, Denbighshire. Originally a pretty but generally unremarkable stone cottage with a mere five rooms, the house was expanded into a large Gothic residence by its two most devoted inhabitants. Eleanor Butler and Sarah Ponsonby had both grown up in wealthy society families in County Kilkenny, Ireland. The family of The Right Honourable Lady Eleanor Butler, elder of the two women by some sixteen years, had arrived in Ireland with the Norman invasion of the twelfth century and had lived at Kilkenny Castle since 1391. Eleanor spoke French fluently, having been educated at a French convent and counted Anne Boleyn among her illustrious antecedents. Sarah Ponsonby's background was slightly less impressive, but equally as upper-class and stifling. Lady Caroline Lamb was a distant cousin and Sarah's temperament was closer to that of Lord Byron's erstwhile lover than her family might have liked. Orphaned by the age of 7, Sarah was eventually informally adopted by her late father's cousins, Sir William and Lady Betty Fownes of Woodstock, County Kilkenny.

The two women met in 1768, when 29-year-old Eleanor was asked if she might keep a 'friendly eye' on the teenage Sarah, who was at boarding school near to Kilkenny Castle. Their joint love of novels and French philosophy drew them together and Sarah is said to have described Eleanor to friends as being 'uncommonly handsome'. As their friendship grew, the pair started planning a future together 'in delightful retirement and seclusion'.

Each had been expected to marry a suitable young man and to keep the family names both respectable and wealthy. However, neither Eleanor nor Sarah were prepared to do any such thing. There has never been a lack of strong-willed young women in the world, but in the late 1700s it was rare that any of them actually managed to escape the claustrophobic plans set in place for them by their families. Eleanor and Sarah were a different matter entirely. Sarah (who Eleanor often called Sally) attempted to escape from her school by leaping from a window while carrying a pistol and her dog, Frisk, but was caught sleeping in a barn and returned to her educational prison. By 1778, things were getting desperate. Sarah had no dowry and her adopted family were clear that they wished to find her a wealthy husband as soon as possible.

At the same time, Sarah's adoptive father William had made inappropriate advances towards her in the hope of taking her as a replacement wife should Lady Betty's ailing health prove fatal, but Sarah refused to make any accusations public, for fear of upsetting her foster mother. One can only assume that she also wished very much to leave the family home – but not via a society wedding. Eleanor – by now approaching 40-years-old – was under pressure from her own family to find herself a husband, their frustration compounded by the fact that she had already turned down several offers of marriage. Concerned by the deep attachment she had made to Sarah, the family eventually felt they had no option but to arrange for Eleanor to be removed to a convent in Calais.

A second escape was attempted and this time the women were more successful, reaching Waterford before Eleanor's father caught up with them and forced them to return to Kilkenny. By now, however, it was clear to everyone that Sarah and Eleanor were never going to acquiesce to society's expectations. When Eleanor escaped yet again and was caught living secretly in Sarah's rooms, it was eventually agreed that the pair would be given a small allowance and left to their own devices, on condition that they leave Ireland and save their families from the inevitable gossip. The two women crossed the Irish Sea from Waterford to Milford Haven and travelled around the Welsh countryside for some weeks, before eventually settling in Llangollen, North Wales, in the autumn of 1778. In 1780 they bought a cottage overlooking the village, named it Plas Newydd, and arranged for Sarah's family's maid, Mary Carryl, to join them as housekeeper.

Despite the dramatic beginnings to their relationship, neither Eleanor nor Sarah ever admitted to it being anything other than a close friendship (and clearly enjoyed the fact that the other residents of Llangollen let them live their lives without any awkward questions). They are sometimes described as having had a 'Boston Marriage', in which a relationship is conducted for convenience, rather than any level of sexual attraction or even love. Their stand against society's judgment was certainly admired by many and they became firm favourites of many of Britain's literary and artistic greats. Visitors to Plas Newydd are said to include Mary Shelley, the Duke of Wellington and Sir Walter Scott (contrary to common assumption there is no evidence that Lord Byron ever visited 'The Ladies of Llangollen', as they became known, but he certainly knew of them, mentioning them by name in a letter to his friend Elizabeth Pigot in 1807). Wordsworth wrote of Plas Newydd and its unusual residents in 1824:

> To Lady Eleanor Butler and the Honourable Miss Ponsonby, Composed in the grounds of Plas-Newydd, Llangollen

> A stream to mingle with your favorite Dee
> Along the Vale of Meditation flows;
> So styled by those fierce Britons, pleased to see
> In Nature's face the expression of repose,
> Or, haply there some pious Hermit chose
> To live and die — the peace of Heaven his aim,
> To whome the wild sequestered region owes
> At this late day, its sanctifying name.
> Glyn Cafaillgaroch, in the Cambrian tongue,
> In ours the Vale of Friendship, let this spot

Be nam'd, where faithful to a low roof'd Cot
On Deva's banks, ye have abode so long,
Sisters in love, a love allowed to climb
Ev'n on this earth, above the reach of time.

When Eleanor and Sarah first moved into Plas Newydd it was decidedly unimpressive, but they improved and developed both the house and the land it still stands in until it became a picture-perfect chocolate box dwelling, nestled in fairytale gardens. Plas Newydd's renown was such that Queen Charlotte requested a visit in order to view the house and gardens, later supposedly persuading King George III to grant the ladies a royal pension. A fifteenth-century statuette of the Virgin Mary belonging to Sarah and Eleanor sold at auction in 2009 is believed to have been a gift from the Prince Regent.

Sarah, Eleanor and Mary Carryl – together with a succession of beloved dogs (most of which were named 'Sappho') – lived together in Plas Newydd for the rest of their lives. When Mary died in 1809, Sarah and Eleanor had a three-sided monument to her memory installed outside St Collen's Church in Llangollen. Eleanor died in 1829 at the age of 90, and a second side of the monument was duly inscribed with her details. Sarah Ponsonby lived on at Plas Newydd until her death in 1831 at the age of 76, and the final, third side of the Llangollen monument was duly inscribed:

She did not long survive her beloved Companion LADY ELEANOR BUTLER, with whom she had lived in this valley for more than half a century of uninterrupted friendship.

Chapter 23

Comfortably Numb

These turdy-facy-nasty-paty-lousy-fartical rogues, with one poor groat's-worth of unprepared antimony, finely wrapt up in several scartoccios, are able, very well, to kill their twenty a week, and play; yet, these meagre, starved spirits, who have half stopt the organs of their minds with earthy oppilations, want not their favourers among your shrivell'd sallad-eating artizans, who are overjoyed that they may have their half-pe'rth of physic; though it purge them into another world, it makes no matter.

From *Volpone* by Ben Jonson, 1605

'In Xanadu did Kubla Khan, a stately pleasure-dome decree'

From *Kubla Khan* by Samuel Taylor Coleridge, 1816

It's fair to say that unlicensed medics have always existed and always been viewed with suspicion – if only by those more qualified. By the turn of the eighteenth century, quacks were a part of general life in Britain. The word itself is shortened from 'quacksalver', a translation of the sixteenth-century Dutch *kwaksalver*, which was originally used to describe someone who cured ailments with home remedies. It soon became a catch-all description for anyone who sold unproven – and often potentially dangerous – remedies to those who had no option but to rely on the recommendations of anyone who could offer potential solutions.

Many would have viewed the remedies borne by a visiting quack as being preferable to formal medicine, even if they'd been able to afford the latter. Treatments at the time were yet to bear anything other than the vaguest similarities to those we recognise today – even the most expensive of private physicians would still have relied on blood-letting and leeches as potential cures for all manner of sickness and disease. Additionally, in the days before accurate diagnostics or even any real understanding of how diseases worked within the human body, most would have no idea that they were seriously – or even terminally – ill until it was too late for anything to be done. Often, what the sick believed to be an illness in itself would merely have been a symptom of some deeper, darker malady lurking beneath the surface. With this in mind, it's easier to understand why the majority of remedies were aimed at what we today would consider the most minor of issues. Smallpox and consumption (now more commonly known as tuberculosis or TB) were rife, as was cholera. This was an age before public sewerage systems, or even an awareness of why they might be necessary. Diarrhoea – today considered a minor irritation which involves nothing more than a quick visit to any decent grocery store for a solution – killed, and quickly.

Laudanum was a tincture of opium that had been popular since the late seventeenth century and is – in theory at least – still available on prescription to this day. Back in the late 1700s and early 1800s, a remedy for stomach upsets and coughing which also had the side effect of both inducing sleep and calming the nerves was always going to be popular. The very accessibility of laudanum is also the reason it was the downfall of so many – rather like Valium in the 1970s and alcohol today, laudanum was so socially acceptable that it was very easy to fall into accidental addiction.

The widespread accessibility of laudanum also made it a common option for those who wished to end their own lives. It was easily accessible for middle-class and aristocratic women who saw no other way out of their cloistered existence. Suicide was considered a criminal act and an insult to God himself – those who tried and failed could be prosecuted for attempted 'self-murder' – but it must have occasionally seemed the best option. Laudanum just made it that little bit more civilised.

Opium has been around for millennia and was mentioned in the Sumerian clay tablet of 2100 BC. In the sixteenth century, Swiss alchemist and philosopher Paracelsus mixed a tincture of opium with alcohol and named his creation 'laudanum'. It isn't known for certain where Paracelsus got the name from, although it's thought it might be from the Latin for 'to be praised'. Laudanum was certainly praiseworthy on many levels, but even when it was being used 'correctly', most of those who took it had no idea of just how addictive it could be.

In the late seventeenth century, English physician Thomas Sydenham refined laudanum into a standardised recipe and began marketing it as a 'cure-all', the popularity of which rapidly attracted imitators who wanted in on this potentially lucrative new market. Soon many supposedly different 'secret' formulations were doing the rounds, some more effective than others. We now consider many drugs to be 'unacceptable' only because we are judging on the back of centuries of medical research and development. In the early nineteenth century, if there was a product in the cupboard that calmed nerves and helped to soothe digestive disorders, it's likely it would be used for pretty much every ailment that occurred in the household – even a fretting, teething baby who isn't sleeping. In the years before drugs were tested for safety, there was little understanding as to the side effects many of these products actually had; it is quite likely that many babies were sedated to the point of never waking up again. The same went for adults, of course – both men and women could find themselves in the grip of laudanum addiction, without even understanding what addiction actually was.

Some were in a comfortable enough position in life to be able to use laudanum as a recreational drug, rather than as a medicinal remedy. Percy Bysshe Shelley certainly took his laudanum usage further than was potentially safe – and was warned against doing so by his personal physician – but he did it on sparse enough occasions for it to never become a major problem in his life. Or, perhaps more likely, he had the wealth and lifestyle to make a laudanum habit easy and thus less noticeable. The infamous trip to the Villa Diodati during which Shelley, Byron and their friends created such literary magic was, in essence, a bunch of twenty-somethings intent on indulging in a drug-fuelled holiday with a side order of creative carnage.

Others weren't so lucky. Samuel Taylor Coleridge was the foremost poet of his time, whose influence on his peers was huge. Wordsworth regularly took advice from Coleridge about his own work and adapted his own writing style accordingly. But Coleridge's confidence in himself was lacking; he suffered bouts of crippling depression and anxiety throughout his life and came to rely on laudanum as a salve for his frantic mind. It has often been suggested that Coleridge may have been bipolar, in the days before the term was even known (interestingly, he is also thought to have been the first person to use the word in its modern guise, in 1810).

He certainly made some unlikely decisions in life that appeared to have no rational reason behind them at the time, including dropping out of Cambridge in 1793 in order to enlist with the army under an assumed name – he struggled through military training for several months before his brothers rescued him, blaming his actions on 'insanity'. But Coleridge's drug use was, if anything, beneficial to his writing career, at least in the early days. He famously wrote *Kubla Khan* in 1797, while in an opium haze (although it was unknown until Byron persuaded Coleridge to finally publish it in 1816).

Coleridge's friendship with Wordsworth was strong enough that he eventually moved in with William and his sister Dorothy at their home in Grasmere, in the Lake District, but the months he spent with the Wordsworths were difficult ones – for his hosts. Coleridge was picky about what he ate, had frequent nightmares that would wake the other occupants of the house and his laudanum dependency was increasing exponentially. He married, but he and his wife Sarah separated in 1808 and in 1810 Coleridge had a serious quarrel with William Wordsworth that all but ended their friendship. Although Coleridge knew his drug use was by now a real problem, he felt it was necessary in order to cope with his failing health (while ignoring the fact that the laudanum was probably *causing* some of the issues – he would later undergo regular enemas in order to ease the constipation caused by his use of opiates). Coleridge's closest friends knew he was in trouble, but appeared unable to grasp the depths of his addiction, nor why he couldn't just shake himself out of it. The implication was that Coleridge's dire situation was salvageable if only he made the effort, and that his not doing so was a intentional fault on his own part.

In 1814, Coleridge was taken in by John and Mary Morgan, old friends of author Robert Southey, who was one of Coleridge's longest serving and most steadfast confidantes. There is an air of frustrated resignation in the correspondence that flew back and forth between Southey and Joseph Cottle (publisher of both men's work) at the time. In a letter dated 17 April 1814, Southey talks of plans for friends to club together and subsidise Coleridge's living expenses:

In truth Cottle his embarrassments & his miseries of body & mind are all owing to one accursed cause: – excess in opium, of which he habitually takes more than was ever known to be taken by any person before him. The Morgans with great effort succeeded in making him wholly leave it off for a time, & he recovered in consequence health & spirits. He has now taken to it again. Of this indeed I was too sure before I heard that his looks bore testimony of it. Perhaps you are not aware of the costliness of this drug. In the quantity which he takes it would consume more than the whole annuity which you propose to raise. A frightful consumption of spirits added to this, – in this way bodily ailments are produced, & the wonder is that he is still alive. [...] He is at this moment as capable of exertion as I am, & would be paid as well for whatever he might please to do. [...] He promises & does nothing.

Both men wrote directly to Coleridge at various times, expressing their sorrow at both his condition and what they saw as his lethargic unwillingness to do anything about it. This approach clearly did nothing to help Coleridge and only made the situation worse, causing him to both berate them for their lack of understanding while also bemoaning his inability to direct his own fate in the unmistakable way of addicts throughout the ages. After receiving Southey's letter quoted above, Cottle wrote to Coleridge directly, pleading with him to give up opium 'from this moment' and to use 'the ample abilities which God has given you'. In an era before addiction was more widely understood, it's unlikely that it would have ever occurred to either Cottle or Southey that Coleridge by this time had little to no control over his addiction. Coleridge wrote a heartfelt response, in which he attempted to explain to Cottle that he was living through a nightmare of his own – unintentional – doing, and that his freely admitted addiction was not by choice.

You have poured oil in the raw and festering Wound of an old friend's Conscience, Cottle! but it is Vitriol! ... For years the anguish of my spirit has been indescribable, the sense of my danger staring, but the conscience of my GUILT worse, far far worse than all! I have prayed with drops of agony on my Brow, trembling not only before the Justice of my Maker, but even before the Mercy of my Redeemer. 'I gave thee so many Talents. What hast thou done with them'? ... It is false and cruel to say ... that I attempt or have ever attempted to disguise or conceal the cause. On the contrary, not only to friends have I stated the whole Case with tears & the very bitterness of shame; but in two instances I have warned young men, mere acquaintances who had spoken of taking Laudanum, of the direful Consequences, by an ample exposition of it's tremendous effects on myself ... I may say, that I was seduced into the ACCURSED Habit ignorantly. I had been almost bed-ridden for many months with swellings in my knees – in a medical Journal I unhappily met with an account of a cure performed in a similar case ... by rubbing in of Laudanum, at the same time taking a given dose internally—It acted like a charm, like a miracle! I recovered the use of my Limbs, of my appetite, of my Spirits.

Coleridge goes on to explain in greatly dramatic detail of how the drug-induced relief eventually subsided and he took laudanum again, eventually becoming enslaved to it; not because he enjoyed the experience, but because he couldn't bear the physical effects of *not* doing so – 'effects were produced, which acted on me by Terror & Cowardice of PAIN and sudden Death, not (so help me God!) by any temptation of Pleasure, or expectation or desire of exciting pleasurable Sensations.'

Coleridge himself clearly had an understanding of the mentally paralysing effect of addiction, illustrated in his attempt to explain later how futile it was for his friends to assume that he had power over his own behaviour:

my Case is a species of madness, only that it is a derangement, an utter impotence of the Volition, & not of the intellectual Faculties—You bid me rouse myself—go, bid a man paralytic in both arms rub them briskly together, & that will cure him. Alas! (he would reply) that I cannot move my arms is my Complaint & my misery.—

Southey still couldn't understand why Coleridge 'refused' to give up drugs and return to work. He wrote again to Cottle after reading Coleridge's response:

You may imagine with what feelings I have read your correspondence with C. Shocking as his letters are perhaps the most mournful thing which they discover is that while acknowledging the guilt of the habit, he imputes it still to morbid bodily causes, whereas after every possible allowance is made for these, every person who has witnessed his habits, knows that for the greater & infinitely the greater part, – inclination & indulgence are the motives.

Despite his friends' concerns, Coleridge wasn't a lost cause just yet. Late in 1814 he placed himself under the care of a physician and began to piece his life back together again. He undertook translation work and produced his autobiography, the lengthy and rambling *Biographia Literaria*, in 1817. Coleridge died in 1834 at the age of 61, having never reached the literary heights promised by his earlier work.

Coleridge was far from being the most notable casualty of opium in literary circles. Although it only just squeaks into the Regency timeline, *Confessions of an English Opium Eater* by Thomas De Quincey is perhaps the work that best illustrates the complicated relationship that many of the literary establishment had with drugs during a time of intellectual development. Written while De Quincey was living in Covent Garden, the now legendary account of his troubled relationship with opium was first published anonymously (in two parts) in 1821 in the *London Magazine* and was such a success that it was released in book form in 1822. De Quincey was unknown and in debt when he first wrote *Confessions*, but it would be the work for which he would become (in)famous.

> Oh just, subtle, and mighty opium! that to the hearts of poor and rich alike, for the wounds that will never heal, and for 'the pangs that tempt the spirit to rebel', bringest an assuaging balm! eloquent opium, that with thy potent rhetoric stealest away the purposes of wrath, and to the guilty man for one night givest back the hopes of his youth, and hands washed pure of blood; and to the proud man a brief oblivion for
> wrongs unredress'd and insults unavenged.

Born in Manchester in 1785, De Quincey's father Thomas Quincey died when Thomas junior was around 8 years old. His sister Jane had died when he was 4 and another older sister, Elizabeth, died a year before their father. Some time after that, his mother Elizabeth moved the family to

Bath and added the 'De' to their surname. When Thomas began to show signs of academic excellence (it's said that he could speak both Latin and Greek fluently by the age of 13), she removed him from his school and sent him one she considered to be inferior, apparently in order that he didn't get ideas above his station. Already showing a literary awareness beyond his years, Thomas became fascinated with the story of Thomas Chatterton, a precocious poet revered by writers such as Keats and Coleridge, who had died of suicide at the age of 17. But even Chatterton paled in De Quincey's mind in comparison to William Wordsworth, whose ballad *We Are Seven* he later described as 'the greatest event in the unfolding of my own mind'.

Eventually sent to Manchester Grammar School in order to study for a scholarship to Oxford, De Quincey ran away somewhere around the age of 17, determined to find a way of meeting Wordsworth. Rapidly losing his nerve at the thought of meeting such an icon of literature, De Quincey instead made his way to Chester. His family eventually caught up with him, but he somehow persuaded them to let him try an experiment in which he would live as a 'tramp' on the roads and tracks of Wales. His solitary journey was funded by an uncle who gave him an allowance of one guinea a week, but this was stopped when De Quincey failed to keep his promise of making sure the family always knew of his whereabouts. Rather than give in and return home to possible punishment, De Quincey travelled on to London where, lacking any income, he lived on the streets in the day and at night slept in the empty house of a moneylender who had refused to give him a loan, but took pity and offered him a roof instead. Befriending a teenage prostitute called Ann, De Quincey came to rely on her for support and company and was devastated when she disappeared while he was out of town attempting to borrow money. For the rest of his life, De Quincey was in the habit of scanning the streets every time he visited London, in the hope of spotting Ann's face in the crowd. He writes of 'Ann of Oxford Street' in *Confessions*:

Oh, youthful benefactress! How often in succeeding years, standing in solitary places and thinking of thee with grief of heart and perfect love, how often have I wished that, as in ancient times the curse of a father was believed to have a supernatural power and to pursue its object with a fatal necessity of self-fulfilment, even so the benediction of a heart pressed with gratitude might have a like prerogative—might have power given to it from above to chase, to haunt, to waylay, to overtake, to pursue thee into the central darkness of a London brother, or (if it were possible) into the darkness of the grave, there to awaken thee with an authentic message of peace and forgiveness, and of final reconciliation!

It was on one of these trips in 1804, while a student at Worcester College, Oxford, that the bereft De Quincey was offered his first taste of opium, as a salve to the dramatic emotional pains he was wont to create around him (although some reports suggest it might have been to ease the pain of neuralgia, which De Quincey may have developed after accidentally being hit across the head with a cane while at Manchester Grammar School). Developing a habit of venerating people and then finding them unable to live up to his expectations – Wordsworth among them, having finally met his hero in 1807* – opium was both De Quincey's salvation and his escape. Despite having seen what opium had done to Coleridge, who had by now been scooped up by De Quincey into his collection of inspirational and potentially useful friends, his use of the drug increased exponentially, even through the birth of his son (and the later marriage to the boy's mother, De Quincey not seeing any reason to live by the accepted social standards of the time). At its peak, De Quincey was taking up to 480 grains of opium per day, the equivalent of 12,000 drops of laudanum – in context, an adult's medical use of laudanum at the time would be unlikely to exceed much over 100 drops per day.

De Quincey took on the editorship of the *Westmoreland Gazette* in Kendal in 1818, but was so hopeless at meeting deadlines that he resigned in the face of complaints from the newspapers owners in late 1819. Visiting London in 1821 in order to sell works by other writers which he had translated from German, De Quincey was asked to contribute his thoughts on opium to the *London Magazine*, his personal habits clearly no longer a secret from anyone.

Confessions of an English Opium Eater was published in two parts, in the September and October issues of the *London Magazine* of 1821. Wildly popular from the start, *Confessions* opened up a world of literary contacts for De Quincey, but it is questionable as to whether anything he wrote afterwards was through choice and inspiration, or merely in order to make money. De Quincey's life was complicated by debt from an early age – he was loaned a small amount of money by a bookseller when he was 7 years old in order to buy books and was both excited and repulsed by the idea of there theoretically being no limit to how many books he might own.

De Quincey claimed that *Confessions* was an attempt to warn people of the dangers of opium, but from the start, critics expressed concern that he failed to posit enough of a negative view, and potentially risked others copying his behaviour. Only two years after the first publication of *Confessions*, an anonymous response was published, which had the snappy title, 'Advice to opium eaters, with a detail of the effects of that drug upon the human frame, and a minute description of the sensations of a person who has been in the habit of taking opium.' In it, the author discusses the reasons why opium could be a tempting prospect, but makes sure to balance it with a hefty dose of fear-mongering:

> some persons (though few in number) cannot take the smallest quantity of either Opium or Laudanum, without effects of a most injurious nature. One of these persons, (a gentleman in the prime of life,) has assured me, that when the physicians have given him (as a composing draught) a mixture containing only eight or ten drops of laudanum, a short time after he has taken it he finds himself greatly distressed, he starts up in his bed, is full of uneasiness, has spontaneous and rather convulsive motions, and is oppressed with terror and melancholy. Another person, a friend of mine, not twenty-five years of age, was driven into a state of raving delirium by five drops of Laudanum, and remained for some hours in a state requiring personal coercion. Sometimes it will cause death, even when not in very large quantities, as was the case with the French poet, M. de Voltaire, who, unable to procure sleep, took a dose of Opium, which proving too much for his enfeebled state, sent him to that sleep from which he professed to believe he should never awake.

England was awash in opium at the time, with its more common sister laudanum used for any and all manner of ailments in both adults and children. Well-founded concerns were beginning to mount up in opposition to what had once been seen as a wonder drug for all. In order to deflect such commentary, De Quincey inserted an appendix when the work came out in book form, which gave some information on the perils of addiction and his own struggles through withdrawal. His levels of usage fluctuated hugely throughout his life, but De Quincey never gave up opium entirely.

> I do not readily believe that any man having once tasted the divine luxuries of opium will afterwards descend to the gross and mortal enjoyments of alcohol, I take it for granted that those eat now who never ate before and those who always ate, now eat the more.

* De Quincey published *Literary and Lake Reminiscences* in 1834, in which he described his meetings and connections with many of the 'Lakes' poets in close and sometimes acerbic detail. Wordsworth was among those who was furious at De Quincey's descriptions of him, which included the assertion that Wordsworth was, 'upon the whole, not a well-made man. His legs were pointedly condemned by all female connoisseurs in legs.'

Chapter 24

Life's A Gas

In 1799, 20-year-old English chemist (and future president of the Royal Society, the world's oldest independent science academy) Humphry Davy was deep into a series of experiments with newly recognised gases. Davy hoped to prove that nitrous oxide, discovered by Joseph Priestley in 1772, had potential for use as a pain-relieving anaesthetic during surgery, the developments of which were being hampered by the tendency for patients to die of shock during procedures.

James Watt – inventor of the Watt steam engine and one of the founding fathers of the Industrial Revolution – built Davy a portable gas chamber in order to help with his experiments in administering nitrous oxide. It didn't take Davy long to discover that, as well as making the world a temporarily happier place, nitrous oxide made him laugh – a *lot*. After many weeks of trying the gas on himself with no discernible negative side effects, Davy decided to start gathering the opinions of others. His social sphere at the time was impressive, with some of his 'guinea pigs' being very well known names indeed. The volunteer would sit in a chair and hold their nose, while at the same time breathing through their mouth from a green bag that contained the nitrous oxide. They were asked to record their thoughts and experiences afterwards, for Davy's research.

Samuel Taylor Coleridge

The first time I inspired the nitrous oxide, I felt a highly pleasurably sensation of warmth over my whole frame, resembling that which I remember once to have experienced after returning from a walk in the snow into a warm room. The only motion which I felt inclined to make, was that of laughing at those who were looking at me. My eyes felt distended, and towards the last, my heart beat as it were leaping up and down. On removing the mouth-piece the whole sensation went off almost instantly.

The second time, I felt the same pleasurable sensation of warmth, but not I think in quite so great a degree. I wish to know what effect it would have on my impressions; I fixed my eyes on some trees in the distance but I did not find any other effect except that they became dimmer and dimmer, and looked at last as if I had seen them through tears. My heart beat more violently than the first time. This was after a hearty dinner.

The third time I was more violently acted on than in the two former. Towards the last, I could not avoid, nor indeed felt any wish to avoid, beating the ground with my feet; and after the mouth-piece was removed, I remained for a few seconds motionless, in great extacy.

The fourth time was immediately after breakfast. The first few inspiration affected me so little that I thought Mr Davy had given me atmospheric air: but soon felt the warmth beginning about my chest, and spreading upward and downward, so that I could feel its progress over my whole frame. My heart did not beat so violently; my sensations were highly pleasurably, not so intense or apparently local, but of more unmingled pleasure than I had ever before experienced.

Thomas Wedgewood

July 23, I called on Mr Davy at the Medical Institution, who asked me to breathe some of the nitrous oxide, to which I consented, being rather a sceptic as to its effects, never having seen any person affected. I first breathed about six quarts of air which proved to be only common atmospheric air, and which consequently produced no effect.

I then had 6 quarts of the oxide given me in a bag undiluted, and as soon as I had breathed three or four respirations, I felt myself affected and my respiration hurried, which effect increased rapidly until I became as it were entranced, when I threw the bag from me and kept breathing on furiously with an open mouth and holding my nose with my left hand, having no power to take it away though aware of the ridiculousness of my situation. Though apparently deprived of all voluntary motion, I was sensible of all that passed, and heard every thing that was said; but the most singular sensation

I had, I feel it impossible accurately to describe. It was as if all the muscles of the body were put into violent vibratory motion; I had a very strong inclination to make odd antic motions with my hands and feet. When the first strong sensations went off, I felt as if I were lighter than the atmosphere, and as if I was going to mount to the top of the room. I had a metallic taste left in my mouth, which soon went off.

Before I breathed the air, I felt a good deal fatigued from a very long ride I had had the day before, but after breathing, I lost all sense of fatigue.

Peter Roget

(who would go on to compile *Roget's Thesaurus*) certainly had an interesting time of it:

I suddenly lost sight of all the objects around me, they being apparently obscured by clouds, in which were many luminous points, similar to what is often experienced on rising suddenly and stretching out the arms, after sitting long in one position.

I felt myself totally incapable of speaking and for some time lost all consciousness of where I was, or who was near me. My whole frame felt as if violently agitated; I thought I panted violently; my heart seemed to palpitate and every artery to throb with violence; I felt a singing in my ears; all the vital motions seemed to be irresistibly hurried on, as if their equilibrium had been destroyed and every thing was running headlong into confusion. My ideas succeeded one another with extreme rapidity, thoughts rushed like a torrent through my mind, as if their velocity had been suddenly accelerated by the bursting of a barrier which had before retained them in their natural and equable course. This state of extreme hurry, agitation, and tumult, was but transient. Every unnatural sensation gradually subsided; and in about a quarter of an hour after I had ceased to breathe the gas, I was nearly in the same state in which I had been at the commencement of the experiment.

I cannot remember that I experienced the least pleasure from any of these sensations.

Davy published his findings as 'Researches, Chemical and Philosophical: Chiefly Concerning Nitrous Oxide', in 1800, describing how nitrous oxide causes euphoria (he was the first to use the term 'laughing gas') and also works as an analgesic. Davy suggested the use of nitrous oxide as pain relief/anaesthesia during surgical operations, but his ideas weren't immediately taken up by the medical community. Instead, Davy moved on to other research projects, while laughing gas enjoyed a brief popularity as a recreational drug. In the present day, Davy's name is most famously associated with the safety lamp he invented in 1815. The Davy Lamp's design was simple – its flame was contained within a fine mesh canister which prevented it igniting gases in its vicinity – and its impact was huge. The lamp reduced mining fatalities while also allowing seams to be dug out at far greater depths, thus speeding up British industrial development. The design of the torch for the 2012 London Olympics was based on a Davy Lamp.

Despite his scientific background, Davy was terrified of premature burial and had always insisted that his body should be laid out for some time before interment, to be sure he was actually dead. Unfortunately he died of a stroke in May 1829 while visiting Geneva, where it was law for burial to take place immediately. There is a memorial to Davy on the north wall of the chapel of St Andrew in Westminster Abbey.

Devil In The Bottle

'I remember when all the decent people in Lichfield got drunk every night and were not the worse thought of`.'

Samuel 'Dr' Johnson, in 'The Journal of a Tour to the Hebrides, with Samuel Johnson, LL.D.' by James Boswell, 1785

The term 'alcoholism' wasn't coined until 1849, when Swedish physician Magnus Huss first used the term to describe the physical consequences of long-term heavy drinking. Before then a person with a heavy drinking habit would be described as a 'habitual drunkard', but even then only if it clearly negatively impacted their lives or the lives of those around them. The medical establishment already understood that prolonged heavy drinking could eventually have a deleterious effect on a person's health, but the alcohol addiction itself was not yet fully understood.

Alcohol in all its forms was commonplace, the general rule being that no one cared how much or how often you drank, just so long as you continued to function well enough in your daily life. One of the most notorious drinkers of the period only just squeaks into the Regency period, as much of his activity took place after King George IV came to the throne. But despite still only being in his teens when Prince George became King, John 'Mad Jack' Mytton still made his mark. Born into a wealthy Shropshire family in 1796, Jack was heir to the family seat of Halston Hall, Whittington. His father died when Jack was only 2 years old, leaving him the vast estate, along with an annual income of £10,000 (equivalent today to approximately half a million pounds). A 'difficult' child by any standards, one can only assume that Mytton's wealth exacerbated his outrageous behaviour. Expelled from both Westminster and Harrow schools in quick succession, the young squire proceeded to make the lives of a string of private tutors as hellish as possible (on one occasion he left a horse in his tutor's bedroom for no apparent reason other than finding it entertaining).

In 1816, Jack was given a place at Trinity College, Cambridge. Considering his profound lack of effort when it came to using his intellect, one can only assume that money spoke louder than academic achievement. It's alleged that among the luggage he took with him to Trinity was a large case containing 2,000 bottles of port in order to sustain him in his studies. Unfortunately this plan seems to have failed, because Mytton left Trinity without gaining his degree (in fact there is no firm evidence that he ever actually undertook any studies whatsoever).

Returning to Halston Hall, Jack Mytton determinedly made a career out of behaving as outrageously as possible, with little care for the expense incurred. Edith Sitwell wrote of him in *English Eccentrics*, '... money fell like rain, dripped and melted like rain.' He ran two packs of foxhounds and often became so excited by the thrill of the chase that he would strip off his clothes and ride naked, even through snow and floods. His favourite horse, Baronet, was allowed to wander around the grand house at will and would allegedly curl up to sleep in front of the fireplace with his master. If Jack and Baronet had been out riding for a long time and felt the need for rest before continuing home, they would go to the door of any cottage they might be passing, where Jack would request a space for both himself and Baronet be made by the fire. His belief that animals were his equals occasionally backfired – for the animals, if not the squire himself. A horse named Sportsman once dropped dead after Jack – with all kind intentions – got him to drink a bottle of mulled port.

Jack's first wife Harriet could have had little idea of what she was letting herself in for when she wed the wayward country gent in 1818. His behaviour towards his young wife was undoubtedly callous, but whether he intended it to be so is uncertain – Jack Mytton had clearly long lost any real idea of what constituted reasonable behaviour. His close companion Charles Apperly (better known as the racing correspondent Nimrod) defended his friend as best he could. On hearing a tale of Mytton throwing Harriet's pet dog into the fire, Nimrod explained that Jack 'merely took it up in his arms, threw it halfway up to the drawing-room ceiling, and caught it, without injury.' When Jack was accused of attempting to drown Harriet, Nimrod explained, 'Nonsense; he was never mad enough to do that. He merely, one very hot day, pushed her into the shallow of his lake at Halston, a little over her shoes.'

Harriet's drama-filled marriage wasn't to last long – she died two years after their wedding, shortly after giving birth to their daughter, Harriet Emma.

While still married to Harriet, Mytton decided to tip his hat at politics, standing as Tory candidate for Shrewsbury in 1819. He won the seat, but his victory perhaps had less to do with his campaigning (in which he stated his concerns that his past activities might be held against him, but that he vowed to uphold good standards of conduct in the future) and more that he had offered £10 (approximately £500) to anyone who agreed to vote for him. He celebrated his win by throwing himself through the front window of the Lion Hotel in Shrewsbury town centre in order to give a victory speech in front of gathered supporters.

Mytton's Parliamentary career was short, by any standards. His first attendance in June 1819 was also to be his last; he stayed only half an hour before excusing himself and claiming boredom. Upon being asked whether he would consider contesting the seat again in 1820, Mytton allegedly claimed that 'a proper and punctual attendance to his parliamentary duties was incompatible with his present pursuits'.

Rather than learning from the error of his ways, Jack went on to marry a second time, in October 1821. His new wife Caroline was clearly a determined lady, as she managed a whole nine years of cohabitation – and five children – with the errant squire before running away and leaving her husband estranged for the rest of his life (although she didn't manage to escape entirely – after her death in 1841, she was buried next to Jack in the Mytton family plot).

Mytton's spendthrift ways were too much even for an income as grossly swollen as his, and by 1831 he was in dire financial trouble. He sold much of his estate and fled to France, taking with him a young woman he had apparently met on Westminster Bridge in London. 'Susan' was paid the handsome sum of £500 per year for her companionship and stayed with Mytton for the rest of his life. Mytton's behaviour grew ever more erratic while in France and on one occasion he very nearly killed himself when he set fire to his own nightshirt in an attempt to frighten away a bout of hiccups. As a frantic servant beat out the flames, a triumphant Mytton declared, 'the hiccup is gone, by God!' For reasons unknown – perhaps he finally ran out of money – Mytton returned to Britain in 1833. By now utterly penniless, he found himself in the King's Bench debtor's prison in Southwark, where he died the following year, at the age of 37. It was a long way from the rolling Shropshire countryside.

His cardinal virtue was benevolence of heart; his besetting sin a destroying spirit, not amenable to any counsel, and an apparent contempt for all moral restraint.

Nimrod

Chapter 25

The Human Zoo

Regardless of how poverty-stricken they might be, or how terrible the quality of their home lives, humans still look for entertainment in their spare time – and things were no different during the Regency. Rural folk enjoyed country fairs, perhaps competing to catch a greased pig, or racing tups (rams). Those with more money in their pocket might attend the opera, or a dance held by those friends with large enough houses to accommodate such an event.

Madame Tussaud's exhibition of waxworks came to London for the first time in 1802, when the collection was shown for a short time at the Lyceum Theatre in Covent Garden (often noted as being the first theatre in Britain to be lit by gaslight in 1817, which is actually incorrect – in reality the honour belongs to the East London Theatre in Stepney, who were using gas-powered illuminations by 1816). Tussaud's renowned collection of wax figurines went on to tour the country, but it would be another twenty years before her talents were widely recognised by the public.

The Georgian and Regency eras covered a period in which humanity was still very much unconvinced that all were equal, with those at the top of the food chain generally believing that some – i.e. themselves – were more equal than others. This was a time in which slavery was one of the biggest industries in the British Empire and in households of reasonable means would have at least one or two servants of their own. The difference between a slave and a servant was often infinitesimally small – even a member of household staff was all but the property of their master or mistress and beholden to their whims and cruelties. Of course there were many households in which the servants were treated well and with kindness, but there was invariably a distinct hierarchy among the residents of the house.

This sociological background perhaps goes some way to explaining why many of the denizens of the Regency had little or no compunction in using their fellow humans as entertainment and/or education. Parents would take their children on a tour of the local asylum to show them what might happen if they did not conform to society. Patients who, to modern eyes, were clearly suffering serious mental health issues were viewed as somehow having failed themselves. There was a perceived shame in being 'too weak' to survive in a world that expected you to look after yourself without the state providing any form of safety net (other than incarceration in the worst conditions imaginable). Those who were wealthy enough to have a full retinue of servants might purchase a young black boy from a consignment of slaves and use him both as a houseboy and also as a living, breathing anthropological exhibit for visiting guests.

Regardless of the frankly dubious beliefs and political systems being promoted by many through the last years of the eighteenth century and the beginning of the nineteenth, there would always be those who brought with them a breath of open-minded fresh air to British culture.

In 1825, English author Henry Crabb Robinson wrote of William Blake, while struggling to describe his new friend in his diary, 'Shall I call him Artist or Genius – or Mystic – or Madman?' Robinson's eventual conclusion was simple – 'probably, he is all'.

While never having been involved in scandals notable enough for historic reference, nor having taken any damning secrets to his grave – he was outspoken enough to verbalise even his most random thoughts to anyone who would listen, with little embarrassment – William Blake still manages to epitomise the cultural shift in Britain during the Regency period. The eighteenth century had seen the Age of Enlightenment bring reasoned philosophy and scientific argument to Europe and was believed by many to be a huge step forward for humanity on a cultural level, questioning centuries of religious infrastructure and the co-dependent intertwining of church and state. Blake's beliefs stood counter to those of the Enlightenment; he believed that even the application of science and reason should come second to individualism and the pursuit of personal freedoms.

Blake was a committed Christian (while being hostile to most forms of organised religion), and a devoted seeker of true romantic love (who quite possibly desired to extend that affection outside the boundaries of his own marriage). When he met Catherine Boucher in 1781, he was recovering from the breakdown of a relationship which had ended when his proposal of marriage was refused. Boucher was with a group of people to whom Blake told his sorry tale and responded sympathetically that she pitied him. 'Then I love you for that', replied Blake.

Although the term 'pity' at the time meant a far more sincere sympathy that it would imply in modern parlance, it's still a very interesting conversation. Catherine's openly confessed empathy appealed to Blake's desire for freely expressed emotions and regard for fellow humans. The pair were married within the year.

Catherine devoted herself almost entirely to her husband's wellbeing. She helped him to get dressed each morning and assisted with his print-making. She was also completely lacking in judgment about those flights of fancy that Blake's contemporaries were already describing as his 'madness' – visions of angels and demons that he had been seeing almost his entire life and which he accepted as being utterly real.

Blake firmly believed in 'free love'. This wasn't the later movement of the twentieth century, which is forever associated with hippies and public nudity, but the right to be free in oneself to love (both physically and emotionally) anyone a person might choose, regardless of marital status or approval of either church or government. Blake disagreed with the expectation of chastity outside of marriage, and doesn't seem to have been particularly fond of the concept of chasteness *within* marriage, either. He believed sex to be a good and healthy thing and bemoaned those religious doctrines that sought to override carnal urges. In *The Marriage of Heaven and Hell*, Blake wrote, 'Those who restrain desire, do so because theirs is weak enough to be restrained.'

Now seen as the first true Romantic poet, Blake paved the way for those such as Byron and Shelley to walk 'England's pastures green' in his unappreciated footsteps. One of the most unacknowledged and undervalued thinkers of the Regency was, perhaps, its most important.

You never know what is enough unless you know what is more than enough.

William Blake, *The Marriage of Heaven and Hell*, 1790

Bibliography

Listings are for the books I have read and/or referenced while writing this book. Older or newer versions (sometimes by other publishers) may be available.

Bondeson, Jan, *The London Monster*, Tempus Publishing, 2003

De Quincy, Thomas, *Confessions of an English Opium Eater*, Oxford University Press, 2003

Dickens, Charles, (ed.), Grimaldi, Joseph, *The Memoirs of Joseph Grimaldi*, Good Press, 2019

Dowden, Edward, *The Life of Percy Bysshe Shelley*, Routledge & Kegan Paul Ltd, 1969

Hall, Draper, *Mr Gillray: The Caricaturist, a Biography*, Phaidon Press Ltd, 1965

Higgs, John, *William Blake vs The World*, Weidenfeld & Nicolson, 2021

MacCarthy, Fiona, *Byron: Life and Legend*, John Murray, 2014

McGann, Jerome J. (ed.), *Lord Byron: The Major Works*, Oxford World's Classics, 2008

Nelson, Lord Horatio, *The Letters of Lord Nelson to Lady Hamilton, Vol. I.*, public domain.

Quennell, Peter, *Byron*, Collins, 1974

Raine, Kathleen, *William Blake*, Thames and Hudson, 1970

Shelley, Mary, *Frankenstein; or, The Modern Prometheus*, Wordsworth Editions Ltd, 1999

Southey, Robert, *The Life of Nelson*, Grange Books, 2005

Syson, Lydia, *Doctor of Love: James Graham and His Celestial Bed*, Alma Books, 2008

Wilson, Harriette, *The Memoirs of Harriette Wilson, Volumes One and Two Written by Herself*, The Library of Alexandria, 2009

Index